■ The Indiana State Constitution

The Oxford Commentaries on the State Constitutions of the United States
G. Alan Tarr, Series Editor

Professor G. Alan Tarr, Director of the Center on State Constitutional Studies at Rutgers University, serves as General Editor for this important new series which in its entirety will cover each of the 50 states. Each volume of The Oxford Commentaries on the State Constitutions of the United States contains a historical overview of the state's constitutional development, plus a section-by-section analysis of the state's current constitution. Other features included in the volumes are the text of the state's constitution, a bibliographic essay, table of cases, and index. This series provides essential reference tools for those investigating state constitutional development and constitutional law.

The Indiana State Constitution

William P. McLauchlan

THE OXFORD COMMENTARIES ON THE STATE
CONSTITUTIONS OF THE UNITED STATES
G. Alan Tarr, Series Editor

Oxford University Press, Inc., publishes works that further Oxford University's objective of excellence in research, scholarship, and education.

Oxford   New York
Auckland   Cape Town   Dar es Salaam   Hong Kong   Karachi   Kuala Lumpur   Madrid   Melbourne
Mexico City   Nairobi   New Delhi   Shanghai   Taipei   Toronto

With offices in
Argentina   Austria   Brazil   Chile   Czech Republic   France   Greece   Guatemala   Hungary   Italy
Japan   Poland   Portugal   Singapore   South Korea   Switzerland   Thailand   Turkey   Ukraine
Vietnam

Copyright © 2011 by William P. McLauchlan

Published by Oxford University Press, Inc.
198 Madison Avenue, New York, New York 10016

Oxford is a registered trademark of Oxford University Press
Oxford University Press is a registered trademark of Oxford University Press, Inc.

All rights reserved. No part of this publication may be reproduced, stored in a retrieval system, or transmitted, in any form or by any means, electronic, mechanical, photocopying, recording, or otherwise, without the prior permission of Oxford University Press, Inc.

_____

Library of Congress Cataloging-in-Publication Data

McLauchlan, William P.
 The Indiana State Constitution / William P. McLauchlan.
   p. cm. — (The Oxford commentaries on the state constitutions of the United States)
 Includes bibliographical references and index.
 ISBN 978-0-19-977932-1 ((hardback) : alk. paper)
 1. Constitutions—Indiana. 2. Constitutional law—Indiana.
 3. Constitutional history—Indiana. I. Indiana. Constitution (1851) II. Title.
 KFI34011851.A6 M378   2011
 342.77202—dc22   2011002408

_____

1 2 3 4 5 6 7 8 9
Printed in the United States of America on acid-free paper

Note to Readers
This publication is designed to provide accurate and authoritative information in regard to the subject matter covered. It is based upon sources believed to be accurate and reliable and is intended to be current as of the time it was written. It is sold with the understanding that the publisher is not engaged in rendering legal, accounting, or other professional services. If legal advice or other expert assistance is required, the services of a competent professional person should be sought. Also, to confirm that the information has not been affected or changed by recent developments, traditional legal research techniques should be used, including checking primary sources where appropriate.

(Based on the Declaration of Principles jointly adopted by a Committee of the American Bar Association and a Committee of Publishers and Associations.)

You may order this or any other Oxford University Press publication by
visiting the Oxford University Press website at www.oup.com

To David Fellman
Vilas Professor of Political Science
University of Wisconsin
1964–1978

a Scholar and a Gentleman,
a Fine Teacher

■ CONTENTS

Series Foreword by G. Alan Tarr   xv
Acknowledgments   xvii

PART ONE ■ The History of the Indiana Constitution

The 1816 Constitution	4
The Constitution of 1851	12
Subsequent Amendments to the 1851 Constitution	17

PART TWO ■ The Indiana Constitution and Commentary

Article I: The Bill of Rights   37

Section 1. Inherent and Inalienable Rights	38
Section 2. Natural Right to Worship	39
Section 3. Freedom of Religious Opinions and Rights of Conscience	41
Section 4. Freedom of Religion	42
Section 5. Religious Test for Office	43
Section 6. Public Money for Benefit of Religious or Theological Institutions	43
Section 7. Witness Competent Regardless of Religious Opinions	44
Section 8. Oath or Affirmation; Administration	44
Section 9. Right of Free Thought, Speech, Writing and Printing; Abuse of Right	45
Section 10. Truth in Prosecution for Libel	46
Section 11. Unreasonable Search or Seizure; Warrant	47
Section 12. Courts Open; Remedy by Due Course of Law; Administration of Justice	48
Section 13. Rights of Accused in Criminal Prosecutions	49
Section 14. Double Jeopardy and Self-Incrimination	51
Section 15. Persons Arrested or Confined; Treatment	53
Section 16. Excessive Bail or Fines and Cruel and Unusual Punishment	53
Section 17. Right to Bail and Unbailable Offenses	55
Section 18. Penal Code Founded on Reformation	55
Section 19. Right of Jury to Determine Law and Facts in Criminal Cases	56

Section 20. Trial by Jury in Civil Cases ... 57
Section 21. Right to Compensation for Services and Property ... 59
Section 22. Privileges of Debtor; Imprisonment for Debt ... 60
Section 23. Equal Privileges ... 60
Section 24. Ex Post Facto Laws and Impairing Contracts ... 61
Section 25. Effect of Laws ... 62
Section 26. Suspension of Operation of Law ... 62
Section 27. Suspension of Habeas Corpus; Exception ... 63
Section 28. Treason Against State; Definition ... 63
Section 29. Treason Against State; Proof ... 63
Section 30. Conviction; Effect ... 64
Section 31. Right to Assemble, to Instruct and to Petition ... 64
Section 32. Bearing Arms ... 65
Section 33. Military Subordinate to Civil Power ... 65
Section 34. Quartering of Soldiers ... 66
Section 35. Titles of Nobility and Hereditary Distinctions ... 66
Section 36. Freedom of Emigration ... 66
Section 37. Slavery and Involuntary Servitude ... 67

Article II: Suffrage and Elections ... 69

Section 1. Free and Equal Elections ... 69
Section 2. Voting Qualifications ... 70
Section 3. Members of Armed Forces; Residence ... 70
Section 4. Residence; Absence from State ... 71
Section 5. Repealed ... 71
Section 6. Disqualification for Bribery ... 71
Section 7. Repealed ... 72
Section 8. Conviction of Infamous Crime ... 72
Section 9. Holder of Lucrative Office; Eligibility ... 72
Section 10. Collectors and Holders of Public Money; Eligibility ... 73
Section 11. Pro Tempore Appointment; Term of Office ... 74
Section 12. Freedom from Arrest of Electors; Exceptions ... 74
Section 13. Election Methods ... 75
Section 14. Time of Elections; Judges of Courts; Registration of Voters ... 75

Article III: Distribution of Powers ... 77

Section 1. Three Separate Departments ... 77

Article IV: Legislative ... 81

Section 1. General Assembly; Composition; Style of Law ... 81
Section 2. Senate and House of Representatives; Membership ... 82
Section 3. Senators and Representatives; Tenure ... 83

Section 4. Vacancies in General Assembly	83
Section 5. Legislative Apportionment	84
Section 6. Repealed	85
Section 7. Senators and Representatives; Qualifications	85
Section 8. Legislative Immunity; Exceptions	86
Section 9. Sessions of General Assembly	87
Section 10. Selection of Officers; Rules of Proceedings; Adjournment	87
Section 11. Quorum	88
Section 12. Journal; Entry of Yeas and Nays	88
Section 13. Open Session and Committee Meetings	89
Section 14. Discipline of Members	89
Section 15. Contempt by Non-Members; Punishment	90
Section 16. Legislative Powers	90
Section 17. Bills; Raising Revenue	91
Section 18. Reading and Passage of Bills	92
Section 19. One Subject Acts; Exceptions	92
Section 20. Acts and Resolutions; Plain Language	93
Section 21. Repealed	93
Section 22. Local and Special Laws; Restrictions	94
Section 23. General and Uniform Laws	95
Section 24. Right to Sue the State	96
Section 25. Passage of Bills and Resolutions; Signing	97
Section 26. Protest by Members; Entry of Dissent on Journal	97
Section 27. Public Laws	98
Section 28. Effective Dates of Acts	98
Section 29. Compensation of Members; Conditions	99
Section 30. Holding of Public Office; Eligibility	100
Article V: Executive	**101**
Section 1. Governor; Term of Office	101
Section 2. Lieutenant Governor; Term of Office	102
Section 3. Election of Governor and Lieutenant Governor	102
Section 4. Method of Voting	102
Section 5. Tie Vote	102
Section 6. Contested Elections of Governor and Lieutenant Governor	103
Section 7. Qualifications of Governor and Lieutenant Governor	103
Section 8. Ineligible Persons	103
Section 9. Term of Office; Commencement	104
Section 10. Vacancies and Disabilities; Succession	104
Section 11. President of the Senate	106
Section 12. Commander-in-Chief	106

Section 13. Messages by Governor to General Assembly ... 107
Section 14. Presentment of Bills for Signature; Veto Power ... 107
Section 15. Administrative Officers and Departments ... 109
Section 16. Laws Faithfully Executed ... 109
Section 17. Pardons and Reprieves; Exceptions ... 110
Section 18. Vacancies; Filling during Recess ... 111
Section 19. Repealed ... 112
Section 20. Meeting Place of General Assembly ... 112
Section 21. Functions and Duties of Lieutenant Governor ... 112
Section 22. Compensation of Governor ... 112
Section 23. Compensation of Lieutenant Governor ... 113
Section 24. Dual Holding of Office ... 113

Article VI: Administrative ... 115

Section 1. State Officers; Secretary; Auditor and Treasurer; Election ... 115
Section 2. County Officers; Clerk of Circuit Court; Auditor, Treasurer, Sheriff, Coroner and Surveyor; Election ... 116
Section 3. Election or Appointment of Other County and Township Officers ... 117
Section 4. County Officers; Qualifications ... 117
Section 5. State Officers; Residence ... 118
Section 6. Local Officers; Residence ... 118
Section 7. State Officers; Removal Methods; Impeachment ... 118
Section 8. State, County, Township and Town Officers; Impeachment and Removal ... 119
Section 9. County, Township and Town Offices; Vacancies ... 119
Section 10. Powers of County Boards ... 120
Section 11. Repealed ... 120

Article VII: Judicial ... 121

Section 1. Judicial Power ... 121
Section 2. Supreme Court ... 123
Section 3. Chief Justice ... 123
Section 4. Jurisdiction of Supreme Court ... 124
Section 5. Court of Appeals ... 125
Section 6. Jurisdiction of Court of Appeals ... 125
Section 7. Judicial Circuits ... 126
Section 8. Circuit Courts ... 127
Section 9. Judicial Nominating Commission ... 127
Section 10. Selection of Justices of the Supreme Court and Judges of the Court of Appeals ... 128

Section 11. Tenure of Justices of the Supreme Court and
          Judges of the Court of Appeals   129
Section 12. Substitution of Judges   130
Section 13. Removal of Circuit Court Judges and
          Prosecuting Attorneys   131
Section 14. Repealed   131
Section 15. No Limitation on Term of Office   131
Section 16. Prosecuting Attorneys   132
Section 17. Grand Jury   132
Section 18. Criminal Prosecutions   132
Section 19. Pay   132
Section 20. Repealed   133
Section 21. Repealed   133

Article VIII: Education   135

Section 1. Common Schools System   135
Section 2. Common School Fund   136
Section 3. Principal and Income of Fund   137
Section 4. Investment and Distribution of Fund Interest   138
Section 5. Reinvestment of Unused Interest   138
Section 6. Preservation of Fund by Counties; Liability   138
Section 7. State Trust Funds Inviolate   139
Section 8. State Superintendent of Public Instruction   139

Article IX: State Institutions   141

Section 1. Institutions for the Deaf, Mute, Blind, and Insane   141
Section 2. Institutions for Juvenile Offenders   142
Section 3. County Asylum Farms   142

Article X: Public Finance   143

Section 1. Property Assessment and Taxation   143
Section 2. Public Debt; Payment   145
Section 3. Appropriations Made by Law   146
Section 4. Receipts and Expenditures; Publication   146
Section 5. State Debt; Requirements   146
Section 6. Corporation Stock and Subscription by Counties;
          State Assumption of County Debts   147
Section 7. Wabash and Erie Canal   148
Section 8. Income Tax; Levy and Collection Authorized   148

Article XI: Corporations   151

Section 1. Banks; Banking Companies and
          Moneyed Institutions; Incorporation   151

Section 2. General Banking Laws; Exception	152
Section 3. Registry by State of Votes	152
Section 4. Banks and Branches of Banks; Charter	153
Section 5. Bank Branches Mutually Liable	153
Section 6. Repealed	153
Section 7. Redemption of Bills and Notes	153
Section 8. Holders of Bank Notes	154
Section 9. Interest Rates	154
Section 10. Repealed	154
Section 11. Trust Funds; Investment in Banks with Branches	155
Section 12. State as Stockholder in Banks; Prohibition	155
Section 13. Corporations Other Than Banking; Creation	156
Section 14. Liability of Stockholders	156

Article XII: Militia — 157

Section 1. Membership	157
Section 2. Commander-in-Chief	158
Section 3. Adjutant General	158
Section 4. Conscientious Objectors	158
Section 5. Repealed	159
Section 6. Repealed	159

Article XIII: Municipal Debt — 161

Section 1. Limitations on Debt; Excess; Exceptions	161
Section 2. Repealed	162
Section 3. Repealed	162
Section 4. Repealed	163

Article XIV: Boundaries — 165

Section 1. Boundaries of State Established	165
Section 2. Jurisdiction and Sovereignty	166

Article XV: Miscellaneous — 167

Section 1. Nonconstitutional Officers; Appointment	167
Section 2. Term of Office	168
Section 3. Holding Over of Office Pending Successor	168
Section 4. Oath of Affirmation of Office	169
Section 5. Seal of State	169
Section 6. Commission Issued by State	169
Section 7. Areas of Counties	170
Section 8. Repealed	170
Section 9. State Grounds in Indianapolis	170
Section 10. Tippecanoe Battle Ground	170

Article XVI: Amendments   **171**

   Section 1. Constitutional Amendments; Procedure   171
   Section 2. Multiple Amendments; Separate Vote   172

Table of Cases   173
Index   185
About the Author   189

■ SERIES FOREWORD

In 1776, following the declaration of independence from England, the former colonies began to draft their own constitutions. Their handiwork attracted widespread interest, and draft constitutions circulated up and down the Atlantic seaboard, as constitution-makers sought to benefit from the insights of their counterparts in sister states. In Europe, the new constitutions found a ready audience seeking enlightenment from the American experiments in selfgovernment. Even the delegates to the Constitutional Convention of 1787, despite their reservations about the course of political developments in the states during the decade after independence, found much that was useful in the newly adopted constitutions. And when James Madison, fulfilling a pledge given during the ratification debates, drafted the federal Bill of Rights, he found his model in the famous Declaration of Rights of the Virginia Constitution.

By the 1900s, however, few people would have looked to state constitutions for enlightenment. Instead, a familiar litany of complaints was heard whenever state constitutions were mentioned. State constitutions were too long and too detailed, combining basic principles with policy prescriptions and prohibitions that had no place in the fundamental law of a state. By including such provisions, it was argued, state constitutions deprived state governments of the flexibility they needed to respond effectively to changing circumstances. This—among other factors—encouraged political reformers to look to the federal government, which was not plagued by such constitutional constraints, thereby shifting the locus of political initiative away from the states. Meanwhile, civil libertarians concluded that state bills of rights, at least as interpreted by state courts, did not adequately protect rights and therefore looked to the federal courts and the federal Bill of Rights for redress. As power and responsibility shifted from the states to Washington, so too did the attention of scholars, the legal community, and the general public.

During the early 1970s, however, state constitutions were "rediscovered." The immediate impetus for this rediscovery was former President Richard Nixon's appointment of Warren Burger to succeed Earl Warren as Chief Justice of the United States Supreme Court. To civil libertarians, this appointment seemed to signal a decisive shift in the Supreme Court's jurisprudence, because Burger was expected to lead the Court away from the liberal activism that had characterized the Warren Court. They therefore sought ways to safeguard the gains they had achieved for defendants, racial minorities, and the poor during Warren's tenure from erosion by the Burger Court. In particular, they began to look to state bills of rights to secure the rights of defendants and to support other civil-liberties claims that they advanced in state courts.

The "new judicial federalism," as it came to be called, quite quickly advanced beyond its initial concern to evade the mandates of the Burger Court. Indeed, less than two decades after it originated, it has become a nationwide phenomenon. For when judges and scholars turned their attention to state constitutions, they discovered an unsuspected richness. They found not only provisions that paralleled the federal Bill of Rights but also constitutional guarantees of the right to privacy and of gender equality, for example, that had no analogue in the U.S. Constitution. Careful examination of the text and history of state guarantees revealed important differences between even those provisions that most resembled federal guarantees and their federal counterparts. Looking beyond state declarations of rights, jurists and scholars discovered affirmative constitutional mandates to state governments to address such important policy concerns as education and housing. Taken altogether, these discoveries underlined the importance for the legal community of developing a better understanding of state constitutions.

Yet the renewed interest in state constitutions has not been limited to judges and lawyers. State constitutional reformers have renewed their efforts with notable success: since 1960, ten states have adopted new constitutions and several others have undertaken major constitutional revisions. These changes have usually resulted in more streamlined constitutions and more effective state governments. Also, in recent years political activists on both the left and the right have pursued their goals through state constitutional amendments, often enacted through the initiative process, under which policy proposals can be placed directly on the ballot for voters to endorse or reject. Scholars too have begun to rediscover how state constitutional history can illuminate changes in political thought and practice, providing a basis for theories about the dynamics of political change in America.

William P. McLauchlan's excellent study of the Indiana Constitution is the latest volume in the series, The Oxford Commentaries to the State Constitutions of the United States, which reflects this renewed interest in state constitutions and will contribute to our knowledge about them. Because the constitutional tradition of each state is distinctive, the volume begins with the history and development of the Indiana Constitution. It then provides the complete text of Indiana's current constitution, with each section accompanied by commentary that explains the provision and traces its origins and its interpretation by the courts and by other governmental bodies. Finally, the book concludes with a table of cases cited in the history and the constitutional commentary, as well as a subject index.

G. Alan Tarr

■ ACKNOWLEDGMENTS

Several people have contributed to the work on this volume. Among the most important is Professor G. Alan Tarr, series editor, who first suggested the idea that I might undertake this project. His patience, his scholarly judgment, and his "eye" have greatly improved the final product. Bob Bauman, my attorney, provided much more important support than mere legal advice. Professor Robert Browning provided a number of references for this work, plus some perspectives on Indiana that were quite valuable. The librarians in the Indiana Supreme Court Law Library and those connected with the Indiana Historical Bureau helped in a number of ways that only they could provide.

Several students contributed mightily to this effort through research and through their thoughts and discussions regarding the materials in this work. Roy Anderson and Christy Short did a good deal of research on parts of this book. I hope their efforts were worth it to them, because their thinking and extra effort are evidenced in this volume. Trevor Beldon and Jennifer Hoelzel, perhaps the epitomes of Dean's Freshman Scholars, brought an energy and enthusiasm to the research and the subject that was refreshing, but also enlightening. May neither of them lose that taste for the topic or for scholarship in general. The vision of David Caputo, Dean of the School of Liberal Arts here at Purdue, should be commended for the support and the climate that made this possible.

PART ONE
The History of the Indiana Constitution

The history of the current Indiana Constitution is largely in two parts. A constitutional convention unilaterally adopted the Constitution of 1816 as a prelude to statehood.[1] The second part of the history began in 1851, when the voters of the state replaced the original 1816 Constitution with a new one drafted by a constitutional convention. The 1851 Constitution is still in place, with some 90 amendments, replacements, or repealed provisions. These have included minor, necessary technical corrections, and fundamental revisions that restructure institutions, define rights more clearly, or outline new policy procedures. Yet, despite these changes, the 1851 Constitution remains operational today, largely with the original provisions and some "modernized" sections or articles.

The longevity of this constitution speaks generally to the conservative political perspectives held by many in the state. In addition, the procedure for amending the constitution made it very difficult to amend until the 1930s, when a more moderate interpretation of the process facilitated some amending. That means the analysis of this constitution is largely a story of judicial interpretation and the political difficulties of changing the original document. There have been no

---

[1] The original version of this and other documents relating to Indiana constitutional development can be found in the multivolume work: Charles Kettleborough, *Constitution Making in Indiana: A Source Book of Constitutional Documents with Historical Introduction and Critical Notes* (Indianapolis: Indiana Historical Bureau, 1971).

changes or interpretations of some of the sections of the 1851 Constitution. It is as if these original provisions were conclusive, and there has been no need for any amplification or adjustment of them. At the other extreme, sections or whole articles have been replaced or modernized. However, most of the provisions in the constitution have changed somewhat in wording or meaning.

THE 1816 CONSTITUTION

The striking features of the original constitution under which Indiana entered the union in 1816 are that it reflected a then-modern approach to constitutionalism, supposedly a Jeffersonian or Republican approach to the organization of government. It was not a unique or peculiar constitution, original in all its features. Rather, it was very much like other state constitutions of the time. The document was general rather than specific. This constitution emphasized a set of broad principles rather than technical specifics that the drafters, who were Jeffersonian Republicans, felt the organic act should include. It was these general provisions about the structures and powers of government that the framers thought would permit adjustment or adaptation of the constitution in the future. That is not unlike the orientation of the 1787 version of the United States Constitution. The result of this generality was that the state was able to function under the Indiana Constitution of 1816. It is not clear that the original document was masterful and successful, but it was satisfactory for purposes of the westward expansion and development in the state at the time.

The antecedent events leading to the 1816 Constitutional Convention began with the Northwest Ordinance of 1787.[2] The Northwest Territory formed the basis for the creation of the Indiana Territory in 1800,[3] and President John Adams appointed William Henry Harrison the first territorial governor.[4] This began the "first stage" of territorial government in presentday Indiana, in 1800. That phase involved an appointed territorial governor with nearly complete power over the lawmaking functions of government. In addition, local judges, appointed by the governor, insured the implementation of policies and the enforcement of laws in the territory.

The 1800 enactment recognized that the original Northwest Territory was too ungainly for government because of its size, and that it was too large to foster the development of individual states. The Northwest Territory became two separate territories at that time. The first, eastern part eventually became the State

---

[2] 32 *Journals of the Continental Congress*, 334–343. Much of this discussion derives from John Barnhart and Donald Carmony, *Indiana: From Frontier to Industrial Commonwealth*, vol. I (New York: Lewis Historical Pub. Co., 1954). Hereinafter cited Barnhart & Carmony.

[3] *Annals of Congress*, 6th Cong., 1 Sess., 645, 649, 1489–1500.

[4] Barnhart & Carmony, vol. I, 95.

of Ohio in 1803. The western part of the territory encompassed everything else northwest of the Ohio River, east of the Mississippi River, south of the Canadian border, and west of present-day Ohio. Subsequent modifications of the boundaries of the "Indian Territory" occurred as Michigan separated into its own territory in 1805,[5] and Illinois became another separate territory in 1809.[6]

Indiana officially passed into the second territorial stage in 1804.[7] For this representative stage of development, the legislature had the political or governing authority. Efforts to obtain Indiana statehood began energetically in 1811, but the failure of the territory to meet the minimum population of 60,000 (set by the Northwest Ordinance[8]) and the eruption of the War of 1812 with Britain sidetracked these initial efforts at full-fledged statehood.

The Indiana legislature submitted another memorial to Congress in 1816, after the 1815 census indicated the presence of 63,897 people in the territory. This memorial sought authority to hold a constitutional convention, and it specified several features of authority that the Territorial Legislature requested the U.S. Congress to include in its approval. These regarded the generation of public revenue.[9] Congress approved the election of delegates to a constitutional convention on May 13, 1816.[10] That convention was to convene on June 10, 1816. This congressional approval was in conjunction with a similar enabling act for Mississippi. This seems to have been the first instance of the "twin state" process, allowing for the simultaneous statehood of two states, one slave (Mississippi) and one free (Indiana).

The constitutional convention drafted the constitution in Corydon, the first capital of the state. This first Indiana Constitution drew heavily from the existent Ohio and Kentucky constitutions. The Indiana version used much of these documents verbatim, with a few minor exceptions. The major provisions of the document included an explicit tripartite governmental structure with a dominant legislature that would meet annually. The governor served for a three-year term, and that officeholder could hold the office for only six out of every nine years.

---

[5] *Acts Passed at the Second Session of the Eighth Congress of the United States*, 241–243.

[6] *Annals of Congress*, 10th Cong., 2 Sess., 1808–1810.

[7] Barnhart & Carmony, vol. I, 107.

[8] *Annals of Congress*, 12th Cong., 1 Sess., 607, 749, 1247.

[9] The 1815 Memorial sought to give Indiana 7 percent of the sale of public lands, one section of each township for the support of public education, and the reservation of three full townships for an academy, a college, and a state capital. The memorial also explicitly specified the intention to be a free state.

[10] The Enabling Act of 1816 specified several features that were to be included in the constitution of the state:

- The boundaries of the state were outlined, with concurrent jurisdiction over the Wabash River, with Illinois.
- One U.S. representative until the next general census.

In addition, the Enabling Act also specified the boundaries of the state-to-be.

Acts Passed at the First Session of the Fourteenth Congress of the United States, 59–61.

The legislature could override gubernatorial vetoes by a simple majority vote in both houses. Members of the bicameral legislature served for annual terms in the case of the House of Representatives and three years in the case of senators. The state supreme court headed the judicial system, and the circuit courts had general jurisdiction over legal issues. The General Assembly could create additional, inferior courts. The governor of the state appointed the judges of the supreme court, but this required the advice and consent of the state senate. All judges served for seven-year terms, as long as they behaved "well." The president of the circuit courts (the presiding officer) was appointed jointly by both houses of the legislature, and the voters of the jurisdiction selected the remainder of the circuit courts by popular ballot.

The first article of the 1816 Constitution contained the Bill of Rights, and that article afforded the people of Indiana many of the rights contained in the U.S. Constitution. "The People" explicitly had inherent political power in this constitution. This made the people of the state the political sovereigns. There were freedoms of worship, speech, press, peaceable assembly, and the right to bear arms. There were also a number of procedural protections for persons accused of crimes, as well as protections from unreasonable treatment relating to bail, punishments, and searches and seizures. The wording of these differed from the Bill of Rights in the U.S. Constitution; that is largely due to the Indiana Constitution following the model of other midwestern states, such as Ohio and Kentucky. However, the origins of these protections were also evident from the U.S. Constitution or the Declaration of Independence.

All white males 21 years of age or older who had resided in the state for a year had the right to vote. Eighteen- to 45-year-old white males, who resided in the state, made up the militia. "Negroes, Mulattoes and Indians" were explicitly excluded from membership in the militia. The constitution prohibited slavery and involuntary servitude, according to an interpretation of the constitution by the Indian Supreme Court. The actual wording of the constitution would allow earlier indentures (i.e., before 1816).

One significant contribution of the 1816 Constitution was the liberal provision for a "general system of education, ascending in a regular graduation, from township schools to a state university, wherein tuition shall be gratis, and equally open to all." The qualifying words, "as soon as circumstances will permit" (Article IX, section 2), left this promise unfulfilled by the General Assembly until it was replaced in the 1851 Constitution. However, the principle of free public education stands as a clear mark of interest in and the importance of an educated electorate. The drafters had no underlying reasoning for this provision. Rather, the earlier state constitutions served as models for this part of the Indiana organic act.

The Constitution of 1816 became effective immediately upon the signature of the convention delegates, on June 29, 1816. The people of Indiana did not ratify it. They had no opportunity to vote on the constitution, even though the constitution explicitly indicated "the People" possessed inherent sovereign political power in the state. The first election of legislators and the governor occurred in August of 1816.

Provisions of the 1816 Constitution that caused some controversy included the location of the state capital in Corydon until 1825, when the General Assembly could select any site it wanted. The usual competition for the capital eventually resulted in the selection of a neutral location, Indianapolis. It had no built-in beneficiaries, and it was close to the geographic middle of the state.

Another point of concern was the form of voting provided for in the 1816 Constitution. For the first five years of the operation of the constitution, voting was by secret ballot. In 1821, the General Assembly had the opportunity to change the form of voting to a voice vote, which some people favored. However, if there was no change in 1821 by the legislature, then the secret ballot would remain in place, not subject to any other legislative alteration. In 1820, the legislature decided that the voters should indicate their preference on this issue, but there is no record of the vote. Either there was no vote taken in 1820 or the change in voting was defeated. In 1821, the General Assembly had to face the issue anyway, but it adjourned without acting on it. The issue largely disappeared from public debate, perhaps because it was not open to change and people saw value in a secret rather than a public vote.

The 1816 Constitution contained no provision for amending the document, and that created much of the controversy that surrounded it. There was a provision in the constitution that every twelve years the voters of Indiana (called "Electors") would be given the opportunity to express their preference on calling a constitutional convention. If a majority of all the voters at the election voted for a convention, the General Assembly was to provide for the election of convention delegates. There was an exception in the 1816 Constitution that prevented any subsequent constitutional convention from permitting slavery or involuntary servitude in Indiana (Article VII, section 1). Apparently, this prohibition was required by the Northwest Ordinance.

The first question that arose under this constitutional provision was whether the legislature was limited to providing the voters with the choice only once every twelve years, or whether the call for a convention could be presented more often. This resulted in a great deal of debate and discussion, as well as disagreement, generally along party lines. The Democrats supported the view that the authority to call a convention involved the politically sovereign people who could amend their constitution whenever they wished. Thus, the legislature could seek to call a convention whenever it thought appropriate. The Whigs, on the other hand, viewed the wording more restrictively and supported the rigid, only-once-in-twelve-years rule. The Democrats largely controlled the General Assembly during the 1820s and 1830s, so the submission of calls was more frequent than once in twelve years, and the proposals for calls were even more frequent. Actual calls for a constitutional convention were presented to the voters five times in the span of 26 years—1823, 1828, 1840, 1846, and 1849. There were another fourteen attempts during this same period in the legislature to call a convention—1820, 1821, 1826, 1827, 1829, 1830, 1831, 1833, 1835, 1836, 1841, 1844, 1845, and 1847—but these were all voted down in one or both houses. Table 1 indicates the votes of the people on convention calls and the major issues where these are evident.

A great many broad and narrow issues provided arguments for changing the 1816 Constitution. They focused on fiscal matters, specific mechanisms for governance in the constitution, and local issues. It is accurate to say that two primary issues caused the most concern about the 1816 Constitution over the period of its existence. First, some criticized the annual sessions of the legislature as unnecessary, and most importantly, too expensive. The proponents of moving to biennial sessions of the legislature frequently argued that the General Assembly cost too much money and did too little of importance to justify annual meetings.

The other frequent item of discussion involved this problem, and may have caused it: the need for a change in the process of removing local officials. The 1816 Constitution required impeachment by the General Assembly for their

TABLE 1 *Record of Proposed Calls for Constitutional Conventions in Indiana between 1823 and 1851*

Year	Vote for Convention	Vote against Convention	Notes
1823	2,601	11,991	—Biennial legislative sessions
			— The governor's authority to call special or emergency sessions of the legislature
			—Abolition of the office of associate judge
			—Local officer removal by circuit courts
			—Circuit courts granting divorces
			—Popularizing supreme court judge selection
			—General Assembly fixing the time and place of meetings
1828	10,092	18,633	—Biennial legislative sessions
			—Local officer removal by circuit courts
			—Voice voting
1840	12,666	62,714	No particular issues
1846	32,468	27,123	—Biennial (or triennial) legislative six-week sessions
			—Abolition of associate judgeships
			—Modernizing the judiciary
			—Modernizing the judiciary
			—Reform of the probate system
			—Abolition of local and special legislation
			—Prohibiting the legislature from granting divorces
1849	81,500	57,418	No particular issues

removal, and charges of fraud, criminal behavior, or just political skullduggery were raised against a good many local officials. Impeachment processes took a great deal of the state legislature's time and attention, and distracted it from substantive policy considerations. Some observers felt that another constitutional process for removal (perhaps involving courts) would work better for dealing with these kinds of local problems.

The first convention call, in 1823, was the most widely and hotly debated in the legislature and the popular press. That was partly because this call was *not* at the twelve-year period (which would occur in 1828), and many were uncertain about the authority of the legislature to seek to call a convention so early. Others debated it because there was concern that the press for a convention was coming from Kentucky interests focused on the slavery issue. However, this last point was clearly an implicit undertone in the 1823 debate. The popular vote for the convention in 1823 was overwhelmingly negative.

The 1828 call was constitutional, if only because it was the twelfth year after the beginning of the constitution. However, there were no clear issues that sparked the call and, in fact, there were distractions that led to the defeat of the call. The national Jacksonian Democracy movement was quite visible in 1828, and the call for the convention seemed lost in comparison. There was no major controversy to attract voters' attention to the convention, and the call was rejected by a wide margin.

The next call for a convention, again at the twelve-year point, in 1840, also disappeared in the national concerns of the time. There were no specific or unique issues that underwrote the call, and the popular vote on the convention was clearly negative. It seems the 1840 call was largely the result of the requirement in the constitution rather than any pressing issues. (However, from the number of efforts that failed in the legislature [five] during the 1830s, clearly few individuals or legislators thought there were problems with the constitution that needed correcting.)

The 1846 call was very striking for several reasons. First, some of the issues, both old ones like the biennial session of the legislature and newer issues like concerns over local and special legislation, were in evidence. Eventually, these issues would undergird the drafting of the new, 1851 Constitution, since they had become more significant problems for many in the state. There was much activity among other states of the union to amend their constitutions at this time, so this effort in Indiana was part of a larger movement or effort at constitutional modernization. The national issues involving Oregon and Mexico were confounding issues, but they were nevertheless present at the time.

The most interesting or surprising feature of the 1846 call was that it won a majority vote among the electors in 1846. This presented a question that would plague the state for nearly a century, under two different constitutions with different amending procedures. The problem was that the 32,468-to-27,123 vote in favor of the constitutional convention was only a plurality. It was *not* an absolute majority of all the voters in Indiana (126,969 electors). The actual provision of the 1816 Constitution read:

> if there should be a majority of all the votes given at such election, in favour of a convention, the Governor shall inform the next General Assembly thereof, whose duty it shall be to provide, by law, for the election of the members to the convention, . . . (Article VIII)

There are three questions that this provision and the 1846 vote generated.

First, can the General Assembly submit a call for a constitutional convention other than in the twelfth year? The practice and convention of some 30 years indicated that it could, but since the voters of Indiana had finally voted "yes" on a call that was out of sequence, the question arose again. No one actually challenged the practice or the outcome on this ground at the time, even though it concerned some observers.

Second, there is the question of what "majority" of votes the 1816 constitutional provision required to support the actual calling of the convention. The possible answers to this question ranged from the plurality of those voting on the call to a majority of all voters casting votes in the election. The second answer would have required a majority of all the voters casting votes in the election. That answer would have defeated the call in this case. A third answer required an absolute majority of all the electors, whether they voted in the election or not. The call for a convention clearly failed by that measure. There was no agreement among observers in 1846 about which answer would govern the legislature's actions after the election of 1846.

The third question was whether the General Assembly could refuse to call the convention by *not* passing the necessary enabling laws, regardless of what the popular vote on the call was. The wording of the constitutional provision might be "recommendatory." That means the legislature did not have to take action or even consider the popular vote on the issue as binding on their actions.

The voters dealt with an original convention call presented by a Democratic majority in 1846. After the election of 1846, the Democrats lacked a majority in either house. The House of Representatives postponed consideration of the enabling legislation for a convention, and the Senate tabled an identical proposal. This 1846 call for a constitutional convention ended in the legislature, after the popular vote yielded a mixed or unclear picture of the people's preferences, and the partisanship in the legislature prevented further action.

This trouble with amending the constitution did not end the problems or the concerns about constitutional change. The pre-1851 era involved efforts at state building and economic development; some of these endeavors were more successful than others. However, the geographic distance, the lack of developed transportation systems, and the early settlement patterns along the Ohio and Wabash rivers rather than in the interior of the state left Indiana an emerging entity with little significance in national politics, and limited internal cohesion or capability.

One set of forces pushing Indiana toward revision on its constitution at this time was several specific events or "problems" in addition to the perennial ones that have been discussed already. Many advocated that these problems should have a direct constitutional remedy. The problems arose from the state's extensive Internal Improvements Act of 1836 which caused the state to overextend itself with a debt of over $10 million by the 1840s. The eventual economic repercussions led many to advocate a constitutional prohibition against the state's engaging in deficit spending, and a prohibition against assuming the debts of private investors or companies. In addition, there was a general reluctance to allow local governments to become indebted either.

Another set of concerns involved the multiplicity of local and special legislation that siphoned off a great deal of the General Assembly's time. Repeated and frequent efforts in the state legislature to deal with local traffic regulations and ordinances was an obvious effort at "micromanagement" that many observers felt was not necessary for the legislature. Many thought this an acceptable activity for the state legislature, but others thought it beneath their dignity and a waste of state resources in light of the broader policy concerns facing the state.

The governor asked the legislature for a convention call to deal with the problems of the costs and delay regarding local and special legislation, the biennial session of the legislature, and prohibitions against public debt. The governor thought the twelve-year rule on convention calls was not binding, and the people could vote on another proposed convention right after the 1846 vote. The Democratic Party supported a call for a convention, and it controlled both houses of the legislature as well as the governorship. The opposition, the Whigs, were in such disarray that there was no effective opposition to the position taken by the Democrats.

Thus, in 1849 the people had another opportunity to call a constitutional convention. The vote in that election was 81,500 in favor and 57,418 against the proposal. Given the number of voters in the state at the time, the majority in favor was an absolute majority, so the earlier questions about the required majority did not arise. The 1849 General Assembly, again controlled by Democrats, provided for the election of 150 delegates to the convention.

TABLE 2 *Delegates to the Indiana Constitutional Convention of 1851*

	Democrats	Whighs
Senate Districts	33 (66%)	17 (33%)
House Districts	62 (62%)	38 (38%)
Total	95 (63.3)	55 (36.6)

Although the Whigs were a party in decline, they adopted a set of resolutions indicating the kinds of changes they advocated for the convention to consider:

- The direct election of all legislative and judicial officers.
- The expansion of suffrage to all native and naturalized citizens 21 years or older.
- The prohibition on public debt, except through direct vote by the people.
- Additional funds to the common school fund.
- The abolition of local legislation.
- A reduction in the number and salaries of officials.
- A homestead exemption from forced sale.

This action incensed the Democrats because the Whigs apparently stole or claimed a good many of the issues that Democrats favored. The Democrats approved a similar list of proposals but denied they were Whig principles. The Whigs argued that the convention should not be partisan. Other segments of leadership in the state also advocated a nonpartisan convention. However, in the end, the only way to characterize the Constitutional Convention of 1851 was in partisan terms. Table 2 indicates its partisan makeup:

There is one important note to make of the operation of the 1816 Constitution and the problems or difficulties in amending it. The legislature did try (unsuccessfully) to obtain amendments with specific legislative enactments. Then voters could consider those without a convention. The two substantive problems of most concern in this regard were the biennial legislature issue and the removal of local officials. This informal process, first advocated in the mid-1820s, suggested the legislature could enact a statute to amend the constitution. The voters would consider these enactments at the next election. Those laws the voters adopted or approved would be the basis for the next legislature constituting itself as a constitutional convention to adopt the people's wishes as they had just voted.

The House explicitly rejected this complicated procedure, even if constitutional, in 1826. However, advocates tried this mechanism and others like it repeatedly before 1851. This suggests the difficulties that some saw with the 1816 Constitution. Many devoted a great deal of time and energy to overcoming the 1816 amending process. These efforts to circumvent the process also provided a basis for attempts to change the 1851 Constitution.

THE CONSTITUTION OF 1851

The constitutional convention delegates were apportioned among Senate and House districts. The convention met from October 7, 1850, through February 10, 1851, The constitutional convention organized itself along partisan lines, with the Democrats clearly dictating the result or outcome whenever they thought it important. The convention organized itself into 22 committees to construct and draft various provisions of a constitution. However, items considered by a committee had to come from the entire convention, by referral. There was widespread agreement on a variety of issues or problems that required attention by the convention. However, there was not always the same agreement on the best solution for each problem. Agreement on these problems focused on:

- The need for as many offices as possible, both state and local, to be directly and popularly elected.
- The need to expand the franchise to include native and naturalized citizens.

There was less agreement but widespread attention paid to several issues:

- Biennial legislative sessions and legislative powers.
- Local and special legislation.
- The impeachment and removal process for local officers.

The ways used to address these issues provide the basic outline of the 1851 Constitution. However, some of the new provisions did not solve the problem, and other provisions generated unanticipated difficulties that would continue for some time. The delegates addressed a variety of the specific concerns that held their attention. They borrowed their solutions from then-modern state constitutions such as Illinois and Wisconsin because many thought the way to modernize Indiana's organic act was to adopt the modern constitutions of neighboring states. If those instruments did not contain the "right" solution or any solution at all, the Indiana framers drafted their own provisions.

The voters of Indiana approved the 1851 Constitutional Convention's work, on August 4, 1851, by a vote of 82,564 to 26,755. In addition, the voters voted separately on the issue of a Negro and Mulatto exclusion provision. The voters displayed a clear preference for excluding slaves from the state, adopting that provision overwhelmingly (Article XIII).[11] The Constitution of 1851 took effect November 1, 1851. In general, the constitution was Jacksonian, moving to democratize many aspects of government. It expanded the franchise to "every white male citizen of the United States, of the age of twenty-one years and

---

[11] The provision, since removed from the constitution, read:

Section 1. No Negro or Mulatto shall come into or settle in the State, after the adoption of this Constitution.

Section 2. All contracts made with any Negro or Mulatto coming into the State, contrary to the provisions of the foregoing section, shall be void; and any person who shall employ such Negro or Mulatto, or otherwise encourage him to remain in the State, shall be fined in any sum not less than ten dollars, nor more than five hundred dollars.

Section 3. All fines which may be collected for a violation of the provisions of this article, or of any law which may hereafter be passed for the purpose of carrying the same into execution shall be set apart and appropriated for the colonization of such Negroes and Mulattoes, and their descendants, as may be in the State at the adoption of this Constitution, and may be willing to emigrate.

Section 4. The General Assembly shall pass laws to carry out the provisions of this article.

upwards" (Article II, section 2). Most strikingly, the franchise was extended to male noncitizens, as well, who declared their intention to become citizens. This suffrage expansion reached nonproperty owners as well as noncitizens, but it obviously did not reach women or blacks. Article II, section 5 explicitly prohibited Negroes and Mulattoes from voting, but there was not explicit treatment of women. The provision did not include any residency requirement and that became a point of controversy. A qualified voter could vote anywhere in the state, and subsequent practice led to repeated efforts to amend the constitution to prevent electoral fraud and abuse by various individuals and groups.

The 1851 Constitution reduced the legislature to a biennial body (Article IV, section 9) with a limited session of 61 days (Article IV, section 29). This session limit was a point of debate, because some felt that the biennial session alone would limit the expense of state government enough. However, the advocates believed that limiting the length of the session was necessary to insure that the annual sessions held previously did not exceed the cost and the time that the biennial sessions had displayed under the 1816 Constitution. The constitution specifically prohibited the General Assembly from enacting local or special laws (Article IV, section 22). This was a focused effort to prevent the state legislature from spending any more time and energy on matters of local concern. This was a frequently cited problem with the original constitution. Many would regret this new prohibition after its adoption, but the advocates thought it essential to keeping the state legislature's attention on matters of state concern. The state could not go into debt or engage in deficit spending (Article X, section 5). This reflected the concerns some had about the Internal Improvements fiasco of the 1840s. In addition, the General Assembly was prohibited from assuming the debt of any county or other governmental unit, or any corporation (Article X, section 6).

These provisions are restrictions on the actions and authority of the state legislature. They reflect popular reaction to various efforts (and failures?) of the General Assembly under the 1816 Constitution, or the Constitution of 1816 itself. However, the Constitution of 1851 also authorized the General Assembly to enact general legislation relating to the welfare of the state and its citizens (Article IV, section 16). In that regard, the new constitution did not differ from its predecessor. It certainly did not prevent the legislature from performing the usual or traditional work of a popularly elected representative body. In fact, that was clearly the expected function for the General Assembly under the new constitution.

The other, particular features of the new constitution included term limitations on elected executive officials. These eventually became viewed as too severe. However, at the outset, the governor served a four-year term, but was *not* eligible for reelection to a second, consecutive term (Article V, section 1). The state's executive branch included the governor, the lieutenant governor (also a four-year term), the secretary of state (two-year term), the auditor, and the treasurer of the state (two-year term) (Article VI, section I).[12] The latter of these officials could serve no more than four years in any period of six years. Interestingly, the constitution specifies a number of elected county offices. That constitution alizes those offices, rather than making them subject to legislative enactments. The county offices that were specified included:

- clerk of the circuit court (four years).
- county auditor (four years).
- county recorder (four years).
- county treasurer (two years).
- county sheriff (two years).
- county coroner (two years).
- county surveyor (two years).

In addition, the General Assembly could create additional offices if necessary (Article VI, section 3).

These offices also had limited terms, as specified above (Article VI, section 2). None of these officials could serve more than two terms out of three consecutive periods. This "opened" the local political system through more elections and increased the turnover of officeholders. This would insure turnover in local offices that was infrequent under the 1816 Constitution. That would prevent individuals or political factions from holding power for long periods of time, without at least replacing the officeholders with new people.

The judiciary, structured in Article VII of the constitution, differed from that created in 1816. The clerk of the supreme court became a statewide, elected office with a four-year term (Article VII, section 7). However, this official could serve as many terms as desired. There would be a supreme court, with three to five members (Article VII, sections 1 and 2). Their terms of office were for six years, if they "behave well." The constitution authorized the General Assembly to divide the state into as many "districts" as there were judges on the supreme court, in as nearly equal population as could be accomplished. Each of these districts elected one supreme court judge through at-large elections (Article VII, section 3). There was no limitation on the number of terms a judge could serve. The selection process differed from gubernatorial appointment with the advice and consent of the Senate under the 1816 Constitution. The circuit courts were the primary court of general, original jurisdiction. The General Assembly had power to establish additional inferior courts as it deemed appropriate.

---

[12] Two additional, elected state officers were indicated (specified) elsewhere in the constitution: clerk of the supreme court and superintendent of public instruction. Article VII, section 7 and Article VIII, section 8.

The constitution required the supreme court, "upon decision of every case, [to] give a statement in writing of each question arising in the record of such case, and the decision of the Court thereon" (Article VII, section 5). This provision relates to a general antagonism toward the legal profession and the judiciary in 1851. It also appears focused on requiring formal explanation for court decisions.[13] The jurisdiction of the supreme court, both appellate and original, was under the control of the General Assembly (Article VII, section 4). "Every person of good moral character, being a voter, shall be entitled to admission to practice law in all Courts of justice" (Article VII, section 21).[14]

The 1851 Constitution made some progress beyond the 1816 version of the provisions for public education. There was no loophole in the wording that required the General Assembly to provide for a "general and uniform system of Common Schools, wherein tuition shall be without charge, and equally open to all" (Article VII, section 1). Therefore, the legislature could not delay the creation of a public school system. There are other differences between this provision and that of the 1816 Constitution. After 1851, the emphasis was on elementary and secondary education institutions. There was no reference to institutions of higher learning (universities) in the new constitution. This requirement may reflect the underdevelopment of public education in Indiana in 1851; the realization that the state education system should not emphasize a higher education system, or the existence, since 1817, of Indiana University; so there was little continuing need for such attention. There may have been a recognition that the need was for basic education rather than higher education of the populace. The constitution provided for the election, for two-year terms, of a state superintendent of public instruction, with no limit on the number of terms that official could serve (Article VII, section 8).

The constitution included an amending process, but it would become a major source of controversy under the new organic act (Article XVI, section 1). Many thought the constitutional convention provision of the 1816 Constitution was a central flaw in the original organic act. They had repeatedly sought (1) clarification of whether the full twelve years must expire before the General Assembly could propose a convention, and (2) to convene constitutional conventions throughout the 1820s, 1830s, and 1840s without success. There remained the inherent amending power of a constitutional convention although there was no provision for it in the 1851 document. Although there were a number of attempts at calling a convention, a constitutional convention never gained sufficient electoral support.

---

[13] Comment, "Written Opinions in Cases Affirmed by the Appellate Court," 4 *Indiana Law Journal* 200 (1928). This comment indicates the narrow interpretation the supreme court placed on this provision of the constitution in order to avoid the purpose of the constitutional provision.

[14] Interestingly, the constitutional convention rejected an amendment to this provision requiring that lawyers possess the "requisite qualifications."

The amending process provided in the constitution requires that amendments originate in the General Assembly. If a majority of the members of two successive General Assemblies agree, the proposal will be submitted to the voters at the next general election. Ratification of a proposed amendment by a majority of voters would then amend the constitution. While this process seems straightforward and more workable than a convention, its actual operation has proven that amending the constitution is very difficult.

This amending provision does not allow for the calling of a constitutional convention as a method for constitutional change, but that did not prevent subsequent political actors from seeking to call a convention to amend or revise the constitution. The widespread basis for such convention efforts was the underlying principle that the people of Indiana, possessing political sovereignty, could always amend or revise their constitution. However, the silence of the 1851 Constitution about the constitutional convention meant that calling a convention required the same procedure as provided in the 1816 organic act.

Since this mid-nineteenth-century modernization of the Indiana Constitution in 1851, there have been no comprehensive revisions of the Indiana Constitution. Despite calls for constitutional conventions[15] and extensive efforts at individual and broader revisions of the constitution, there have been no extensive changes or even examinations of the document that is now over 140 years old. Indiana operates with a constitution that is old. However, efforts at modernization or change are plentiful. This has yielded a number of idiosyncratic and unique modifications. Some systematic efforts to modify the 1851 Constitution have been (1) technical corrections, (2) specific changes to accommodate a particular need or to deal with a specific problem, or, in one or two cases, (3) somewhat comprehensive changes to provisions of the constitution such as the judicial article (Article VII) or the article on Negroes and Mulattoes (Article XIII).

SUBSEQUENT AMENDMENTS TO THE 1851 CONSTITUTION

Actual changes to the 1851 Constitution occurred rarely and sporadically during the first 100 years of its existence. Yet, efforts at amending the constitution were frequent, widespread, and diverse. It is striking how frequently efforts to amend the constitution failed, particularly early in its existence. The variety of procedures used to attempt formal changes on the constitution is surprising because the constitution clearly contains a process for amendment. There are a great many people who believed that the constitutional problems in this document require modernization, reformation, clarification, or replacement. However, the difficulty in amending the constitution and the confusion over the amending

---

[15] For example, see Louis E. Lambent and E. B. McPheron, "Modernizing Indiana's Constitution," 26 *Indiana Law Journal* 185 (1951). These advocates call for extensive constitutional revisions but not necessarily by constitutional convention.

process contributed greatly to the lack of change. The amending process has not been very successful in achieving frequent or comprehensive updates of the constitution. However, in some respects that difficulty was intentional and is consistent with general constitutional theory.

The early problems that generated repeated efforts at change included:

- The uneven and brief terms of local officials required their regular turnover or their repeated seeking of reelection.
- The biennial legislative sessions were too infrequent to permit the legislature to complete all its work.
- There was continuing effort to get local or special legislation for some interests.
- The common school fund and other funding questions arose under the constitution.
- The method of selecting judges, the number of supreme court judges, and the authority of the courts presented problems.
- Limitations on local taxing powers and issues of home rule drew attention.
- Many advocated a variety of changes in the franchise.
  —The right of noncitizens to vote.
  —The lack of a residency requirement.
  —The right of women to vote.
  —The right of Negroes to vote.

Some of these concerns clearly reflect the continuing debate over particular problems or circumstances that generated concerns before the drafting of the 1851 Constitution. Most of these changes reflect views of those who lost particular debates when the convention drafted the constitution in 1851 or who thought that the new provision in the constitution was not as beneficial as the original 1816 method. In addition, some provisions of the new constitution needed clarification or definition. This process involved both judicial interpretations and simple practice by state institutions.

For example, Article IV, section 21 of the constitution specifies that any statute that amends or changes an existing law "shall be set forth and published at full length." The supreme court interpreted this, in an 1854 decision (*Langdon v. Appelgate*, 1854), to mean that the entire statute, in its original and its amended form, must be printed. This decision automatically invalidated 42 of the 155 acts adopted by the 1853 session of the General Assembly, because the full text of the original statute had not been printed. The confusion and awkwardness of this interpretation eventually led the court to reinterpret this article in *Greencastle Turnpike Co. v. State* (1867) not to require the printing of the original version of the law, as long as the entire new version (the amendment) appeared in print.

Another example of this involved the Common School Fund provision of the constitution (Article VIII). Reading the first section of this article, literally, means a restrictive limit on local funding of schools. The provision requires "a general and uniform system of Common Schools." The restrictive perspective of this provision was exactly the interpretation given the phrase by the state supreme court in 1854 (*Greencastle Township v. Black*). The court invalidated a state law enacted in 1852 that allowed local voters to adopt local school assessments above those provided for by the state under the Common School Fund. The court held that the constitution prohibited that local taxing effort, because such local action would defeat the "uniform system" of schools required by the state constitution.

This decision generated popular pressure for a constitutional amendment to change the wording of the article or allow for local option taxes for school funding some other way. However, that amendment was unnecessary when the 1867 General Assembly adopted the 1852 statute over again, despite its having been declared unconstitutional by the court. No one challenged this new statute in Indiana courts and so the judiciary did not have the opportunity to reassert its interpretation of the constitutional provision. The state practice has long been to allow broad local funding differences, so it is unlikely that the original interpretation of the constitution is operative (*Quick v. Springfield Township*, 1856).

There were two sets of efforts at amending the constitution that ran parallel in the period since the adoption of the 1851 Constitution. The calling of a constitutional convention appears repeatedly in these efforts. Even though there was no provision for a convention in the 1851 Constitution, many expected that such a convention was legitimate. This effort arose most visibly in the early 1870s after the amending process had been repeatedly unsuccessful. Many participants began to doubt that they could succeed by using the Article XVI process. The convention issue largely centered on partisan interests. The Democrats, often in control of one or both houses of the General Assembly, opposed calling a convention because the 1851 Constitution was largely their work. The Republicans were successful in getting the convention call through both houses and out to the people for a vote only twice, once in 1859 and again in 1914. In both of these occasions, voters rejected the call for a convention.

Most of the public argument against the convention focused on cost of the process, not that the convention was impermissible or unnecessary. Many observers felt the 1851 Constitution needed changes. However, a good many argued that the appropriate (best, cheapest, most efficient, only, or wisest) way of making those constitutional changes was by means of the amendment process in Article XVI of the constitution.

The predominant way to change the 1851 Constitution was the amending process provided in Article XVI. This amendment proved to be difficult in operation for several reasons. First, the process requires that two successive General Assemblies adopt the same proposed amendment(s) before they can be submitted to the people. This was not always possible or easy, especially given partisan differences from one legislature to the next. Sometimes the two houses of the legislature were controlled by different political parties. Thus, getting a proposed amendment through two sessions of the legislature was not an easy task. However, this difficulty was intentional and understandable.

The second problem connected to the amending process proved to be the most difficult. It involved what constituted a "majority of said electors [voters]" who were to "ratify" the proposed amendment. In fact, these few words produced the most controversial and peculiar litigation in Indiana constitutional history. It has also been the foundation of major difficulties in achieving changes in the constitution until recent decades. The fundamental issue is, on what basis is the majority calculated. The three interpretations of this affect the outcome of the amending process differently.

The first interpretation is the easiest way to achieve amendment. It bases the "majority" on the votes cast for and against the proposed amendment in any election. Thus, if a majority of votes cast on the amendment were in the affirmative then the amendment is ratified and the constitution changed. This "majority" would simply require a majority vote in the affirmative for adopting the amendment.

A more difficult "majority" requires a majority of the voters voting *in the election*, not on the amendment, to approve the amendment. That meant that regardless of the number of votes cast for and against the proposed amendment, a "majority" required a majority of the total voters voting in the election. For example, the total vote for governor could be much larger than the number of voters voting on the amendment issue, but the vote for governor determines the "majority." Only a few of the voters voting in the election might vote on the amendment issue. This requirement is something of a middle position between the extreme interpretations of "majority." It depends on the total voter turnout for an election. That will probably be a higher requirement than on the votes cast for the amendment. However, it is lower than an absolute majority of eligible voters.

The third interpretation of this constitutional provision requires that an absolute majority of the voters eligible to vote in Indiana must approve the amendment. This view disregards how many electors voted in the election, or how many voted on the amendment. This makes any amendment very difficult to ratify because the number of eligible voters is higher, perhaps much higher, than those voting in any given election and certainly higher than those voting for any amendment. A majority based on that total number of voters is very difficult (impossible?) to achieve.

The supreme court of Indiana has held different views at different times. Actually, the court has only held the first two of these views. However, the wording of the court's opinions has not clarified the question. In 1872 the voters of Indiana voted on the first proposed amendment to the 1851 Constitution. This proposal would prevent the state from assuming any debt arising from the construction of the Wabash and Erie canals. The state faced great political pressure from the creditors of the bankrupt canal company to assume (guarantee) its private debt. There was obviously substantial opposition to the assumption of any of this debt. The legislature in 1871 adopted the proposed amendment. The next legislature, a special session called in 1872 to consider much unfinished business left over from the 1871 session, was a separate General Assembly from the first one to propose the amendment. As a result, it could approve the amendment for submission to the people even though it was not the regularly scheduled session, due in 1873. When the proposal finally reached the voters in 1873, their vote to adopt the amendment was 158,400 for and 1,030 against. This overwhelming majority was not an absolute majority of the electors in the state or a majority of those voting in the last general election. However, the governor declared the amendment adopted, and there it stood.

In 1880, in *State v. Swift*, the supreme court reviewed the ratification process used for the canal amendment and approved the process and the governor's declaration of the result. The court held that a "majority" of the electors meant a majority of those voting in the election. This is the second interpretation discussed above. However, if the state officials (here the governor and the secretary of state) decided the ratification issue, by proclaiming ratification, then the constitutional change becomes effective. It is a settled issue or *res adjudicata*. Thus, the acceptance of the vote by the governor stood even though the actual "majority" did not meet the constitutional requirement, as interpreted by the supreme court in that case.

The problem of the "majority" arose simultaneously with another matter in 1880. The voters of Indiana voted on a set of seven constitutional amendments relating to the voting rights of blacks and Mulattoes, the schedule for holding general elections, allowing the counting of people of color in the census, a change in the power of the legislature to create appellate courts as well as inferior or trial courts, and the rotation of vacancies on the supreme court. In the 1880 general election, the proposals all received majority votes, but none received a majority of all the votes cast in that election for township officers, the only other office up for election at that time. However, the real question that arose was how many electors there were in the state at the time of this election. No one could say, so the strict enforcement of the "majority" requirement was impossible, since the election was not held concurrently with a census. The number of electors could be the number at the last census (in 1880, a majority would be 255,515 given the count in 1877). If the electors were the count of those voting in the last general election, then the majority required for these proposals was 217,004. If the requirement depended on the number voting in the 1880 election, then the required majority on any proposed amendment was 190,386. (This was the view taken by the court in *Swift*.) None of the interpretations or count of voters yielded a "majority" for any of the amendments. The supreme court's interpretation in *State v. Swift* required a majority of the total votes cast in that election, so none of the proposed amendments achieved ratification. All seven had received more affirmative votes than votes against, but that was inadequate.

An additional feature of the *Swift* opinion was that these amendments were in limbo because they had not been adopted or rejected in 1880. Therefore, they remained pending before the voters. Thus, without two successive General Assemblies readopting them, the voters could vote on them again. The status of these proposals blocked any additional amendments that the legislature wished to consider. The clear indication of the Court in *State v. Swift* was that no new amendments could be presented to the voters until these seven had been removed from consideration by an act of the legislature. As an alternative, the voters could vote against these proposals if the legislature decided to resubmit them. This "pendency" of amendments that did not receive a majority of votes in the election, and that the voters did not reject them outright, constituted a continuing problem with the amending process for more than 30 years to come. The usual practice was for the next legislature to withdraw an amendment that did not receive a "majority" by formal action so other proposals could be made.

The General Assembly immediately approved the resubmission of the seven amendments to the voters at a *special* election. In the special election, the proposed amendments were the only items on the ballot. So if someone voted at all, it was on that proposal and that insured that any amendment receiving a majority of votes became ratified. In 1881, all seven of the proposed amendments obtained a majority of the votes of the electors. This experience indicated a way in which amendments might be obtained more easily—submit them in a *special* election where the amendment was the only issue, so that voters voting on the amendment met the definition of a "majority," no matter how low the voter turnout. While this was *not* the end of problems with the amending process, this solution did overcome the immediate difficulty of approving these seven amendments. It also yielded some closure on the issue as long as the legislature would hold *special* elections for proposed amendments.

A substantive discussion of these 1881 adjustments in the constitution illustrates the practical, as well as the fundamental, problems that the amending process presented. Article XIII of the 1851 Constitution originally provided that:

- No Negroes or Mulattoes could settle in the state after the adoption of the constitution.
- No contracts could be made with Negroes and Mulattoes.
- Any contracts that were made would be crimes subject to penalties.
- All fines collected under this prohibition would fund efforts to colonize Negroes and Mulattoes who were willing to resettle elsewhere.

Other portions of the original constitution prohibited blacks from voting. These provisions of the constitution were obsolete as a result of the Civil War and the adoption of the Civil War amendments to the U.S. Constitution. The state supreme court had declared these segments of the state constitution null and void in 1866, because they were repugnant to the U.S. Constitution

(*Smith v. Moody*). However, it was not until 1881 that Indiana was able to repeal the 1851 provisions successfully. The initial effort to repeal Article XIII began in 1872, but various political and procedural difficulties repeatedly prevented the successful removal. The eventual (successful) repeal occurred at the same time as the municipal debt provision was added (Article XIII, section 1) because there was widespread support for limitations on municipal tax rates. The delay between the original proposal in 1872 and the eventual repeal in 1881 indicates both the politics of the time and the extreme difficulty of amending the state constitution.

Table 3 indicates the number of amendments or other changes (repealed provisions) in the constitution by decade. This display illustrates the limited number of amendments and the slowness with which formal constitutional change has occurred in this state. What is striking here is the infrequency of early, successful constitutional changes despite the continual pressure and the widespread proposals to change the constitution.

One of the striking features of this tabulation is that the flow of changes in the Indiana Constitution has not been constant or even. Despite a number of efforts (almost a continual flow of proposed amendments in the first fifty years), the changes have been infrequent, have come in spurts, and have only recently been numerous. There are substantial gaps of time between changes to the constitution. The difficulty in amending the constitution partly accounts for the

TABLE 3 *Number of Amendments and Repealed Provisions in Relation to the Indiana Constitution, Categorized by Decade*

Decade	Amendments	Repeals	Total Changes
1850	0	0	0
1860	0	0	0
1870	1	0	1
1880	7	5	12
1890	0	0	0
1900	0	0	0
1910	0	0	0
1920	1	0	1
1930	2	1	3
1940	1	2	3
1950	2	0	2
1960	2	1	3
1970	35	*	35
1980	25	7	32

*The repeals in this decade involve replacements of some of the sections in Article VII with alternatives. The sections not overwritten by new sections were repealed in effect. A count of these as repeals would be inaccurate.

gaps in amending it. The late nineteenth and early twentieth centuries clearly produced few corrections of the constitution or solutions of problems. As experience developed with the 1851 Constitution, some changes either in wording or in the provisions of the organic act were likely. Yet, these problems did not result in many changes at all.

The most significant reason for that difficulty is the amending process. While the early difficulties with this provision have been discussed, (1) the members of the 1851 Constitutional Convention intended that constitutional changes would occur, given their earlier experience with the 1816 provision for constitutional conventions, (2) the drafters did not wish to make it too easy to amend the constitution, for fear that partisan political preferences would be placed in the organic act, thus giving one faction a permanent political advantage.

In addition to the amendments in 1881, attempts at expanding the franchise to include additional voters surfaced. There were several issues relating to the right to vote that drew attention. The first was the continuing election fraud problems produced by the lack of a residency requirement in the constitution. Voters could vote anywhere they chose in the state. There were few examples of mass migrations into or out of electoral districts because of the lack of residency requirements. However, cases of trucking in groups of voters and fraudulent acts such as duplicate voting appeared. Voters did not have the opportunity to consider these because the discussion did not produce proposed amendments.

Another issue of this sort was women's suffrage. The proposal to extend the franchise to women appeared a number of times in the legislature starting in 1865, but voters rejected it until 1921. The linkage of this franchise issue with proposals to add a prohibition amendment or a local option provision usually meant a rejection at the polls because of the opposition to prohibition in the General Assembly or among the voters. Another reason for the failure was probably the strength of the opposition to this substantive change in the right to vote in some quarters.

Another frequent proposal to change the constitution was the "lawyers' amendment." Article XII, section 1 produced frequent challenges from the Indiana Bar Association because the original constitution permitted anyone of "good moral character" to be admitted to practice law in the state.[16] From 1851, this provision was a source of concern for lawyers and others that this specification permitted unqualified, untrained, or incompetent people to practice law.

---

[16] See Bernard C. Gavit, "Can Indiana Constitutionally Impose Educational Prerequisites for Admission to the State Bar Examinations?" 9 *Indiana Law Journal* 357 (1934). Comment, "Admission to the Bar as Provided for in the Indiana Constitutional Convention of 1850–1851," 1 *Indiana Law Journal* 209 (1926). The comment indicates that the origin of this provision in the 1851 Constitution was a strong antilawyer bias among a number of the delegates to the convention and an almost humorous (or comical) effort to impose this specific, open-ended provision on the "lawyer class," which was not in favor among many of the convention delegates in 1850–1851.

Since the legislature had a number if not a majority of lawyers, the General Assembly regularly considered amendments to this provision. This change appeared in the legislature in 1881, 1885, 1889, 1897, 1901, 1903, 1905, 1907, 1909, 1917, 1919, 1921, 1927, and 1929. Under the *Swift* ruling of the supreme court, the voters of Indiana rejected this proposed amendment only twice, in 1891 and 1900. The proposal did not always take the same form. Sometimes it just removed this provision from the constitution. On other occasions, it authorized the General Assembly to set qualifications for practicing law in the state.

In 1900, the Indiana voters did not reject or adopt the lawyers' qualification amendment. They reached the middle ground that was clearly problematic since *State v. Swift* (1880). The amendment in 1900 received an affirmative vote, but the margin of victory was not sufficient to yield a "majority" of electors supporting the amendment as required by the *Swift* interpretation. The supreme court decision in *In re Denny* (1900) exacerbated this state of limbo. The court, in regard to litigation arising from the failure to adopt the lawyers' amendment, determined that the proposed amendments (the other provided for an increase in the size of the supreme court) were again neither rejected nor adopted, just as the seven 1880 amendments in *State v. Swift*. Rather, they were still pending, and had to either be removed from consideration by the legislature or resubmitted to the voters. Having gotten this particular proposal to the electors, a number of legislators were reluctant to withdraw it again.

This pendency problem was finally disposed of with the supreme court's decision in 1913 in the case of *In re Boswell*. In that case the court held that a proposed amendment that was *not* ratified by a "majority" of the electors was rejected, and automatically removed from further consideration unless it was reinitiated in the legislature. Thus, the limbo created some 50 years earlier in the *Swift* opinion about pending amendments was removed from the amending process in Indiana.

By 1930, the state bar association and the courts had made exhaustive and repeated efforts at changing the "moral character" provision of the constitution, without success. A rough count of these efforts indicates that between 1881 and 1930, the change was proposed fourteen times in the legislature and *not* ratified by the voters less than four times. In usual fashion the lawyers' amendment was again before the voters in 1930, but this submission was declared unconstitutional by the attorney general. So, in 1932, the voters, as usual, did not ratify it by the necessary majority. (The vote on the amendment was 439,949 in favor, and 236,613 against. This was only a plurality, and the amendment was thought rejected as indicated by the *Boswell* holding.) However, an individual was denied admission to the bar because he failed to meet a newly imposed education requirement for admission. When he sued, the Indiana Supreme Court reversed itself and over fifty years of precedent and practice in *In re Todd* (1935). The court held that the plurality vote for the amendment achieved ratification.

An amendment becomes part of the constitution if "it receives a majority of those votes cast for and against its adoption."

This reinterpretation of the requirement for amending the constitution had profound results, as Table 3 above indicates. Clearly, the flow of adopted amendments after 1935 was substantially greater than before that time, although not immediately. In 1935, two amendments were added by the *Todd* decision, not only the lawyers' qualifications requirement, but an income tax amendment which had been repeatedly rejected by voters during the 1920s. It may well be that the supreme court reached the conclusion that the original interpretation was no longer workable, or perhaps had never been realistic. Faced with the regular and repeated rejection of the lawyers' amendment, the court may have decided to do something; the only thing it could do was change its interpretation of the "majority" requirement. It could also be that early events in the 1910s involving issues of constitutional amendment, and repeated failures to adopt various proposals for constitutional modernization in the 1920s were considered impossible hindrances to governance of the state in the depression years.

One example of a major and systematic, if idiosyncratic, failure to change the constitution occurred in 1911.[17] The General Assembly, at the behest of the governor, sought to circumvent the burdensome amending process altogether by preparing and adopting a proposed constitution as if it were a statute, with the voters given the chance for final approval over its adoption in a referendum.[18] The approval of each provision in this new constitution would have given the legislature a clear basis for then constituting itself as a constitutional convention (elected in the same election) and ratifying those constitutional provisions approved by the voters in the election, in the form of a new state constitution.

However, this circumventing effort was held to be unconstitutional by the supreme court in *Ellingham v. Dye* (1912).[19] The court's reasoning for its decision was that a draft of a new constitution, which this surely was, was beyond the power of the legislature to enact as if it were a statute. The legislature only has the power to "make, alter, or repeal laws," not the power to amend the constitution. The court claimed that it was interpreting the amending provision of the constitution (Article XVI, section 1) to reach this conclusion. The State Board of Election Commissioners was enjoined from submitting this proposed state constitution

---

[17] Ray Boomhower, "'To Secure Honest Elections': Jacob Piatt Dunn, Jr., and the Reform of Indiana's Ballot," 90 *Indiana Magazine of History* 311 (1994), passim.

[18] The 1851 Constitution did not contain the referendum and initiative provisions later added to many state constitutions during the Progressive Era. In Indiana, there had only been only two attempts to add the initiative and referendum. The first in 1897 was postponed as premature because there were pending amendments that barred this one from immediate consideration, and the second in 1899 when the proposal was postponed indefinitely in the Senate.

[19] The U.S. Supreme Court dismissed an appeal of this for want of jurisdiction in *Marshall v. Dye*.

to a vote of the electors. Governor Marshall, a primary advocate of this method and this proposal, reacted to this court decision in striking language.[20]

After the *Dye* decision, the legislature called a constitutional Convention by statutory enactment in 1917. The supreme court invalidated this call for the convention on the basis of the provision of the original 1816 Constitution that required that a convention required the people give their approval for any convention call before the legislature could issue the call (*Bennett v. Jackson*, 1917).[21] The legislature could not call a constitutional convention directly. Rather, the question must be put to the people of the state for their vote, and no convention can be called if the popular vote is not in favor of a convention, according to the court. The supreme court did explicitly recognize the validity of a convention as a means of constitutional amendment in *Bennett*. This, in itself, was a significant change, for the process of a constitutional convention had been left out of the 1851 Constitution, and the supreme court had been silent on the issue up to this point. However, once again a subterfuge process for conducting a major and exhaustive revision of the constitution came to naught in 1917. The high court indicated that the constitution could be altered or replaced by such a constitutional convention, in addition to the procedure outlined in Article XVI, but not by either the Marshall effort in 1911 or the convention method tried in 1917.

At the point when the court decided *In re Todd* in 1935, the process of constitutional amendment was not particularly clear or well-defined. However, there are several points that can be outlined as established by that time about the operation of the Indiana Constitution. These include the following:

- Any number of amendments can be proposed or considered at a time as long as they are separated on the ballot.
- An absolute majority of votes must be given for each proposed amendment (26 in the Senate and 51 in the House) before the amendment is approved by the General Assembly.
- These votes must be recorded.
- The amendment must be approved by two successive, but different, legislatures before it can be submitted to the people, even if one of those is a special session of the legislature.

---

[20] The proposed constitution has been referred to as the Marshall Constitution because of his public and private efforts at constitutional reform. See Boomhower, *supra* note 18. In informing the General Assembly that he was pursuing an appeal to the U.S. Supreme Court, the governor stated:

> I should have totally disregarded the decision of the [state] Supreme Court, defied its authority, thrown its sheriff out my window, called out the militia to defend my position and submitted the question to the people regardless of the [state Supreme] Court. (*Senate Journal, Sixty-Eighth Session*, 11, January 9, 1913).

[21] *Bennett v. Jackson* (1917). This holding is interesting because it was a judicial interpretation of a constitution that had not been in effect for some 65 years at the time the decision was reached.

- A "majority of the electors" requires that a majority of voters voting in an election must approve the proposed amendment. (This was changed in the *Todd* decision in 1935.)
- Once an amendment has been voted on by the electors it is either ratified, if it receives a majority, or it is rejected.

These points were both self-evident and hard-won elements of constitutional change in Indiana. The process had been difficult at best, and the number of amendments proposed and adopted in the period before 1935 was minimal at most (nine amendments, either additions or changes, and five sections repealed). This is most striking when it is compared with the widespread concerns of the nineteenth century, from the time of the creation of the 1851 Constitution. Specific problems regarding any number of narrow and technical features of the constitution had received criticism but no remedies were adopted. Major issues relating to the franchise and the powers of government were also barely addressed by the amending process. At the point when the Supreme Court decided *Todd* in 1935, it is possible to view the constitution as continuing to function, but as largely inadequate to the needs for aggressive or positive state government in the period of the 1930s.

The changes in the constitution that have occurred since the 1935 decision have been more numerous, and somewhat more comprehensive. However, despite the changes displayed in Table 3, there was no immediate flood of amendments after 1935, and it was only in the decades of the 1970s and 1980s that the number of changes increased appreciably. There were continued efforts at comprehensive and systematic constitutional change, with efforts to call constitutional conventions, but there was very little success.

The voters of Indiana were presented with the opportunity to convene a convention on the 1930 ballot. This proposal was rejected by a majority of electors (the vote was 355,546 in favor and 439,461 against), but the discussion surrounding this call for the convention was interesting and surprisingly modern.[22] That debate indicated, from the perspective of the convention advocates, that the 1851 Constitution was grossly out-of-date, and that it reflected a Jacksonian perspective of government.[23] The view was that authority from the constitution was (in 1930) inadequate for governing a modern, industrial state. The effort to modernize the state government required that the substantial flaws in the 1851 document should be remedied or completely replaced. The argument for the

---

[22] For substantive discussions of the issue, see Hugh E. Willis, "Revision of the Indiana Constitution," 5 *Indiana Law Journal* 329 (1930); Albert Stump, "Indiana Should Call a Constitutional Convention," 5 *Indiana Law Journal* 354 (1930); and James W. Noel, "In Re: Proposed Constitutional Convention," 5 *Indiana Law Journal* 373 (1930). These articles form a symposium regarding the 1930 convention call.

[23] Stump, "Indiana Should Call a Constitutional Convention."

convention was that a systematic and comprehensive revision of the constitution was necessary rather than the repeated episodic efforts at piecemeal change.

The major flaws in the 1851 Constitution included both old points that had been made from nearly the outset in 1851, such as the inadequacy of biennial sessions of the legislature with severe (unrealistic) limits on the length of sessions at 61 days. In addition, there were fundamental problems with the structure and complexity of the judicial and executive branches of government that made governance impossible to the advocates of change. The advocates felt that piecemeal constitutional change or the failure to change at all through amending the existing constitution required a comprehensive revision, done by a constitutional convention.

Those opposing the call for the convention in 1930 were institutional conservatives and advocates of traditional, limited government. Their arguments went to the purpose of constitutions, which was to preserve individual liberties and rights, while restricting the power of government to intrude and expand into new areas of people's lives.[24] This set of arguments carried the day in terms of Indiana voters in 1930. However, the Indiana discussion preceded the federal government's growth into economic regulation and the expansion of rights and liberties that emerged from the New Deal and World War II. Interestingly, the current debate within states and at the federal level (in the 1990s) about the size and authority of government clearly parallels the constitutional convention discussion in Indiana in 1930.

Although it did not result in a successful effort to amend the constitution in 1950, there was a significant call for systematic and comprehensive revision for the constitution from the academic arena.[25] This article presented an extensive and devastating series of indictments of the 1851 Constitution. The advocates claimed that the state constitution needed widespread attention in order to modernize it, and they claimed that the age of the constitution alone was fatal. However, they also outlined a variety of specific problems with the constitution that they felt only a systematic revision could address. These included:

- The *amending process* made it very difficult to change the fundamental law of the state.
- There are severe restrictions on the size, structure, length, and procedures of the *legislature*, making it difficult for the General Assembly to perform its constitutional duties.
- The state's *executive* agencies and offices were disorganized, irresponsible, uncontrolled, and not integrated.

---

[24] Noel, *supra* note 22 articulates this view.

[25] Louis E. Lambent and E. B. McPheron, "Modernizing Indiana's Constitution," 26. *Indiana Law Journal* 185 (1951).

- The *courts* faced severe administrative inefficiency and were subject to partisan politics.
- The strict limitations on *local government* prevented the adequate and independent governance of municipalities.
- There was also a *mixture* of financial and bill of rights matters that needed to be corrected.

These problems were identified as widespread among state constitutions in general, and the article focused on the nature of these problems within Indiana. It argued that on each of these dimensions, Indiana's organic act needed serious and extensive correction. It did not advocate any particular solutions to these problems, and it did not claim that one of the methods of constitutional amendment (convention or a series of amendments) should be adopted. However, this extensive indictment probably would require a constitutional convention. The essay, though not successful, was a loud call for change in the academic forum most attended by the state's policy makers and the legal profession.

There were scattered and frequent efforts at change until the 1970s. This is partly due to the difficulty of amending the constitution before 1935. Yet, Table 3 shows there were no more successful efforts at constitutional change even after it became easier to amend the constitution in 1935. In 1970, however, a major set of revisions in the constitution was adopted. These changes involved a complete restructuring of the Judicial article (Article VII). The changes focused on several basic features in the judiciary. Some of these had been points of concern for over a century, such as the methods of selecting judges. Others were more modernizing efforts at creating a new and more operable judicial system.

First, an intermediate level appellate court was created. The supreme court was allowed to allocate appellate jurisdiction to this court as it deemed appropriate. That could relieve the supreme court of some of its workload, and as its appellate business changed, the supreme court had the discretion to afford appellate review to any set of cases, temporarily. Second, the amendments changed the process by which the judges of the state supreme court were selected. The amendments replaced the geographic "districts" where they must reside and compete on a partisan ballot with a merit selection system for high court seats. That same selection process was provided for the selection of courts of appeals judges as well. Partisan elections remain the means of judicial selection at the trial court level.

This set of amendments clearly focused on modernizing the judicial system of the state. That was the result of deficiencies in the capability of the supreme court to hear and decide all the appeals that arose from the trial courts in the state.[26] It also reflected problems that the antiquated judicial structure created

---

[26] Randall T. Shepard, "Changing the Constitutional Jurisdiction of the Indiana Supreme Court: Letting a Court of Last Resort Act Like One," 63 *Indiana Law Journal* 669 (1988). Note that this article

for the handling of the types of litigation that were then occurring, some 120 years after the 1851 Constitution began operation.

The modification of the selection process was undoubtedly intended to insure the selection of meritorious appellate court judges throughout the state and was advocated by a judicial reform commission.[27] That objective dictated a merit process involving the judicial nominating commission, appointment by the governor from a list of three candidates, and then a retention ballot at the next general election at least two years after the appointment. If approved, the judge retains office for a ten-year term, subject, at the end of that period, to another retention election. That replaces the partisan ballot, six-year term provided in the 1851 Constitution for supreme court judges. The length of a judge's tenure was clearly increased substantially with these changes.

Another change in 1970 was the number of judges on the supreme court. Under the original constitution, the supreme court was composed of three to five members, as determined by the General Assembly. The size of the court was changed in 1970 to range from four to eight members. Clearly, one of the needs in the 1970s was, at least, the capability to expand the size of the highest state court, as well as changing its jurisdiction. Rather than fixing the number of supreme court judges in the constitution, the parameters were specified for the General Assembly, which could make adjustments as it deemed necessary.

There were also various amendments adopted in the 1980s. These may warrant noticing just because they are the most recent constitutional changes. They do not reflect the same kinds of changes as discussed above, but they reflect that some broad constitutional change can be accomplished. These more recent amendments have been systematic modifications, but these are largely wording changes. Some of these are significant, such as the elimination of the masculine pronoun "he" in a number of provisions. However, these most recent changes do not restructure government. They do not change the powers of government, and they do not alter the processes by which governmental institutions proceed and exercise authority. However, they may be significant in terms of personal liberties and rights, and they make their constitutional rights more modern or expansive.

A primary reason for the paucity of amendments until recently is the series of Indiana Supreme Court decisions interpreting the "majority" requirement in Article XVI. These interpretations ended in 1935 with the court's "capitulation" or adoption of the minimalist definition of "majority." The original interpretation resulted in the failure of a number of proposed amendments, submitted to the voters after two consecutive legislative sessions had approved the amendment. The probable reason for this problem is that candidates for public office

---

advocates the adoption of another, more recent constitutional amendment. However, this analysis does indicate the nature and purpose of the 1970 amendments to the judicial article.

[27] Malcolm L. Morris and A. James Barnes, "The Indiana Judicial System: An Analysis and Some Renewed Proposals for Reform," 44 *Indiana Law Journal* 49 (1968).

attract voters' interest and attention, but there is little interest in constitutional amendments. As a result, voters do not all vote on amendment questions. So even though a majority of those voting on the proposed amendment might approve it, that rarely constituted a majority of all voters participating in the election. The restrictive interpretation also produced the bottleneck in the flow of amendments to the voters because of those amendments neither ratified nor rejected. This was reversed in 1913.

The eventual interpretation of the amending process in 1935 by the Indiana Supreme Court was that a proposed amendment was ratified by the voters if it received a majority of the votes cast for or against the proposal. That interpretation resulted in two immediate changes to the constitution—the Income Tax amendment (Article X, section 8), and the removal of the requirement of "good moral character" for lawyers, retroactively to 1932. That interpretation means that from 1935 on, amending the Indiana Constitution was as easy as it could be under the 1851 provision. The earlier, more restrictive interpretation of Article XVI can be blamed for the limited number of amendments to the Indiana Constitution before 1935. In fact, of the eleven proposed amendments that cleared the first hurdle, approval by two successive General Assemblies between 1930 and 1960, all were approved by the voters of the state. None of them would have been adopted using the original *Swift* rule.

However, it would be incorrect to place all the blame for the slow constitutional change on the amending process. Very few proposed amendments have been approved by two successive General Assemblies. This is the result of both partisan and substantive differences in successive legislatures. This does constitute a substantial difficulty in moving proposed amendments out to the people for their ratification.

There have always been legitimate concerns about the ease of amending a constitution. The limited success of amending the Indiana Constitution seems to be the extreme form of protecting against easy amendment. The stream of constitutional amendments since 1935 has also been sporadic, except for the 1970 changes in the judicial article and the 1984 changes in various provisions.

One of the striking aspects of the history of the Indiana Constitution is the narrowness of the interpretations placed on its provisions. It is rare that a state court opinion interprets a section of the constitution in terms of constitutional theory or philosophy. Court decisions generally treat constitutional questions as narrow, restricted issues much like matters of statutory interpretation. The words of the constitution are treated as clear and definitive; the only issue involved is the application of those words to the case or the facts before the court. While that permits the constitution to function, a recognition of its broader dimensions might produce more understanding.

This restrictive approach to constitutional interpretation is certainly not unique or out of the ordinary. However, it means that the substantive content of the constitution does not develop much beyond the literal words in the documents.

There have been some major interpretive innovations, as in the *In re Todd* case in 1935. However, that interpretation was the only one possible that produced the results sought—the removal of the lawyers' section. This interpretation of Article XVI was the only one left, the only one not adopted earlier by the court. Given the long, earlier experience and failure of the amending process, the interpretation in *Todd* was probably inevitable.

There are other exceptions to this narrow construction of the state constitution, but they are rare exceptions rather than the rule.[28] Rather, the Indiana Constitution has served as a limit on governmental structure, authority, and process. It will continue to be a grant of limited powers for governing which may reflect the political climate of the state. Those limitations are hindrances or faults only if the constitution does not succeed or if the government fails. If the constitution does not permit the accomplishment of public policy goals desired by the people, then it is inadequate. Until then, the age of the constitution and the restrictions in the organic act are both historical artifacts and real operating limitations.

This lack of a broad-ranging discussion of judicial philosophies has not prevented the constitution from working or prevented the state from governing. The development of the constitution has been limited in scope and that development has not been accompanied by a comprehensive or an extensive discussion of judicial, constitutional, or political philosophies. There has been little consideration of interpretative approaches to treating constitutional provisions and to developing their meaning. In that sense, perhaps the general features of the history of the Indiana Constitution, as well as the meaning of specific constitutional provisions, have been of limited breadth and scope. That has made constitutional development in Indiana less exciting or controversial, or less thought-out, than it might have been. However, this limited view of constitutional interpretation has not prevented the constitution from achieving the basic, minimalist goals that may have been the true objective or intention of the framers of the state constitution.

The limited setting in which constitutional interpretation has taken place could also be due to a wide acceptance of this limited view among people that the constitution is immutable and not open to varying interpretations. Such a view is certainly not very observant,[29] and it is not open-minded with regard to what judges actually do when they interpret a constitution. However, this

---

[28] Patrick Baude, "Has the Indiana Constitution Found Its Epic?" 69 *Indiana Law Journal* 849 (1994). This cites a recent supreme court decision as indicating that the court and the constitution may have finally reached an epic. See *Price v. State* (1993).

[29] This view also does not coincide with various doctrines that have developed and changed over time. The earlier discussion of the constitutional amending process in Article XVI and what that required clearly indicates that the supreme court has changed its mind, eventually to a diametrically opposed view of the meaning and operation of the same constitutional provision.

restrictive view that judges "find" rather than "make" the law has been widely accepted through much of American constitutional development by a number of actors. It is generally rejected because of judicial activity and scholarly observation. It seems as if much of the judicial work on the Indiana Constitution reflects the narrow view of finding rather than making law in the course of interpreting or applying the provisions of the constitution, without recognition that the decisions reached by courts have (perhaps major) policy implications. Although the limited view of constitutional interpretation may not be realistic, it still reflects a judicial and political culture widely held in the state and it exhibits the expectations of many of the actors involved in the process of interpreting and governing.

The discussions in Part II focus on specific segments of the Indiana Constitution, what those provisions have come to mean, and what problems or questions remain with the wording and operation of these sections. However, it should be recognized that the narrow issues that have been treated in connection with parts of the constitution do not shed comprehensive or broad light on the issues of constitutional interpretation or the fundamental significance of the constitution as a whole, and its impact (political, judicial, governmental) on the people or their well-being.

PART TWO
The Indiana Constitution and Commentary

Article I
The Bill of Rights

Much of the constitution remains worded as it was initially drafted and adopted in 1850–1851. The discussion in Part I indicates how difficuslt it has been to adopt formal changes to the document, so few have been adopted until recent decades. Thus, much of the original constitution has gradually changed through court interpretations and practice. There have been few systematic amendments and no comprehensive revisions of the organic act of Indiana. However, the Judicial Article (Article VII) was redrafted completely in 1970, and there was an effort, in 1984, to change a set of the provisions to achieve modern consistency.

The comprehensive change made in 1984 needs to be noted here in connection with Article I. The initial wording of these provisions in the 1851 Constitution contained the masculine reference to "men" or the masculine pronoun "he," "him," or "his." These references were all changed to the gender neutral "people" or "person." While this can be viewed as a technical correction of the initial constitution, it is more accurate to recognize that these revisions substantively reflect the intended meaning of the original provision; they reach beyond mere technical or wording changes. Those sections that were changed this way in 1984 are: section 1, section 2, section 4, section 12, and section 21.

It is important to note that with regard to Article I of the Indiana Constitution, there is a good deal of overlap with the federal Bill of Rights and other provisions of the federal Constitution. This provides for points of conflict, differences in interpretation, and premption by the federal Constitution's provision where there is conflict between the two sets of Bills of Rights. Some of the most notable differences or conflicts will be outlined in the following discussion. However, the fundamental basis for resolving this conflict is that the federal Constitution and the U.S. Supreme Court's (or lower federal court's) interpretation of it prevails when a conflict exists. The federalization of the Bill of Rights has also imposed a variety of requirements on all states and their constitutions. However, it is striking to note how few occasions have produced direct and explicit conflicts between the two sets of constitutional provisions.

SECTION 1

Inherent and Inalienable Rights. *We Declare* that all people are created equal; that they are endowed by their *Creator* with certain inalienable rights; that among these are life, liberty, and the pursuit of happiness; that all power is inherent in the people; and that all free governments are, and of right ought to be, founded on their authority, and instituted for their peace, safety, and well-being. For the advancement of these ends, the *people* have, at all times, an indefeasible right to alter and reform their government. (Amended November 6, 1984)

This initial segment of the constitution contains wording similar to parts of the Declaration of Independence. This section clearly outlines the basic, philosophical point that people are created equal, they possess inalienable rights, and that they are political sovereigns with the power to create government to achieve peace, safety, and well-being. The variations between this wording and the Declaration essentially involve the absence of the indictment of the king for his actions. In addition, the wording in the Indiana Constitution is not as detailed and as ordered as the Declaration. That indicates that the framers of the state constitution were more interested in the general concept of liberty than in a litany. Furthermore, this section is not designed to justify independence or rebellion from established authority.

The purpose of government is to attain the ends that people desire. The basic principles articulated here reflect the foundation of popular sovereignty and the dignity of people. These are also articulated in the Declaration. This undoubtedly was a popular, Jacksonian orientation in 1851 on which to found a state constitution. This focuses on the proposition that the people create and can modify or change their government. The right to alter the government has served as the basis for repeated proposals to call a constitutional convention in Indiana. That formal method of constitutional change is not specified anywhere in the constitution, so this introductory provision has been used for that purpose.

The inalienable rights protected or guaranteed here are those rights and liberties inherent in a sense of democracy that derives from the independence of the individual and a concept of natural individual rights that form the basis for political sovereignty and self-government. Thus, life, liberty, and the pursuit of happiness are the categories of rights specified in this section. The specific, substantive content of these involves a variety of liberties ranging from privacy to procreation, travel to holding office, entering into contracts to practicing religion, and engaging in business practices to voting. These rights can be interpreted broadly and expansively (inclusively) in order to insure that the people enjoy a broad, if restrained, form of personal interests, as the wording of this section suggests. Thus, "property" has been grafted onto this provision so that this component of the federal Due Process Clause is part of this section. However, this component of liberty (the right to property) does not enjoy quite the same status as other rights and liberties (*Barrick Realty, Inc. v. City of Gary,* 1973).

This view of the inalienable rights of the People has not been considered as absolute by the Indiana Courts (*State v. Levitt,* 1965). Rather, these rights are subject to legitimate police power restrictions (*Shupe v. Bell,* 1957; *Muncie v. Pizza Hut of Muncie, Inc.,* 1976). Such limits are inherent in the government's duty to promote order, safety, health, morals, and the general welfare of society. Indiana government is no exception to this limiting perspective (*Bruck v. State ex rel. Money,* 1950). The fundamental requirement of this provision is for government to protect these rights of the people from infringement. However, the interpretations placed on this constitutional provision give government a central role in both protecting the rights and limiting these for justifiable (police power) reasons. There is uncertainty about what kinds of limitations are permitted within the outline of this section, but the general principle remains that there are occasions when the freedoms and liberties of people must be curbed in order to permit the functioning of society and government.

Given the fundamental nature of the philosophy contained in this section and the established principles it contains, the general perspective has been in favor of liberty rather than its limitation. There have been only a few such limiting decisions and they have been recent. They focus largely on exigencies or the necessity to insure peace and tanquility. While the judgment of the legislature is crucial to determining when police power should be exercised, it is up to the courts to conclude what is included in this power and what liberty is protected from intrusion (*Peachey v. Boswell,* 1960).

SECTION 2

Natural Right to Worship. All people shall be secured in the natural right to worship *Almighty God,* according to the dictates of their own consciences. (Amended November 6, 1984).

This section grants people the right to worship as they choose. This is somewhat different than the wording of the First Amendment of the U.S. Constitution.

Here, the right to worship is recognized as a natural right, and the object of the right to worship is also specified as *Almighty God* as conscience dictates. The focal point of the protected behavior, *God*, could generate concern, given that some people worship another supreme being or not, but within the structure of a religion. In addition, the explicit recognition of a natural right to worship may also provide a fundamental basis that is lacking in the First Amendment of the U.S. Constitution, where the right is only to be free from congressional interference.

The first difference regarding this right may reflect a relatively narrow vision of this right to worship, since the writers of the Indiana Constitution did not have a broad perspective of worship. Their wording suggests a narrow view of religion. This was not a unique perspective, and this view has not carried the day. The courts have treated this right relatively broadly, not limited to worshipping only ALMIGHTY GOD. Generally, this has developed into the free exercise provision of the state constitution, with a reach not unlike that of the federal constitutional protection.

There have been instances of state interference with religious practice, under this provision. However, from *Lynch v. Indiana State University Board of Trustees* (1978), it is acceptable for the state to intercede if there is a state interest of substantial magnitude that overrides the claimed protection of free exercise. If that sufficient interest is not present, then the state must appear not to deny free exercise of religious belief by its actions. This view suggests that this right to free exercise is not absolute, but rather allows for a balancing of this freedom and the state's interest. It is not at all clear how that balance is to be struck in each case, or what weight each competing interest is to be given in the process of that balancing in particular instances. The courts have been vague on this balance and they have not rendered many decisions that outline the borders of the doctrine.

This provision has given rise to several disputes regarding church property and the protection does not allow a minority of a congregation to dictate the manner in which the majority will worship (*Stansberry v. McCarty*, 1958). While courts might intervene to protect the contractual and property rights of a minority of the congregation, the worship chosen by a majority will not be scrutinized or validated by the judiciary. This reluctance for courts to control church governance or other issues relating to ecclesiastical bodies is well established in Indiana, and it is understandable (*Kompier v. Thegza*, 1938).

This liberty is not so extensive that there are no limits on the manner in which worship is practiced. This section works against substantial state interference with the practice of worship by people. The balance that is struck between free exercise and state regulation under this provision is similar to that developed and applied by the United States Supreme Court under the Free Exercise Clause of the First Amendment of the U.S. Constitution.

SECTION 3

Freedom of Religious Opinions and Rights of Conscience. No law shall, in any case whatever, control the free exercise and enjoyment of religious opinions, or interfere with the rights of conscience.

This section guarantees the free exercise of religion, somewhat like the First Amendment of the U.S. Constitution. Here, however, the rights of conscience are also protected from interference by the government. Lastly, part of this section does relate to the holding of religious opinions. That makes it reiterative of the previous section (section 2) relating to conscience. These guarantees differ from the Free Exercise Clause contained in the First Amendment of the U.S. Constitution. The rights and freedoms guaranteed here pertain to the beliefs and opinions of people in addition to the practices (free exercise) in which people engage in connection with worshipping. This wording is a curious blend of freedom of conscience and belief on the one hand and the free exercise or practice of those beliefs on the other.

The courts have recognized this dichotomy of belief and practice. This freedom is absolute with regard to religious beliefs, but the right to act or practice can be limited. Such religious action or behavior can be regulated by appropriate state law (e.g. *Mitchell v. Pilgrim Holiness Church Corp.,* 1954). The federal Court of Appeals for the 7th Circuit held in *Mitchell* that an Indiana church could be subject to the federal Fair Labor Standards Act for commercial activity it was engaged in completing.

The U.S. Supreme Court has held that the denial of unemployment benefits to a Jehovah's Witness who refused to make tank turrets and who quit his job because of his beliefs was deprived of the right to the free exercise of religion under the provision of the First Amendment of the U.S. Constitution (*Thomas v. Rev. Bd. of the Indiana Employment Security Division,* 1981). The state supreme court had previously held that this individual's right to his religious opinion to the unemployment benefits was not protected by this provision of the state constitution (*Thomas v. Rev. Bd. of the Indiana Employment Security Division,* 1981).

A zoning ordinance that prevented a church from constructing an off-street parking facility in a residential area was held to violate this provision of the constitution, even though it is difficult to grasp how the parking facility involves the free exercise of a religious belief or opinion (*Church of Christ of Indianapolis v. Metro. Bd. of Zoning Appeals of Marion County,* 1978). The state can exercise its police powers in connection with churches only in "reasonable" ways. This state authority is grounded in the promotion of the public health, safety, or general welfare. Such state or municipal regulation would have the burden of establishing that they are reasonable exercises of the police power. Thus, reasonable zoning restrictions based on the government's policy power are not violations of this section of the constitution (*Milharcic v. Metropolitan Bd. of Zoning Appeals of Marion Co.*, 1986).

Any governmental activity that affects the practice of religion must have a secular purpose and have an evenhanded impact. Its primary impact must also be neutral (*Lynch v. Indiana State University Bd. of Trustees*, 1978). Thus, a limitation on someone's religious exercise or expression in a public school setting is not a violation of this provision of the state constitution. That includes the exclusion of nonvaccinated pupils alleging their freedom to exercise religious beliefs as the reason for nonvaccination (*Vonnegut v. Baun*, 1934).

SECTION 4

Freedom of Religion. No preference shall be given, by law, to any creed, religious society, or mode of worship; and no person shall be compelled to attend, erect, or support, any place of worship, or to maintain any ministry, against his consent. (Amended November 6, 1984)

This provision is confusing when read in conjunction with section 2 of this article which specifies that people have the liberty to worship *Almighty God*. As the interpretation and meaning of that earlier section have developed, there is no particular religious preference contained in it. As a result, this section is designed to prevent the preference for any one religion, over any other, by the state. Thus, this section is also a variant on the Establishment Clause of the First Amendment of the U.S. Constitution.

This prohibition of any preference being given to any particular creed, church, or mode of worship is much more direct and specific than the U.S. Constitution. In addition, no one can be forced to attend, support, maintain a ministry, or erect or maintain a church. This part of the section is also more explicit than the Establishment Clause. It clearly bars the state from establishing any religion to the extent that one of these prohibited acts "establishes" a religion. In fact, this wording may be more useful and supportive of the right, since it is more precise. It does not leave quite as much room for interpretation and that could be limiting, but generally, the drafters of section 4 clearly indicated what they did not want the state to become involved in with regard to churches.

This provision is not limited as a bar on the state. It is a blanket prohibition of preference for one religion. Any governmental restraint or limitation must have a secular purpose and be applied to all religious sects, evenhandedly (*Lynch v. Indiana State University Bd. of Trustees*, 1978). As long as the regulation is neutral in its impact and it is intended to have a secular impact, it does not violate this constitutional provision.

SECTION 5

Religious Test for Office. No religious test shall be required, as a qualification for any office of trust or profit.

This provision is a specific component of religious freedom. It prohibits the use of a religious test as a qualification for an office of trust or profit. This prohibition applies to qualification for public office. But it also can be interpreted to apply to any other position. Thus, the wording here could be interpreted to prevent a corporation from requiring a religious test to qualify as an officer of the company. However, the purpose of this provision was to insure that religion would not become involved in the process by which people would be formally selected for holding office.

This ban applies not only to elected office but to the broader category of public employment as well. However, jury membership is not covered by this provision (*Wheeler v. State*, 1970). July membership does not involve holding public office, and so it is not appropriate to bar jury members from being given a religious test. The test involved here related to asking prospective jurors about their feelings on the imposition of a death penalty sentence in a criminal prosecution. This view leads to the conclusion that this provision focuses on public offices, not private office in which profit may arise. The court has had no opportunity to focus directly on whether "profit" includes private office, which can certainly involve "trust."

SECTION 6

Public Money for Benefit of Religious or Theological Institution. No money shall be drawn from the treasury, for the benefit of any religious or theological institution.

This section directly prevents state funds from being used to benefit a religious institution. The wording here is different than the Establishment Clause of the U.S. Constitution in that it is explicitly directed at public support of "institutions" with a religious or theological orientation or connection. This wording is narrower than the Establishment ban of the First Amendment. Here, the wording prohibits the use of public funds to benefit such an organization. Although it never has been interpreted this way, the wording could allow state funding for various religious activities or institutions as long as the intention was not to benefit that activity or institution. That may be virtually impossible to achieve, but it would appear to be an opening in this wording.

Where a public official had paid out moneys from a common school fund to "private, Religious, sectarian and theological institutions" such misspent funds clearly are prohibited by the section, the funds must be reimbursed by the offender (*State ex rel. Johnson v. Boyd*, 1940). However, consistent with the U.S. Supreme Court holding in *Everson v. Board of Education* (1947), the expenditure of state funds to provide free transportation to nonpublic school students is not a violation of this provision of the state constitution (1967 Op. Atty. Gen. No. 3). There has been little interpretation of this section of the Indiana Constitution, but the general view of its meaning is consistent with that emerging from the relevant portions of doctrine under the Establishment Clause of the U.S. Constitution.

SECTION 7

Witness Competent Regardless of Religious Opinion. No person shall be rendered incompetent as a witness, in consequence of his opinions on matters of religion.

This section of the state constitution focuses on the witnesses in court proceedings and it provides that the witnesses' ability to testify is not affected by religious beliefs or opinions. This is a unique feature of the state constitution that focuses on one dimension of free exercise, or religious qualifications. However, it was considered important at the time of drafting, since it was given an itemized place in the constitution. The competency or qualification of witnesses to testify because of their religious opinions certainly can be significant in criminal prosecutions, depending on the witness involved and the evidence that the witness brings to the trial.

This provision has been interpreted to apply to a seven-year-old witness who cannot be tested for competency based on his religious belief (*Johnson v. State*, 1977). This means that the witnesses' Understanding that an oath is a promise to God is not subject to scrutiny under this provision of the state constitution. Furthermore, the religious beliefs of a witness cannot be challenged, but they can be used to challenge the witness's credibility (IC 34-1-14-13). This statutory provision indicates that a lack of belief in a Supreme Being does not make a witness incompetent to testify. Such beliefs are legitimately subject to scrutiny in connection with the witness's general moral character, however.

SECTION 8

Oath or Affirmation; Administration. The mode of administering an oath or affirmation, shall be such as may be most consistent with, and binding upon, the conscience of the person, to whom such oath or affirmation may be administered.

This section of the constitution specifies that any oath or affirmation that is administered by the state is to be developed and applied in a way that is consistent with the personal conscience of the person who is taking the oath or giving the affirmation. That gives the state the opportunity to craft oaths so that they do not offend beliefs or conscience, and this provision indicates that everyone need not take the same oath.

This section also emphasizes that the oath should be developed so that it is binding on the conscience of the individual under oath. That means that one of the objectives of this provision of the constitution is to insure that the oath-taker is placed in circumstances that they feel binds them. This section is focused on insuring that the oath that is administered has a salutary effect; insuring that the oath will have a binding effect. Section 7 relates to insuring that a witness will not be declared incompetent because of any religious beliefs.

The judicial interpretation of this section of the constitution is nonexistent, so there has been little amplification of its meaning. As provided by the statutes of the state (IC 5-4-1-1), every officer and deputy must accept the oath, within ten (10) days of taking office, to support and respect the U.S. Constitution and the Indiana Constitution. If the officer fails to give (take) that oath within the specified time period, the office is automatically vacated and it is open for a new candidate or individual to occupy (IC 5-4-1-1; IC 5-4-1-1.2). By taking an oath of office, one whose election to that office is completely invalid gains no legal status or claim to the office (1933 Op. Atty. Gen. 32). The point of this implementation is that section 8 is connected to taking oaths for office rather than binding witnesses, even though there is no such limitation in the wording of the section.

SECTION 9

Right of Free Thought, Speech, Writing and Printing; Abuse of Right. No law shall be passed, restraining the free interchange of thought and opinion, or restricting the right to speak, write, or print, freely, on any subject whatever; but for the abuse of that right, every person shall be responsible.

This provision operates to grant the right to free thought by whatever means: speech, writing, or print. The reason for the right is to insure the broadest possible dissemination of ideas and discussion of matters of interest and concern. This could be viewed in the context of the marketplace of ideas and people's need to enter that dialogue. That is, this section underlies the expectation that the free and broad interchange of ideas is fundamental to a democracy.

The presumption of this section is that the right will be liberally applied or interpreted. The wording is expansive. In addition, that wording provides a broad right to free speech. This perspective is considered a serious aspect of the section, and it is the fundamental feature of the rights contained in this section (*Gibson v. Kincaid*, 1966).

However, there is a restrictive component in the section. The wording explicitly recognizes that persons can abuse this right. They are to be held responsible for such abuses. The possibility of abuse is recognized but not defined in the constitution. That leaves to the courts and the legislature the duty to develop and implement limitations that are consistent with this broad freedom. These features of free expression are governed by the body of constitutional law that parallels that developed by the U.S. Supreme Court. However, there is state common law that has developed in this connection, suggesting largely that the parameters of this section coincide with the Free Speech portion of the U.S. Constitution. This includes the basic expectation that these rights yield to the government's right to self-preservation from violent overthrow (*State v. Levitt*, 1965).

Speech that damages reputation (libel or slander) constitutes an abuse of this right. This is implied directly in the next section (Article I, section 10). Thus, it can be viewed as an "abuse" under this section. Obscene and foul language is not protected by this section, since that is offensive to society and thus constitutes an abuse of this constitutional provision (*Stults v. State*, 1975; *State v. Kuebel*, 1961). Picketing can be prevented by a local ordinance, since it is not viewed as "true or pure speech," and therefore it can be abused. However, picketing without the use of force, threats, or intimidation is the exercise of free speech, protected by this section (*Roth v. Local Union No.1460 of Retail Clerks Union*, 1939). An ordinance cannot prevent the posting of a "For Sale" Sign on private residential property (1972 Op. Atty. Gen. No. 12). Billboards, even though they are not "pure" speech, can be regulated (*Barrick Realty v. City of Gary*, 1974). However, they are protected to a degree and cannot be prohibited completely by the state (1979 Op. Atty. Gen. No. 29). This coincides with the U.S. Supreme Court's interpretation of the First Amendment's protection of Commercial Speech as protected under the First Amendment, even if it is not absolutely protected (e.g., *Bigelow v. Valentine*, 1976; and *Bates v. State Bar of Arizona*, 1977).

The developed constitutional law on this subject is a combination of state court interpretation and U.S. Supreme Court interpretation of federal First Amendment rights. There are no fundamental differences between the two sets of doctrines, although it is obvious that they did not develop simultaneously or in parallel. Rather, the state courts have generally kept abreast of the U.S. Supreme Court as cases raising similar issues have been presented to the state judiciary for decision under this section of the constitution.

SECTION 10

Truth in Prosecution for Libel. In all prosecutions for libel, the truth of the matters alleged to be libelous, may be given in justification.

This section is related to the previous section (section 9). It provides that in a prosecution for libel (one of the abuses recognized in the previous discussion) the truth of the statement can be given as justification for the statement, no matter how damaging the statement is to the plaintiff's reputation. The plaintiff has the burden of proving the damage of the matter uttered or printed. However, once that burden has been carried, then the defendant has the opportunity to defend the action using the truth of the statements (*Palmer v. Adams*, 1894; IC 34-1-5-1; IC 34-1-5-2). This provision is designed to structure libel actions in relation to the truth of the assertion, and it constitutionalizes that framework.

SECTION 11

Unreasonable Search or Seizure; Warrant. The right of the people to be secure in their persons, houses, papers, and effects, against unreasonable search or seizure, shall not be violated; and no warrant shall issue, but upon probable cause, supported by oath or affirmation, and particularly describing the place to be searched, and the person or thing to be seized.

This provision guarantees that individuals will be free from unreasonable searches and seizures. The wording of this provision is identical to that of the Fourth Amendment to the U.S. Constitution. Although the doctrine that has developed from this provision parallels the Supreme Court's treatment of the Fourth Amendment, there have been periods of time when some discrepancies between the two sets of protections have existed. The case law that has developed in connection with this provision of the state constitution revolves around considerations of defining the words and phrases in this section, developing an outline of what constitutes "Probable cause," and applying the exclusionary rule to evidence that is illegally seized or is otherwise tainted (*State v. Buxton*, 1958). This provision and its protections are to be liberally construed (*Flum v State*, 1923). As an example of the parallel pattern of development of this doctrine with that emerging from the Fourth Amendment of the U.S. Constitution, there is now a good faith exception to the Exclusionary Rule which prevailed for so long (*Blalock v. State*, 1985; and *Moran v. State*, 1993). The state exception was created essentially within a year of the federal good faith exception (*U.S. v. Leon*, 1984).

The right can be waived by the individual subject to the search or the arrest, but not by any third party that may be related to or connected with the investigation or the arrest from which the search or seizure arises (*Maxey v. State*, 1969). Probable cause does not justify a warrantless search and seizure (*Ferry v. State*, 1970). On the other hand, information of criminal activity obtained from an informant, the defendant's use of drug paraphernalia in plain view, or when the arresting officers have probable cause to believe a felony is being committed in their presence, all provide examples of adequate grounds for seizure of the evidence and its use in convicting the perpetrator, without a warrant issuing first (*Johnson v. State*, 1973). There is a limited plain view exception to the warrant requirement (*Hewell v. State*, 1984; *Wood v. State*, 1992). As long as an officer is justified in "observing" from a particular place, he can seize materials that are in plain view from that place (*May v. State*, 1977).

Searches are valid when they are consented to by the individual. Furthermore, once consent is obtained, seizures of evidence cannot be challenged later. There is the requirement that the consent be voluntary in order for it to be valid. No challenge can be raised to the search of property owned by another individual.

There are a good many technical dimensions to this provision. It should be recognized that the extent of these developments revolves around this section of the constitution in relation to its federal constitutional counterpart. Both are seen as fundamental means for persons suspected of crimes to avoid giving evidence without establishing probable cause to the satisfaction of a magistrate. The exclusionary rule, as modified by good faith exception, prevents the use of illegal evidence against the accused. It is generally important as a protection against unwarranted police intrusion or the seizure of personal belongings, unless related to criminal activity, unless supported by probable cause, or unless there are extenuating circumstances that support the circumvention of the warrant requirement. In this way, this section has become a repository for the criminal process doctrines relating to searches, search warrants, and the arrest practices in the state, just as the Fourth Amendment of the U.S. Constitution has developed.

SECTION 12

Courts Open; Remedy by Due Course of Law; Administration of Justice. All courts shall be open; and every person, for injury done to his person, property, or reputation, shall have remedy by due course of law. Justice shall be administered freely, and without purchase; completely, and without denial; speedily, and without delay. (Amended November 6, 1984)

This section provides that the courts of the state are to be open and available to the public for the redress of legal wrongs, to person, property, or reputation. Justice is to be freely and fairly rendered, without delay. This, in effect, is a guarantee that the state will provide an official arena in which the law can be used to resolve disputes or settle conflicts between private parties. This provision is consistent with the later decision by the U.S. Supreme Court in *Ex Parte Milligan* (1866). *Milligan* related to the operation of civilian courts in the State of Indiana.

This provision has become the source of the requirement or guarantee of Due Process of Law, even though the wording of the section certainly does not contain an explicit guarantee of that sort (*Dunn v. Jenkins*, 1978; *Hudgins v. McAtee*, 1992). The "due course" wording in this section has been interpreted to require due process of law, and that has largely occurred within the state judiciary over the years. This expansion of the wording of this section might not coincide with a literal reading of the provision, but the state courts have consistently treated this phrase to require fair procedure or "due process" (e.g., *Warren v. Indiana Telephone Co.*, 1940).

This provision forms the guarantee of a speedy trial as interpreted by the Indiana courts (*Fryback v. State*, 1980). In *Fryback* the state court held that this section, plus the Sixth and Fourteenth Amendments of the U.S. Constitution, imposed the speedy trial requirement on the state. The nature of this guarantee depends on the reason for any delays that occur in the prosecution. Those delays may be warranted (*Wright v. State*, 1992). Under such situations, the supreme court is willing to waive the speedy trial requirement (*Loyd v. State*, 1980). Furthermore, the defendant must show prejudice from the delay before the constitutional requirement can be violated (*Harrell v. State*, 1993). However, absent a clear and convincing reason for the delay, a trial conviction can be rejected on appeal by the failure to conduct the trial speedily (*Bailey v. State*, 1979).

There has developed a great deal of detail in the state courts' interpretations of this provision of the state constitution. That interpretation is also overlaid by the parallel provisions of the U. S. Constitution (the Sixth and Fourteenth Amendments). In addition, section 13 of this article (I) of the state constitution deals with persons accused of crimes and the rights to be afforded them. As a result, the criminal or the accused person is afforded extensive procedural protection. In general, the state courts' interpretations have not varied much from the parallel protections directed by the U.S. Supreme Court based on the Bill of Rights of the U.S. Constitution. That is the case even though the decisions and the substantive law developed by the state and federal courts have not occurred simultaneously in the two judicial systems.

SECTION 13

Rights of Accused in Criminal Prosecutions. In all criminal prosecutions, the accused shall have the right to a public trial, by an impartial jury, in the county in which the offense shall have been committed; to be heard by himself and counsel; to demand the nature and cause of the accusation against him, and to have a copy thereof; to meet the witnesses face to face, and to have compulsory process for obtaining witnesses in his favor.

This section clearly contains the guarantees afforded a person accused of a crime. It is the portion of the state constitution most similar to the Sixth Amendment of the U.S. Constitution, even though there is some variation in wording. This provision addresses the rights of criminals and the criminal justice process. (However, see the preceding section [Article I, section 12] and accompanying text.) The rights guaranteed here, include:

- The right to a public trial.
- The right to an impartial jury.
- Trial held in the county where the offense occurred.

- The right to be heard.
- The right to be represented by legal counsel.
- The right to know the nature of the accusations.
- The right to confront one's accusers.
- The right to compulsory process.

These rights seem basic and fundamental, and they may operate today, regardless of whether they are outlined in a state or a federal constitutional provision. However, when this constitution was drafted in 1851, these rights may have been far less well developed, understood, or applied. They were certainly less developed in the context of the federal Constitution.

This section is very frequently litigated nowadays, although much of the development of the criminal process doctrine based on this provision was probably worked out and applied decades ago. Furthermore, the meaning of most of these segments coincides with the appropriate provision of the federal Constitution's Sixth Amendment. What remains is the interstitial development of answers to specific questions about the application and meaning of these provisions as applied to specific cases conducted by the trial courts in Indiana.

The purpose of the public trial requirement is to insure public scrutiny and knowledge of the judicial proceedings. Such openness is the norm and any exception to that is not favored, but can be justified (*State ex rel. Post-Tribune Pub. Co. v. Porter Superior Court*, 1980). The trial court has recognized discretion in limiting access as long as such limitations further the integrity of the process (*Hackett v. State*, 1977).

The right to an impartial jury requires the removal of any biased jurors, whenever that bias is discovered (*Threats v. State*, 1991). This bias can be actual or evident on the one hand or implied or inferred on the other (*see Irvin v. Doud*, 1961). Such bias is a state of mind rather than a formal or technical evidentiary requirement. This right to an impartial jury does not mean the right to a jury of defendant's choice, nor is there a constitutional right to peremptory challenges to jurors (*Robinson v. State*, 1983).

The doctrine emerging from the requirement of the right to counsel has developed much like that formed from the federal constitutional requirement. For example, the right to legal representation in connection with a charged misdemeanor was first recognized in 1979, when the constitutional provision was recognized as making no distinction between felonies and misdemeanors (*Frazier v. State*, 1979; *Brunson v. State*, 1979). The U.S. Supreme Court had held the Sixth Amendment to include a similar right to counsel in 1972 in *Argersinger v. Hamlin*. The right exists at every stage of the criminal proceeding against an accused (*Monroe v. State*, 1961; *Wizniuk v. State*, 1961). This begins at the time the adversarial judicial proceedings commence (*Young v. State*, 1979).

The rights to confront the witnesses against the accused and to compulsory process have been combined in treatment by the Indiana judiciary. That is not unique or exceptional, but there are few questions that have arisen about compulsory process. Most of the doctrines arising from these rights are instances when some question arises regarding confrontation. The supreme court has devoted much of its attention in this area to recognizing exceptions to the right to confront witnesses (*Ingram v. State*, 1981). The supreme court held in *State v. Owings* (1993) that this right to confront was not coextensive with the Sixth Amendment of the U.S. Constitution. In this case, the state guarantee does not afford a criminal defendant all the rights to confront every witness in all instances of the criminal proceedings.

Any of the rights contained in this section can be waived by the defendant (*State ex rel. Fox v. La Porte Circuit Court*, 1956), but that waiver must be knowingly and intelligently given. Such a waiver requires that the individual be competent to waive the rights provided under this section of the constitution. There is a good deal of variation and technicality relating to the waiver of each of these rights. That is because the scope and nature of them differs a great deal. The courts of the state have been generally reluctant to grant waivers quickly or without careful consideration (*Russell v. State*, 1978).

Although this section is certainly a substantial segment of the rights of the accused, it is often coupled with a broad view of section 12. That combination leads to an extensive set of rights for persons who are involved in the criminal justice system of the state. The specific rights relating to the components of this section have developed in incremental and elaborate fashion that involves a great deal of complexity and specialty. That development has varied somewhat from the parallel components contained in the federal Constitution, but those variations are not numerous or very significant.

SECTION 14

Double Jeopardy and Self-Incrimination. No person shall be put in jeopardy twice for the same offense. No person, in any criminal prosecution, shall be compelled to testify against himself.

This section of the Indiana Constitution provides individuals with protection against double jeopardy and self-incrimination. While these protections are also present in the Fifth Amendment of the U.S. Constitution, the wording in this section is somewhat different, and the self-incrimination protection here is not clearly stated as either a right or a privilege. It is a privilege in the Fifth Amendment. Both of these protections are basic to our system of criminal justice. The drafters of the state constitution followed the explicit lead of the Kentucky and Ohio drafters by including these in a separate section of the Bill of Rights, and coupling them together. There are a variety of double jeopardy issues which indicate that the individual can waive this protection in several situations (*Corley v. State*, 1983).

Most of the cases relating to double jeopardy issues focus on when jeopardy attaches and what the meaning of this protection involves. For example, double jeopardy does not attach if the defendant is found incompetent to stand trial and a mistrial is declared (*Griffin v. State*, 1981). Furthermore, double jeopardy does not attach where a defendant seeks or causes the declaration of a mistrial (*White-head v. State*, 1983), as is also the case with a hung jury. Discharging a jury before the verdict is returned does not place the accused in double jeopardy. The finding of guilt on one provision in an indictment without any verdict on the other counts prevents reinitiation of the prosecution on other charges, because that is considered the equivalent to an express finding of not guilty (*Weinzorpflin v. State*, 1844). However, there is some question of whether this view is still good law, given the age of the precedent. An erroneous acquittal of the defendant works to prevent a new prosecution on the same charges (*State v. White*, 1983). The reversal of a conviction on appeal does not necessarily attach double jeopardy to the charges of a subsequent retrial, since that reversal is based on legal errors in the first trial (*Sumpter v. State*, 1976).

The self-incrimination provision in this section can be waived by the individual (*Appelby v. State*, 1943). However, unless it is intelligently waived, the individual need not provide any evidence that could incriminate himself. This provision applies in both civil and criminal actions (*Wilkins v. Malone* 1860), although civil testimony is protected only if it might subject the person to a subsequent criminal prosecution or penalty. If an individual chooses to testify, then he is subject to cross-examination (*State v. Comer*, 1902). Failure of a defendant to take the witness stand does not constitute any basis for an inference about guilt in connection with the charges (*Barnes v. State*, 1982; *Pitman v. State*, 1982). Such failure to take the stand cannot be commented on by the prosecution (*Holland v. State*, 1983).

The purpose of this protection against self-incrimination is to require the accusing party (criminal prosecutor or civil plaintiff) to provide independent evidence of the allegations and to prove those allegations to the trier of fact with sufficient weight to result in a finding for the plaintiff. The defendant need not provide any of the evidence used by the prosecution or the plaintiff. This is a testimonial right. This means that a witness can only refuse to testify or answer specific questions if the testimony sought will incriminate that individual (*Allen v. State*, 1981).

In *Miranda v. Arizona* (1966), the U.S. Supreme Court held that the Fifth Amendment privilege against self-incrimination operates in the context of suspect apprehension. Thus, the apprehended individual, before charging or arrest, must be informed of the (in)famous "Miranda" rights:

- The suspect has the right to remain silent.
- Anything the suspect says may be used against him in a court of law.

- The suspect has the right to an attorney.
- If the suspect cannot afford an attorney, then one will be provided.

These rights, particularly the first three, preclude the use of any statements made by the individual before those protections have been read to the individual. Certainly no incriminating evidence can be extracted by violence or threats or any other coercive or improper influence. These "Miranda" rights have been added to this provision of the state constitution by the court decision in *Haskell v. State* (1970).

SECTION 15

Persons Arrested or Confined; Treatment. No person arrested, or confined in jail, shall be treated with unnecessary rigor.

This section protects people in custody from unnecessary "rigor" in their confinement. This protection does not have an analogue in the federal Constitution. It reaches more situations than jail, so it protects the individual wherever confinement may occur, including the trial courtroom (*Suter v. State*, 1949). This protects people from the possibility of excessive force or restraint while they are in custody.

"Unnecessary rigor" is not defined in this section, but a variety of circumstances or practices have been considered in this regard. At the same time, the "rigor" necessary to incarcerate a suspect safely is left to the law enforcement, prosecution, prison, and judicial officials charged with duties in the criminal justice system. Thus, there is certainly some discretion in the amount of force or rigor applied to an individual (*Hall v. State*, 1928). That is to be expected because any individual case involves particular facts, circumstances, and requirements to complete confinement (*Bonahoon v. State* 1931). However, this deference by the courts does not extend to all circumstances and all cases (*Kokenes v. State*, 1938). Courts will not accept a confession obtained under circumstances that constitute unnecessary rigor by law enforcement officers involved in the case, that is, a coerced confession.

SECTION 16

Excessive Bail or Fines and Cruel and Unusual Punishment. Excessive bail shall not be required. Excessive fines shall not be imposed. Cruel and unusual punishments shall not be inflicted. All penalties shall be proportioned to the nature of the offense.

This protection insures that cruel and unusual punishment, excessive fines and penalties, and bail will be not assessed against an accused or a criminal after conviction. This provision is analogous to the Eighth Amendment of the federal Constitution, but this section does include limits on the penalties imposed above and beyond the cruel and unusual prohibition. These limits relate to reasonable, compared with excessive, fines or disproportionate penalties. The standard for the reasonableness of a penalty is whether a "reasonable person" would find the sentence to be appropriate (*Carter v. State*, 1984). That standard is not exceptional, given the wording of the last provision in this section. However, the courts have left the determination of reasonableness largely up to those who would otherwise be charged with violation of this provision, that is, the legislature or the judiciary. Thus, there are no external or objective criteria that can be applied as a general rule to make these determinations, and there is no outside institution or "judge" making the assessment of reasonableness.

Determining the penalty for a crime is a legislative act. A court cannot modify a specific penalty imposed by a sentencing court if it falls within the statutory boundaries for that crime. That means that the legislature, rather than the courts, is to determine (define) what complies with the constitutional requirement. Thus, if the legislature sets forth the penalties for a crime, they must be within the "proportional" or reasonable requirement of this section. The matter of legislative judgment in this regard is largely left alone by the courts, since the provision of the constitution does not provide guidance, and the state courts defer to the legislature's judgments about penalties.

The state is permitted under this provision to incarcerate someone, who is sentenced to life imprisonment, on death row given the cruelty and atrociousness of the crime. This incarceration with capital punishment inmates does not constitute cruel and unusual punishment (*Shack v. State*, 1972). If the state fails to provide rehabilitation programs for habitual criminals, sentenced under that statute, there is no violation of the cruel and unusual punishment ban (*Craig v. State*, 1978).

The ban against excessive bail does not require that bail be set for all alleged offenses and perpetrators. Some offenses—murder and treason—are usually not bailable offenses in Indiana (see section 17). The statute on this matter imposes the burden on the accused to show that bail is appropriate. All other offenses are presumed to be bailable (IC 35-33-8-2). However, the purpose of bail is to insure that the accused returns to appear before the court as required under the procedures and charges (*Brown v. State*, 1987). Thus, it is possible that the trial judge may decide that no amount of bail will insure the reappearance and deny bail altogether. That is, the judge can deny bail in order to insure the appearance of the accused. That means there is constitutional right to bail and the statutory presumption is not binding. After conviction for a crime, bail is entirely up to the judge's discretion, without the presumption operating at all (*Critchlow v. State*, 1976). Setting bail is clearly considered to be a matter of judicial discretion.

SECTION 17

Right to Bail and Unbailable Offenses. Offenses, other than murder or treason, shall be bailable by sufficient sureties. Murder or treason shall not be bailable, when the proof is evident, or the presumption strong.

This provision of the constitution establishes that bail is generally to be available, as long as the surety of the bond is adequate. This supports the "presumption" of bail mentioned in the discussion on section 16. The right to bail provided here and the right against excessive bail in the previous section are both founded on the historical tradition that persons accused of crimes are innocent until proven guilty (*Sherelis v. State*, 1983). However, it is also clear that this section makes murder and treason not generally bailable. The wording here does not make this ban absolute. The possibility of bail for these two offenses requires that there is no proof of guilt or a strong presumption of guilt from the evidence at hand. The framers of the constitution intended that if there is little (or no) question as to the guilt of the accused, for either of these very serious crimes, then bail should not be available. How clear the proof or presumption must be is not clear or explicit. Yet, the burden is on the accused to show entitlement to bail in the case of a murder indictment (*Brown v. State*, 1897). Upon the proper showing by an accused, however, bail in a murder case does become a matter of right (*State v. Hedges*, 1912).

The setting of bail in other offenses is left to the "sound discretion" of the trial court (*Hughes v. Sheriff of Vigo County*, 1978). This discretion is limited by the requirements of notice and due process, so that the accused must have the opportunity to participate in a hearing regarding the bail. These requirements are not unique, but rather are reasonable and moderate expectations about the operation of bail in any judicial system.

SECTION 18

Penal Code Founded on Reformation. The penal code shall be founded on the principles of reformation, and not of vindictive justice.

This constitutional provision has no counterpart in the U.S. Constitution. It indicates that the principle motivating the determination of sentences for criminal offenses or penalties in the state's penal code is reform (that means rehabilitation in modern parlance) rather than retribution. This philosophy can be debated, but the constitution settles the debate explicitly with this provision. The debate surfaces most clearly in connection with life imprisonment and capital punishment cases. Neither of these two penalties can arguably be based on reformation or rehabilitation because neither of them admits to the possibility of rehabilitation of the criminal. As interpreted, the death penalty does not violate this provision as long as it was imposed evenhandedly and fairly (*Smith v.*

State, 1984; *Roche v. State*, 1992); nor does a sentence of life imprisonment violate this provision of the constitution (*Lynk v. State*, 1979). The interpretation of this section seems to ride largely on whether the entire criminal code and aggregate philosophy behind penalties was rehabilitative in nature (*Driskill v. State*, 1855).

It is striking that such a philosophical statement would be included in the organic act itself. The section does not grant any rights or liberties, but rather it reflects the philosophical orientation of the drafters of the constitution. It, furthermore, can serve as an interpretive guide for the judiciary in treating other provisions of the constitution and statutory enactments of the state legislature. However, the state courts have not been called on to evaluate the "reformative" dimensions of the state penal code.

This section has given rise to questions about or challenges to jury instructions that are arguably "too vindictive." However, the general features of the penal code are the focus of this philosophical section. Challenges occur to specific criminal sentences on the grounds that the penalty is *not* rehabilitative, but rather is vindictive. It could be a source for challenging the sentences that the legislature imposes, again arguably because they are not rehabilitative. Yet, this constitutional provision has not been a frequent source of challenge.

SECTION 19

Right of Jury to Determine Law and Facts in Criminal Cases. In all criminal cases whatever, the jury shall have the right to determine the law and the facts.

This section specifies a unique function for the jury in criminal cases in Indiana. The fact-finding function of the jury is well established and widely accepted throughout the country and in this state. This role requires the jury to hear and consider the evidence presented in the case in order to determine the guilt or innocence of the accused. The determination of "the law" by the jury, however, does raise some doubt or question about this portion of the section.[1] The jury's function in this regard reflects the predominant Jacksonian view of democracy at the time the constitution was written. That is, the people, and in the case of criminal trials, the jury, should be empowered wherever possible to determine the law, as well as the facts. This contains the possibility of a jury nullifying law which it finds unacceptable in a case. The potential for "mischief" from this provision is pretty clear.

---

[1] See Note, "The Jury's Role Under the Indiana Constitution," 52 *Indiana Law Journal* 793 (1977). *Williams v. State* (1858) characterizes the change that this provision in the 1851 Constitution made in the Common Law jury function.

How this provision operates, in fact, is an open question. It is likely to depend on the wording of jury instructions that are presented to individual juries regarding the law of the subject at trial. In Indiana, jury instructions are expected to provide the jury with the "applicable principles of law" as long as the jurors are not thereby bound with regard to their "right to determine the law for themselves" (*Hart v. State*, 1942). Furthermore, other state court decisions indicate that it is the trial court's duty to "correctly and completely present [the] applicable law to [the] jury so that it will not be misled" (*Rodriguez v. State*, 1979). This discussion hardly captures all the nuances of jury instructions and their wording, in light of this constitutional provision. However, the trial court need not tell the jury to disregard the jury instructions because this constitutional provision gives the jury the right to determine "the law" as well as the facts in a case (*Beavers v. State*, 1957). This suggests that while the jury is the determiner of law as well as fact, there is a major role for the trial judge's instructions to guide the jury's findings in a criminal prosecution. Yet, even with this constitutional wording, the state courts have sought to limit or restrict the jury's lawmaking role. For example, the jury's *power* to substitute its assessment of the law for that given in the court's instruction is not a *right* of the jury (*Candler v. State*, 1977). In the *Candler* case, the court distinguished between the power of the jury to find the law and its right. While this distinction may not be understandable or clear, the court thought it differentiated (and limited) the degree to which the jury could substitute its judgment on matters of law for those of the court.

SECTION 20

Trial by Jury in civil cases. In all civil cases, the right to trial by jury shall remain inviolate.

The right to a jury trial in *all* civil cases is guaranteed by this section of the constitution. This provision contains no monetary minimum such as the Seventh Amendment of the U.S. Constitution does. This section is clear and absolute with regard to its coverage, and there is nothing in this requirement to suggest that there can be exceptions or that any judgment or evaluation need be made about the requirement. It is obviously possible for the parties in a civil suit to waive the requirement (*Randolph v. State*, 1955). However, that waiver must be clear and explicit before section 20 is suspended from operation (*Sheets v. Bray*, 1890).

State statutes provide for the specifics of civil jury organization and operation, but the constitutional provision is the basis for those legislative enactments. By statute, civil juries are to be composed of six jurors with three alternates (IC 34-1-20.5-1). The operation of this constitutional requirement is not quite as straightforward as the wording of the section would imply. However, a civil jury trial must be demanded or else it is considered waived (*Sheets v. Bray*, 1890). The plaintiff's demand for jury trial must be made when the complaint is filed or it is considered waived. Thus, the presumption of a jury trial has been reversed by court interpretations to place the burden on the party desiring a jury trial. That seems completely contrary to the constitutional provision, but the courts have reasoned that the jury is required, but only where it is sought by one of the parties (*Indianapolis Northern Traction Co. v. Brennan*, 1909).

Some civil actions are matters provided for by statute, and there the right to a jury depends on the provisions of the statute and whether a jury trial is afforded by statute. That is, the state supreme court has interpreted the jury requirement to attach only to those actions arising from the common law. That means the legislature can determine for itself, in the case of legal rights of civil action created by statute, whether to permit or require juries. The core of the exceptions is based on a narrow judicial view of "civil" in the constitutional provision. If a right of action arises from a statutory enactment, then the action is arguably not covered by the constitutional requirement.

Thus, in probate trials the presence of a jury to determine the validity of a will is not a state constitutional matter. It is a matter of statutory provision (*Wright v. Fultz*, 1894). This is based on the court's reasoning that some probate issues are not civil, and therefore those are not covered by the constitution, and furthermore, that precludes a jury from the entire proceeding. Neither is a jury required by the constitution in action to foreclose on a mortgage (*Carmichael v. Adams*, 1883). Equitable relief (an injunction) is not guaranteed a jury trial by this section of the constitution (*McKinley v. Britton*, 1913). A petition for habeas corpus is not a civil action so there is no right of a jury trial guaranteed by this section (*Baker v. Gordon*, 1864). Generally, these last two categories of exceptions to the jury trial requirement can be explained in terms of proceedings at law, as opposed to actions involving questions of fact, which is the traditional role that juries play in the judicial system. That is, in neither actions in equity nor habeas corpus petitions would a jury perform its traditional, fact-finding function.

However, in the other kinds of legal actions mentioned—mortgage foreclosures or probate cases—a jury is allowed, because of court interpretations. This seems directly contrary to the constitutional provision. The courts have taken the view that a statutory right of action does not inherently require a jury trial as provided in section 20 of the constitution. However, there is certainly some question about the position of the state courts on this issue. It has been widely and frequently applied, and that practice of the courts has overridden this constitutional provision, but there is still the doubt about the validity of the view held by the state judiciary on this section.

SECTION 21

Right to Compensation for Services and Property. No person's particular services shall be demanded, without just compensation. No person's property shall be taken by law, without just compensation; nor, except in case of the State, without such compensation first assessed and tendered. (Amended November 6, 1984)

This is the takings clause of the Indiana Constitution. It requires that just compensation be paid for a taking, just as the Fifth Amendment of the U.S. Constitution does. However, this state provision contains some differences. First, here a person's "services" as well as property can be taken, and that must be compensated justly. A second difference is that here, the taking can occur before the state assesses and tenders the compensation (*Bd. of Comm'rs of Hamilton County v. Blue Ribbon Ice Cream & Milk Corp.*, 1952). If the state is not taking, then the just compensation must be paid *before* the taking an occur. This last provision applies to private takings such as public utility right-of-ways.

This exception for the state is due to the reluctance of the drafters to require the state to pay for services in advance. (It could also be that most such "takings" cannot be paid for in advance by the state because of a lack of public moneys.) The inclusion of services as well as property may indicate that the drafters recognized that a "taking" of services can be just as significant as a taking of property and both can and should be based on the just compensation requirement. It is not clear what kind of "service" these takings envision, although there has been some litigation that clarified the sense of this services portion of the section. This level of sensitivity may still be operating in the state with regard to such takings. That is illustrated in *Winters v. Mowery* (1993) where the federal District Court held that recipients of child maintenance and spousal support payments had a property interest in the accumulated interest and the state did not own the interest earned from these deposited payments. State retention of the interest on such payments violates the plaintiff's Fifth Amendment right to just compensation under the U.S. Constitution.

Neither attorneys (*Hoey v. McCarthy*, 1890) nor physicians, as professionals (*Buchman v. State*, 1877), can be compelled to perform services without just compensation being provided. To do so would be a taking without compensation. The testimony of witnesses in a criminal prosecution is not a "service" within the meaning of this section of the constitution. Therefore, such testimony does not require just compensation under this constitutional requirement, even though it can be compelled. The development of the takings provision of the constitution has been elaborate and extensive, historically. Its continued development and expansion is likely, given recent developments in the law of takings, particularly in the federal courts (e.g., *Winters v. Mowery*, 1993; *Dolan v. City of Tigard*, 1994).

SECTION 22

Privileges of Debtor; Imprisonment for Debt. The privilege of the debtor to enjoy the necessary comforts of life, shall be recognized by wholesome laws, exempting a reasonable amount of property from seizure or sale, for the payment of any debt or liability hereafter contracted: and there shall be no imprisonment for debt, except in case of fraud.

This section of the constitution guarantees that debtors cannot have their entire wealth garnished or seized. Rather, "wholesome laws" are to insure their "necessary comforts." This is not self-executing, but rather requires the legislature to implement this provision by adopting laws to set out the manner in which this provision will be operationalized (*Green v. Aker*, 1858). This means that while this protection is salutary, it is not considered to be a fundamental or inherent right of people in the state. It does not operate automatically, but depends on positive enactments by the General Assembly to give it meaning. Yet, this provision has a "spirit" to aid the needy and the unfortunate (*Martin v. Louis*, 1935).

In addition, the section means debt cannot be the basis for imprisonment (*State ex rel. Wilson v. Monroe Superior Court IV*, 1983), except in the case of fraud (*Baker v. State*, 1887). This section also does not apply to a criminal defendant who is found guilty and assessed the costs of prosecution (*McCool v. State*, 1864). Such costs are not "debt" within the meaning of this provision. Neither are fines, costs, or forfeitures arising from criminal cases considered to be debts within the meaning of this section of the constitution (*Hardenbrook v. Town of Ligonier*, 1883).

SECTION 23

Equal Privileges. The General Assembly shall not grant to any citizen, or class of citizens, privileges or immunities, which, upon the same terms, shall not equally belong to all citizens.

This section of the constitution does not guarantee citizens privileges or immunities as does the Fourteenth Amendment to the U.S. Constitution. However, it does require that any privileges or immunities that are granted by the General Assembly be equally afforded to all citizens. This is a variant on the Equal Protection Clause of the federal Constitution. Here, the state is obligated to insure equal privileges, while in the federal Constitution states are prohibited from denying equal protection of the laws. This seems designed to insure that if the state distributes benefits it must provide them equally to all citizens.

The Indiana courts have viewed this provision as permitting the state to exercise its political powers by regulating or interfering with the rights of some rather than all citizens (*Selvage v. Talbott*, 1911). So, the state police power is a valid basis for categorizing or classifying people. Particular categories of citizens cannot be arbitrarily excluded from benefits, including jury duty. The arbitrary enforcement or discriminatory enforcement of an otherwise valid law can violate this section as a denial of equal privileges (*Parker v. State*, 1980). This is just the point established by the U.S. Supreme Court in *Yick Wo v. Hopkins* (1886). However, people may be classified reasonably and for a legitimate purpose and then receive different treatment without violating this constitutional requirement (*Johnson v. St. Vincent Hospital, Inc.*, 1980). The *Johnson* case suggests that the classifications made by the General Assembly need not meet a strict scrutiny test in order to be valid. Rather, a "reasonable" connection between the state's objective and the categorization of citizens is all that is required. Such classifications must be based on some fair and substantial relation to the object of the legislation. The idea that drives this requirement focuses on the need to connect any classification with the purpose of the legislature's work. The difference between this and the U.S. Supreme Court's scrutiny of classificatory schemes has not focused on whether the classification scheme was suspect or not. At the state level, there is much less doctrine developed on the basis of this constitutional provision than has arisen in connection with the Fourteenth Amendment.

SECTION 24

Ex Post Facto Laws and Impairing Contracts. No *ex post facto* law, or law impairing the obligation of contracts, shall ever be passed.

These prohibitions combine two protections contained in separate parts of the U.S. Constitution. The state cannot adopt a law which is an *ex post facto* law, and no law can impair the obligation of contract. The law that has developed around these two provisions is fairly straightforward, but important.

The *ex post facto* element means, among other things, that one cannot be tried and convicted for action that was not a crime at the time the acts took place (*Schwomeyer v. State*, 1923). This rule permits subsequent changes in credit for the time already served in prison. This protection applies to matters of criminal laws, but it clearly does not reach civil or private rights. However, little case law development of this provision has occurred. The need to apply or interpret the *ex post facto* protection has not arisen frequently in Indiana, even though the general parameters relating to the *ex post facto* provision have clear meaning. The end result is that the protection is available if a constitutional question arises, but that does not appear to have occurred frequently in the state's history.

The protection against the impairment of contract permits a stable and reliable contractual environment in which people can engage in business transactions. Any exercise of the state police power affecting public health, safety, and welfare is not limited by the bar against impairing contracts (*Central Union Telephone Co. v. Indianapolis Telephone Co.*, 1920). Such legislation, when it affects contracts but promotes the health, safety, or welfare of the public, does not violate this provision of the constitution. The state courts' interpretations of these contractual protections are not as clear or as absolute as the development of the U.S. Constitutional Contract Clause (Article I, section 10, Cl. I). (See *Home Building & Loan Ass'n. v. Blaisdell*, 1934, to the contrary.)

SECTION 25

Effect of Laws. No law shall be passed, the taking effect of which shall be made to depend upon any authority, except as provided in this Constitution.

This provision of the constitution requires that the authority to execute a law must exist in this constitution before the enactment of the law occurs. That means any adopted law must be immediately executable under the existing provisions of the constitution. There is no comparable provision of the U.S. Constitution, although the Necessary and Proper Clause of Article I, section 8 might be viewed in this light. That federal provision is not the same in wording or in meaning as the state constitutional section.

The meaning of this section relates to the execution of state statutes enacted by the General Assembly. For example, a state law relating to the inspection and destruction of diseased cattle derives from the inherent police power of the state to protect public health and safety. The General Assembly has the power to enact such a law even though there is no explicit grant of constitutional authority for that purpose (*Jones v. State*, 1960). This section of the constitution effectively requires that the power to execute a statute be granted in the constitution before enactment of that law can occur.

SECTION 26

Suspension of Operation of Law. The operation of the laws shall never be suspended, except by the authority of the General Assembly.

This section specifies that once enacted, the operation of a law will continue unless that is suspended by an action of the General Assembly. This requires an act of the legislature to suspend the operation of a law that it has already enacted. Thus, neither the governor nor any administrator, and certainly no citizen (*Cain v. Allen*, 1906), can suspend the enforcement of a statute, for any reason. This provision does not permit a permanent or a temporary suspension by any actor except the legislature. Any special statute which arguably does suspend the operation of law is to be strictly construed and scrutinized by any reviewing court (*Highland Sales Corp. v. Vance*, 1962).

SECTION 27

Suspension of Habeas Corpus; Exception. The privilege of the writ of *habeas corpus* shall not be suspended, except in case of rebellion or invasion; and there, only if the public safety demand it.

This section provides that the writ of *habeas corpus* is not to be suspended except when public safety requires it in cases of rebellion or invasion. The purpose of the writ is to protect people from unlawful detention or restraint by government. However, the availability of the writ does not amount to an unlimited permit to abuse the writ (*Shoemaker v. Dowd*, 1953). Furthermore, the issue of the writ when public safety is in jeopardy changes, to require a balance between the writ and the need for public safety or order. The writ of *habeas corpus*, thus, is subject to reasonable regulation by the legislature (*Johnson v. Burke*, 1958). It operates by permitting incarcerated or restrained individuals to petition the courts to examine the validity of the authority for their imprisonment. This writ is independent of the federal Writ of Habeas Corpus, because neither the president nor the U.S. Congress can suspend the writ in a state court, under the general principles of federalism (*Griffin v. Wilcox*, 1863).

SECTION 28

Treason Against State; Definition. Treason against the State shall consist only in levying war against it, and in giving aid and comfort to its enemies.

This section defines treason against the State of Indiana. This definition is closely analogous to the definition of treason against the United States in Article III, section 3 of the U.S. Constitution. Treason requires the individual to levy war against the state or give "aid and comfort" to the enemies of the state. These acts constitute a breach of allegiance toward the state. However, no one can be guilty of treason for merely speaking critically of the state or its policies. This is protected by the rights of free speech and the right to petition government. Treason requires that overt acts of war or overt acts of affording comfort to state enemies must be established (proven) in order for someone to be guilty of this crime.

SECTION 29

Treason Against State; Proof. No person shall be convicted of treason, except on the testimony of two witnesses to the same overt act, or upon his confession in open court.

This provision defines the nature of the proof required to convict someone of treason. This wording is taken verbatim from Article III, section 3 of the U.S. Constitution. Two witnesses, not just one, must give evidence regarding the same overt act. The only other satisfactory basis for conviction for treason requires the accused to confess to the treason in open court. This is a fairly straightforward requirement. There is no indication of the burden of proof that must be met by the prosecution, but it can be assumed to require evidence beyond a reasonable doubt, from at least the two witnesses provided by the prosecution.

SECTION 30

Conviction; Effect. No conviction shall work corruption of blood, or forfeiture of estate.

This section prohibits a conviction for a crime to corrupt the blood of the guilty person. This provision is analogous to part of Article I, section 9 of the federal Constitution that prevents bills of attainder. Thus, the heir and descendants of the criminal cannot be made to pay or suffer from the criminal acts that an individual commits. Furthermore, such a criminal conviction cannot be the basis for the forfeiture of property by the individual.

SECTION 31

Right to Assemble, to Instruct and to Petition. No law shall restrain any of the inhabitants of the State from assembling together in a peaceable manner, to consult for their common good; nor from instructing their representatives; nor from applying to the General Assembly for redress of grievances.

This right insures that people can assemble and petition government for the redress of grievances. Thus, individuals or groups can meet to discuss matters of common concern. They can meet and instruct their elected representatives on matters that concern them. Lastly, they can assemble in order to seek a redress for a grievance they have regarding matters of public concern or public policy. This section is nearly identical to the provision in the First Amendment of the U.S. Constitution guaranteeing the right "peaceably to assemble, and to petition the Government for a redress of grievances."

The right permits the discussion or advocacy of the use of force or the violation of law to redress their concerns (*Communist Party of Indiana v. Whitcomb*, 1974). This interpretation was made by the U.S. Supreme Court and it relates to a combination of this section of the state constitution and the First Amendment of the U.S. Constitution. This right has been interpreted to be the foundation of the right to organize and operate political parties (*Sarlls v. State*, 1929). This section has been interpreted to permit a labor union to picket an employer as long as there were no threats, force, intimidation, fraud, or other unlawful means used in the picketing (*Teamsters, Local No. 364 of the A.F. of L. v. Stewart's Bakery of Rochester*, 1955). In other words, picketing does not violate the "peaceable manner" of assembly that is required by the section. It would appear that any unlawful action relating to the assembly is not protected by this provision. However, except for that determination, assemblies or meetings relating to petitioning government or concerning matters of common concern are protected by this section.

SECTION 32

Bearing Arms. The people shall have a right to bear arms, for the defense of themselves and the State.

This provision guarantees the right to bear arms. This section is worded differently than the Second Amendment of the U.S. Constitution. There is no reference here to the need for a "well regulated militia" as the reason for a right to bear arms. Rather, the reason for the right to bear arms provided in the state constitution is to defend the state or the people of the state. That wording may result in the need for a militia, but there is no explicit reference to a militia as necessary for the defense of the people of Indiana. Exactly what this section means is not well developed, but the qualification that requires the defense of people or the state could be emphasized.

Regulating firearms, such as with licensure requirements, is considered a legitimate state function. According to the courts, this regulation is based on the state's police power to protect the public health, safety, and general welfare (*Matthews v. State*, 1958). Thus, an interest of the legislature in public safety and welfare permits the reasonable regulation of the use of concealed firearms.

SECTION 33

Military Subordinate to Civil Power. The military shall be kept in strict subordination to the civil power.

This statement is an explicit recognition of a principle that is only implied in the U.S. Constitution. There, the president is identified as the commander-in-chief of the armed forces, and that implies civilian control of the U.S. military. In the state constitution, the civilian control is explicitly stated in this section. It may be more direct than is necessary, but it is still clearly stated. There have been no issues relating to this provision, probably because it is so explicit, and because the provision has never been controversial. There has never been any question about the civilian control of the military. There are few circumstances under which this provision would need to be used or come into question.

SECTION 34

Quartering of Soldiers. No soldiers shall, in time of peace, be quartered in any house, without the consent of the owner; nor, in time of war, but in the manner to be prescribed by law.

This section bars the quartering of troops in homes without the consent of the owner, in times of peace. It is identical to the Third Amendment to the federal Constitution. In times of war, however, quartering in civilian homes can take place, but only in a manner that is provided by law. That insures that the General Assembly can provide for such quartering in times of emergency (i.e., war) in a regularized fashion controlled by law. This provision applies to National Guardsmen as "soldiers," in the history of Indiana this exception to the ban (i.e., war) has never occurred.

SECTION 35

Titles of Nobility and Hereditary Distinctions. The General Assembly shall not grant any title of nobility, nor confer hereditary distinctions.

The state legislature, just like the U.S. Congress, is forbidden to grant titles of nobility or hereditary distinctions (see Article I, section 9 of the U.S. Constitution). There have been no legal developments or court interpretations of this provision of the state constitution. That is undoubtedly because the General Assembly has never enacted any provision that could be interpreted as a violation of this section, or brought this provision of the state constitution into play.

SECTION 36

Freedom of Emigration. Emigration from the State shall not be prohibited.

Clearly, this provision prohibits any ban on emigration from the state. Thus, anyone who wishes to leave the state can do so without interference by state law or a state official. The General Assembly has never adopted any legislation which could be interpreted as prohibiting or restricting people from leaving Indiana. However, the section could have become operative in the pre–Civil War era when slavery was a viable issue relating to interstate movement and the like. This coincides with (or supports) the right to travel interstate which the U.S. Supreme Court has recognized (*Edwards v. California*, 1941).

SECTION 37

Slavery and Involuntary Servitude. There shall be neither slavery, nor involuntary servitude, within the State, otherwise than for the punishment of crimes, whereof the party shall have been duly convicted. (Amended November 6, 1984)

This provision clearly reflects the fact that Indiana was a free state at the time of its admission to the union and this section reiterates that that condition will remain in the then-new Constitution of 1851. While slavery and involuntary servitude are explicitly prohibited by the constitution, incarceration as punishment for crimes is not considered to violate this section of the constitution (*Thomas v. City of Indianapolis*, 1924).

The 1984 amendment to this provision involved changes in the wording that were technical or modernizing. The change dealt with removing references to "negro or mullato" and "indenture." It actually removed an antiquated second sentence from this section. The current wording does not change the meaning or the substance of the section at all.

Article II

Suffrage and Elections

SECTION 1

Free and Equal Elections. All elections shall be free and equal.

This provision of the constitution provides for free and equal elections. There is no equivalent provision in the federal Constitution because originally voting and elections were considered to be under state regulation. This requirement of free elections is straightforward. That means that individual voters, or "electors," must be free to cast their votes as they choose to, without regard to constraining influences (*Remster v. Sullivan,* 1905). This is a state right, granted by the state constitution, rather than a federal right based on the federal Constitution (*Gougar v. Timberlake,* 1897). Any deprivation of the right to vote must be based on a legitimate and significant flaw, such as an individual's felony conviction. The courts are not interested in denying the franchise on a technicality that relates only to the letter or words of the law rather than the spirit of a broad interpretation of the franchise, open to everyone, wherever possible (*Dobbyn v. Rogers,* 1948).

The requirement that elections be equal is not so plain or obvious on its face (*State Election Bd. v. Bartolomei,* 1982). However, it appears to capture the expectation that each person's vote would count equally to everyone else's. (*Blue v. State ex rel. Brown,* 1934). This requirement of equality should operate regardless of race, creed, religion, sex, or belief, even though the original provision in 1851 probably was not intended to provide that level of equality, since it preceded the

Civil War and the Reconstruction Amendments to the U.S. Constitution. Some divergence from the "one person, one vote" rule in special districts has been allowed in such settings as school boards or county commission elections. That means that "equal" is not to be applied absolutely to all cases arising under this state provision. Thus, the mathematical precision surrounding the "one person, one vote" rule that has developed in U.S. Supreme Court decisions regarding legislative reapportionment (*e.g., Karcher v. Daggett*, 1983) has not been developed or applied by the state supreme court under this section. Thus, variations from precise mathematical equality in districts is permitted by the Indiana courts under this provision.

SECTION 2

Voting Qualifications. Every citizen of the United States, of the age of eighteen (18) years or more, who has been a resident of a precinct thirty (30) days immediately preceding such election, shall be entitled to vote in that precinct. (Amended March 14, 1881; September 6, 1921; November 2, 1976; November 6, 1984)

The qualifications for voting in Indiana that are specified here reflect current and widespread expectations. The race (1881), gender (1921), and age (1976) of voters were all changed at the times indicated by constitutional amendment. Thus, gradually this provision has been broadened so that the franchise requirements coincide with the changes in the federal Constitution and the franchise has been expanded to reach significant portions of the population. As noted in Part 1, the franchise was originally given to noncitizens who intended to become citizens. That provision was removed as part of the 1921 amendment.

State courts do not consider the right to vote as a natural right, but rather it is treated as a political privilege (*Werber v. Hughes*, 1925; *Gougar v. Timberlake*, 1897; *State v. Goldthait*, 1909). However, once granted, the benefit of the doubt resides with the franchised individual, unless there is a clear specification of limitation or explicit denial of the right to vote (*Werber v. Hughes*, 1925). This privilege cannot be deprived or denied by a board or agency unless the denial of the vote is authorized by a specific statutory provision. The requirements for voting cannot be changed by statutory action of the legislature, but require a constitutional amendment (*Morris v. Powell*, 1890; *State ex rel. McGonigle v. Madison Circuit Court for the Fiftieth judicial District*, 1963).This suggests that while the "right to vote" is a political "right," it has been recognized as of fundamental importance to the individual and it is the basis of the government of the state.

SECTION 3

Members of Armed Forces; Residence. No member of the armed forces of the United States, or of their allies, shall be deemed to have acquired a residence in the

State, in consequence of having been stationed within the same; nor shall any such person have the right to vote. (Amended November 6, 1984)

This section clearly indicated that no one stationed in Indiana while in the armed forces can establish residency for purposes of voting. There have been few questions about this provision, and its purpose seems straightforward. During the Civil War, controversy arose because a number of people were denied the right to vote either because they were present in the state as a member of the armed forces or were out of the state because of that service. Under the court's view of this section, neither category of individual qualified to vote. In 1993, the state legislature considered a proposed constitutional amendment that would strike out this provision of the constitution altogether. It was agreed to by the necessary majorities of both houses of the General Assembly in 1994.

SECTION 4

Residence; Absence from State. No person shall be deemed to have lost his residence in the State, by reason of his absence, either on business of this State or of the United States.

Although this section is not specifically reconnected to voting, that was the original purpose behind this provision. It was intended to insure that persons who were absent from the state for state or federal business would not lose their residency, and thereby their right to vote, for that reason. That insures that someone sent to Washington to represent the state or traveling elsewhere for purposes of state business would retain state residency. The residency requirement for voting is contained elsewhere in this Article. (See Article II, section 2.)

SECTION 5

Repealed. (Repealed March 14, 1881)

This section, repealed in 1881, prohibited any "Negro or Mulatto" from having the right to vote in Indiana. Its repeal followed the adoption of the Fifteenth Amendment of the U.S. Constitution and the declaration by the state supreme court that the provision was "null and void" (*Smith v. Moody*, 1866).

SECTION 6

Disqualification for Bribery. Every person shall be disqualified from holding office, during the term for which he may have been elected, who shall have given or offered a bribe, threat, or reward, to procure his election.

This section prevents persons from holding office if they offered or gave a bribe, a threat, or a reward to obtain their election. This is a self-executing ban on holding public office, which does not require any statutory attention to be operative (*Tinkle v. Wallace*, 1906). This prohibition does not extend to bribes involved in the primary election to secure the nomination to an office (*Gray v. Seitz*, 1904). The court reasoned that the primary election was a mechanism for selecting a candidate to run for office, not electing the officeholder, while the constitutional provision merely insured that an officer could not gain office by bribery. This may not appear very convincing but remains the governing interpretation of this section in the state.

SECTION 7

Repealed. (Repealed November 6, 1984)

This section, repealed in 1984, prohibited anyone from holding an office of trust or profit, if they had given or accepted a challenge to *fight a duel*. Obviously, this recent repeal was a technical correction of the original document, since dueling had been a crime in the State of Indiana for a long time.

SECTION 8

Conviction of Infamous Crime. The General Assembly shall have power to deprive of the right of suffrage, and to render ineligible, any person convicted of an infamous crime.

This section of the constitution gives the General Assembly the authority to ban people from voting if they have been convicted of an infamous crime (*Lucas v. McAfee*, 1940). That means that conviction for such a crime does not automatically disqualify someone from voting, but rather permits the legislature to enact a ban on voting for these offenders. There is no explicit definition of "infamous" contained in the constitution nor has one been developed by the courts. So apparently, the legislature can decide what crimes are sufficiently serious to warrant disfranchisement. The legislature, by statute, disfranchises people while they are in prison, after conviction for a crime. But that does not carry over to postimprisonment (IC 3-7-1-15).

SECTION 9

Holder of Lucrative Office; Eligibility. No person holding a lucrative office or appointment under the United States or under this State is eligible to a seat in the General Assembly; and no person may hold more than one lucrative office at the same time, except as expressly permitted in this Constitution. Offices in the militia to which there is attached no annual salary shall not be deemed lucrative. (Amended November 6, 1984).

This section prevents someone from holding two "lucrative" offices, one in the General Assembly, simultaneously. The one explicit exception is a position in the militia with no annual salary. An officer in the National Guard, even if there is remuneration, is not considered prohibited from holding a legislative seat under this provision (1937 Op. Atty. Gen. p. 252). In addition, a public officeholder who performs *ex officio* duties is not considered to hold two public offices under this section (*McManamon v. Felger*, 1951). If someone holds two such lucrative offices, the first one occupied is considered to be vacated, and the second office occupied, by the offender (1947 Op. Atty. Gen. No. 30). This does not prevent an incumbent officeholder from running for election to another office, and then resigning the first office if elected to the second. It does preclude such an officeholder from holding the old and the new offices simultaneously. This ban includes both elected and appointed office, as long as it involves a significant amount of income (not incidental amounts) for one or both of the offices.

This provision is most directly tested and developed when the issue is whether the person holding lucrative office is vested with some of the functions pertinent to sovereignty or has some power or duty within the legislative, judicial, or executive departments of government. That means, if the officeholder has this kind of power or authority as a result of one office, then he is barred from holding another office with similar functions or powers (1947 Op. Atty. Gen. No. 30). This section also prevents an individual from serving in two capacities but collecting the salary from only one of the offices, while performing the other office without pay (1936 Op. Atty. Gen. p. 155).

The 1984 amendment of this section involved technical changes. It removed specific offices that were not considered "lucrative" such as Deputy Postmaster, where the compensation was less than $90 per year. Furthermore, in counties where the population was less than 1,000, the offices of Clerk, Recorder, and Auditor could be combined and held by two people, without violating this provision under its original wording. The change of this wording in 1984 modernized the prohibition and extended it to reach other offices, but did not change its meaning.

SECTION 10

Collectors and Holders of Public Money; Eligibility. No person who may hereafter be a collector or holder of public moneys, shall be eligible to any office of trust or profit, until he shall have accounted for, and paid over, according to law, all sums for which he may be liable.

This section requires that persons elected to public office must pay over and account for any public moneys they are responsible for at the time they take elected office, that is, leave the office for which they have financial responsibility. This does not prevent people who hold public moneys from running for elected office. They are only required to account for such funds before they can occupy the new office, if they are elected (*Hogue v. State ex rel. Bd. of Comm'rs*, 1902). This provision insures that at the time a turnover in officeholders occurs, there is a complete accounting of public funds.

An individual who converted public funds to his private money is not barred from running for County Auditor, as long as the funds were paid back by the time he occupied the elected office (*Brown v. Goben*, 1890). This case holds that this section does not bar people from running for public office without a full accounting, even if they have converted public funds to private uses. Rather it prevents them from assuming the new office without having accounted for the funds they were responsible for earlier.

SECTION 11

Pro Tempore Appointment; Term of Office. In all cases in which it is provided, that an office shall not be filled by the same person more than a certain number of years continuously, an appointment *pro tempore* shall not be reckoned a part of any term.

This section indicates that persons filling out an unfinished term of office, *pro tempore*, need not count those years as part of their service. That *pro tempore* period is not considered to be part of any term, so that the temporary occupant does not have that partial term counted against any full term they might be elected to later. Thus, if the lieutenant governor was to fill out the unexpired term of the governor, the lieutenant governor would still be able to occupy the office of governor for two full (four-year) terms of office if so elected by the voters (*Carson v. McPhetridge*, 1860). In addition, it would seem this section permits an incumbent who has served the fully allowable term to continue in office, *pro tempore*, until a replacement was designated. However, this point has not been litigated or clarified by the Indiana courts.

SECTION 12

Freedom from Arrest of Electors; Exceptions. In all cases, except treason, felony, and breach of the peace, electors shall be free from arrest, in going to elections, during their attendance there, and in returning from the same.

The section is intended to insure that voters, while voting, will not be subject to harassment or intimidation by arrest or threat of arrest. This immunity does not extend to treason, felony, or breach of the peace allegations, all of which may be directly related to the interruption of the election process (*Andrews v. State*, 1987). Thus, it is understandable that seeking to disrupt the electoral process can be prevented while still protecting voters while they vote under this section.

The only judicial interpretation of this provision indicates that a justice of the peace is not protected from arrest by this section, except if he is conducting a trial (*Gross v. State*, 1917). It is not clear why a justice of the peace would be protected by this provision under any circumstances, but the *Gross* decision indicates that this section does protect officers during their official conduct of business.

SECTION 13

Election Methods. All elections by the *People* shall be by ballot; and all elections by the General Assembly, or by either branch thereof, shall be *viva voce*.

This provision indicates that general elections or other popular elections are to be by written ballot. This is an alternative to the eighteenth-century requirement that voters cast their votes *viva voce* or out loud, and reflects expectation that if people's votes are not publicly known, they will vote free from public intimidation or harassment. This is not an absolute requirement, as the state supreme court held, in 1904, that public elections for a gravel road could require public testimony regarding how each elector (voter) voted on the issue of the building of the gravel road (*Strebin v. Lavengood*, 1904). However, if this case were decided today, it is likely that this single exception would not be upheld.

On the other hand, a vote by one or both houses of the General Assembly is to be by voice vote. The purpose of this provision is to insure that these votes are cast publicly and thus are visible and known to the public. Such a public record of the votes of legislators serves to insure that constituents know how their representatives exercised their judgment and cast their vote on each issue of public concern. Nowadays, voting in the General Assembly is recorded electronically and displayed publicly at the time the vote is taken, but it may not be verbal.

SECTION 14

Time of Elections; Judges of Courts; Registration of Voters. All general elections shall be held on the first Tuesday after the first Monday in November; but township elections may be held at such time as may be pro vided by law: *Provided*, That the General Assembly may provide by law for the election of all judges of courts of general and appellate jurisdiction, by an election to be held for such officers only, at which time no other officer shall be voted for, and shall also provide for the registration of all persons entitled to vote. (Amended March 14, 1881)

This provision sets the day on which general elections will be held in Indiana. This change to the first Tuesday after the first Monday in November occurred with the amendment in 1881. Prior to 1881, the election was held the second Tuesday in October. Prior to the 1851 Constitution, elections were conducted at various times, including August of each year. The importance of regularizing the election in November was so that it would coincide with the practice in other states.

The exceptions to this general requirement involve the election of judges for courts of original (general) and appellate jurisdiction which can be conducted at a time specified by the General Assembly, when no other officer will be elected. This exception has not been interpreted to allow for the election of judges other than by general election, but rather only that the general election of judges can be provided for at times other than the general election day in November (*Taylor v. Mount*, 1898). In fact, the election of judges, and some other public offices, such as school board members, is conducted at the primary election in May, rather than the general election in November.

Article III

Distribution of Powers

SECTION 1

Three Separate Departments. The powers of the Government are divided into three separate departments; the Legislative, the Executive including the Administrative, and the Judicial: and no person, charged with official duties under one of these departments, shall exercise any of the functions of another, except as in this Constitution expressly provided.

This provision of the Indiana Constitution outlines the basic principle that the powers of Indiana state goverement are to be separated—into three branches. While the statement is not particularly striking, it explicitly articulates a principle that is implied in the U.S. Constitution. In that national document the general doctrine has emerged through judicial rulings relating to the delegation of legislative authority and cases involving other overlaps between the functions of the three branches of government.

In Indiana, the doctrine has developed, from the constitutional prescription, that the powers that are outlined in the constitution cannot be blended and that no individual can exercise a blend of these executive, judicial, or legislative powers. This formal statement has been combined with the development of case law that also focuses in part on the issues of the delegation of powers to another branch or institution of government. In addition, the functions and powers exercised by one governmental body, and its incumbent officeholders, cannot be mixed or blended with those of another institution of office (e.g., see *Carlson v. State ex rel. Stodola,* 1966). However, this separation has been applied pragmatically by state courts when they have been faced with apparent violations of this section.

There are several dimensions to the development of the constitutional doctrine regarding this article of the state constitution. First, this provision explicates the separation of power among state governmental institutions. The interpretation of this article has generally been consistent with an absolute view of the separation of powers, that is, a view that the powers of one branch are absolutely separated from those of any other *(State ex rel. Kostas v. Johnson,* 1946). This view is not mutually exclusive with the overlap of checks and balances, but the emphasis by the state courts has been on the separation of powers rather than complementary action of the coordinate branches. The view of the judiciary has focused on a coequal distribution of the power of each of the branches, even though their functions are unique and not comparable *(State ex rel. Black v. Burch,* 1948).

Some cases have focused on the nature of the functions to each of the three branches of government. These interpretations leave to each of the branches, respectively, the powers to legislate, execute, and judge the laws (see, e.g., *Mellot v. State,* 1942; *Branigin v. Morgan Superior Court,* 1967; *City of Mish-waka v. Mohney,* 1973). This simplistic formula has not always yielded precise and clear boundaries among the three branches. Thus, the courts have avoided making a variety of determinations that they consider matters of legislative judgment. Courts also leave open the possibility that a particular combination or overlap of functions or powers will not be a violation of the article of the constitution. That is, the courts have not drawn clear, bright, definitional lines among the three branches of government despite the wording of this article. Rather, they have taken each case separately. There are certainly offices or governmental functions which blend powers or functions. The courts have not gone out of their way to indicate these kinds of institutional arrangements.

A second feature of the development of this constitutional article has focused on the nondelegation doctrine. Thus, the legislature is not permitted to delegate the power to legislate to any other body *Clemons v. State,* 1974). Power given to the governor by statute also cannot be delegated to administrative officers *(Tucker v. State* 1941). In addition, the judiciary cannot delegate its power or functions to judge cases or resolve legal disputes to any other actors, governmental or private (1979 Op. Atty. Gen. No. 24; *Morthland v. Lincoln National Life Insurance Co.,* 1940). This doctrine has expanded to prevent institutions from usurping the power of another branch as well as giving their own power away improperly. Yet, the state courts have followed the federal pattern in upholding delegations of power to boards and agencies as long as the delegation is accompanied by clear directions and policies guiding the administrative action.

The essential feature of this provision is that the explicit separation of powers outlined here has contributed to a differentiation or distribution of governmental power among the governmental bodies in Indiana. That has not resulted, despite the wording of the section or some judicial interpretations, in an extreme or literal separation or the isolation of institutional powers. However, the development of this provision in Indiana has been more explicit or literal than the murky development of the federal doctrine (*Zemel v. Rusk*, 1965).

Article IV

Legislative

SECTION 1

General Assembly; Composition; Style of Law. The Legislative authority of the State shall be vested in a General Assembly, which shall consist of a Senate and a House of Representatives. The style of every law shall be: "Be it enacted by the General Assembly of the State of Indiana" and no law shall be enacted except by bill.

This section establishes a bicameral legislature in Indiana—a House of Representatives and a Senate—and assigns it the legislative power. The remainder of the section specifies the precise manner in which bills will be styled, and further that all enacted laws would be by bill.

The legislature's power is considered to derive from the grant of power from the constitution by the people (*Bennett v. Jackson*, 1917). The legislature has discretion to decide whether to act or not, and that choice is beyond judicial scrutiny (*State v. Haworth*, 1890). Although this view suggests that the legislature's power is not plenary but rather derives from the constitution, the Indiana courts have also deferred to the legislature's interpretation of its power (*Lutz v. Arnold*, 1935). The courts have articulated a mixed view on this basic proposition. As a result, it is probably wisest to treat the power of the General Assembly as granted, rather than plenary.

Yet, the legislature's power is complete and supreme except as limited by the state and federal constitutions. This power allows the legislature to enact any law except those prohibited by the constitution or reserved by the people who retain the fundamental legislative power (*Ellingham v. Dye*, 1912).

The limitations on the legislative power include the constitution and the people (*Pennington v. Stewart*, 1937). Thus, courts can insure that the policy choices of the legislature do not violate the constitution (e.g., *Hollenbauch v. State*, 1859). The explicit constitutional limits on this power are considered primary (*State v. Patterson*, 1914), and the courts consider popular sovereignty as precluding the legislature from acting without limit. Legislation cannot invade the constitutional rights or powers of other public officials (*Hyde v. Bd. of Comm'rs of Wells County*, 1935). The legislature must enact statutes, according to the courts, and that prevents the delegation of legislative functions to either other governmental bodies or nongovernmental agencies or people (*Bissell Carpet Sweeper Co. v. Shane*, 1957). Yet, the discussion above regarding Article III, section 1 suggests that this doctrine is not a fixed or a hard-and-fast rule. The delegation of legal legislative and administrative power to local units of government is permissible. Such grants of power are not self-executing, however, and they require statutory direction and guidance from the General Assembly (*Bryant v. Lake County Trust Co.*, 1972). The same kinds of statutory limits and guides are required of any discretion awarded to administrative agencies (*Schultz v. State*, 1981).

The power to legislate in Indiana is both granted and limited. This is not unique to the state, and rather it indicates the fact that while the legislature possesses a broad grant of power in this section from the people, the courts have continually imposed various limits which confine that power, at least at the margins, if not at the core. As the remainder of this discussion of specific provisions will illustrate, the state has a strong legislative arm and, even though that is limited, it exercises broad authority and discretion in connection with state powers.

SECTION 2

Senate and House of Representatives; Membership. The Senate shall not exceed fifty, nor the House of Representatives one hundred members; and they shall be chosen by the electors of the respective districts into which the State may, from time to time, be divided. (Amended November 6, 1984)

This section specifies the maximum size of the Senate and the House of Representatives at 50 seats and 100 seats respectively. Neither body of the legislature is fixed at the number specified in this provision, but this maximum is the current number of legislators. This section allowed growth in the size of the representative bodies and for adjustments in representation of the people, up to the point of 50 senators and 100 representatives.

This section of the Indiana Constitution also authorizes the General Assembly to establish representative districts. (See Article IV, section 5 below for further discussion of this point.) A 1984 amendment removed "counties" as a unit of representation for either the Senate or the House. Prior to 1984, "Counties or districts" could be the basis upon which each house was apportioned. This 1984 amendment modernizes the basis of representation in both houses and conforms with *Reynolds v. Sims* (1964), in which the U.S. Supreme Court held that counties were not an acceptable basis for division of representatives in state legislatures.

SECTION 3

Senators and Representatives; Tenure. Senators shall be elected for the term of four years, and Representatives for the term of two years, from the day next after their general election. One half of the Senators, as nearly as possible, shall be elected biennially. (Amended November 6, 1984)

This section specifies the terms of office for state senators and representatives. In addition, it staggers the terms of the senators so half the Senate is elected every two years at the general election along with the entire House. The "year" for legislators does not coincide with either the calender year or a 365-day period of time, but rather begins when they take their oath of office, and it ends on the day of the general election (1967 Op. Atty. Gen. No. 1). Legislators do have the option of resigning from the legislature, once they are elected and begin serving their terms of office. They cannot be forced to complete their two or four year terms (*Slenker v. Burch*, 1948).

The 1984 amendment involved a technical correction of the provisions of the section. It changed the wording to provide clearly for staggering the terms of one-half the senators. The original version, which specified an elaborate means of allocating the short and long terms in the first senate by lot, was obsolete. This change did not affect the substantive meaning of this provision.

SECTION 4

Vacancies in General Assembly. The General Assembly may provide by law for the filling of such vacancies as may occur in the General Assembly. (Amended March 14, 1881; November 6, 1984)

This section was completely rewritten in the 1984 amendment. The earlier version required the second session of the General Assembly after the adoption of the constitution to conduct the enumeration that is discussed below in connection with Article IV, section 5, every six years. The current wording relates to the filling of vacancies that occur in the General Assembly. The Opinion by the Attorney General in 1991 was that someone elected to fill a vacant legislative seat must meet the residency requirements specified below in Article IV, section 7 (1991 Op. Atty. Gen. No. 91-15). That is, they must reside in the district for one year prior to election.

SECTION 5

Legislative Apportionment. The General Assembly elected during the year in which a federal decennial census is taken shall fix by law the number of Senators and Representatives and apportion them among districts according to the number of inhabitants in each district, as revealed by that federal decennial census. The territory in each district shall be contiguous. (Amended March 14, 1881; November 6, 1984)

This section outlines the process by which Indiana apportions its legislature after the decennial census. (See the discussion of Article IV, section 4, for the earlier version of this requirement.) The seats are to be arrayed in districts, no longer by counties, and the territory in each district is to be contiguous. This general requirement coincides with the reapportionment decision of the U.S. Supreme Court (*Reynolds v. Sims*, 1964). The legislature has discretion in drawing district lines, as long as no constitutional provision is violated (*Parker v. State ex rel. Powell*, 1892). Apportionment is a legislative function (*Bd. of Comm'rs of Marion County v. Jewett*, 1915), but the governor has discretion to call a special session of the legislature for purposes of redistricting and reapportioning. However, when a constitutional claim is raised about the legislature's actions, then the issue becomes judicial rather than political, and can be resolved by the courts (*Brooks v. State*, 1904). Even if the legislature fails to reapportion itself, the legislation adopted by the unapportioned legislature is still valid (*Patrons of Noble County School Corp. v. School, City of Kendalville*, 1963; *State v. Clark*, 1966). This is clearly a matter of practicality.

The 1881 amendment to this provision removed the phrase "white" preceding the words "male inhabitants," an adjustment in line with the Fourteenth Amendment of the U.S. Constitution. The 1984 amendments completely rewrote the section, to remove all sex-based language (e.g., "male" before "inhabitants"). It also provided that the districts be contiguous, and changed the unit of representation in all cases to districts rather than including "counties." Furthermore, the 1984 amendment provided that the federal decennial census, rather than an "enumeration," serve as the basis for apportionment. These recent changes also make this provision consistent with the changes that were adopted in Article IV, section 2, discussed above.

Clearly, this provision of the constitution has been adjusted to comply with federal apportionment requirements developed by the U.S. Supreme Court.

However, this section still became a source of constitutional challenge in *Davis v. Bandemer* (1986). There a challenge was raised to the 1980 Indiana reapportionment scheme. The claim was that the redistricting involved political gerrymandering that would deny the minority party—the Democrats—the opportunity to become the majority party. The U.S. Supreme Court held that such political criteria for apportioning the state did not violate the federal constitutional requirements of Equal Protection of the Laws.

SECTION 6

Repealed. (Repealed November 6, 1984)

This section was repealed in 1984 to remove a provision that required any Senate or Representative district involving more than one county to be contiguous counties, and prohibited the division of a county for senatorial apportionment. This repeal coincides with *Reynolds v. Sims* (1964). (See the discussion of Article IV, section 2.)

SECTION 7

Senators and Representatives; Qualifications. No person shall be a Senator or a Representative, who, at the time of his election, is not a citizen of the United States; nor any one who has not been for two years next preceding his election, an inhabitant of this State, and for one year next preceding his election, an inhabitant of the district whence he may be chosen. Senators shall be at least twenty-five, and Representatives at least twentyone years of age. (Amended November 6, 1984)

This section specifies the qualifications for state senators and representatives. The age requirements are lower than for U.S. legislators—25 years for state senators and 21 years for representatives. (U.S. Constitution, Article, I, section 2, Cl. 2; Article, I, section 3, Cl. 3.) This difference may well reflect the drafters' judgment in 1851 that there were not a great many residents of Indiana who would qualify for the state legislature if the age limits were set at 35 and 30, respectively. It may also reflect their view that younger people were qualified to serve in the legislature.

In addition to the age qualifications, Indiana legislators must be citizens of the United States, and must have lived in the district they are elected from for one year prior to the election, and in the state for two years before being eligible for election. These requirements reflect the drafters' judgment that residency requirements were appropriate to insure the representativeness of the legislators.However, the requirement is not lengthy in order not to screen out otherwise qualified representatives and senators. Given the mobility and influence of people in the state during the 1830s and 1840s, some residency requirement was acceptable but greater than a year or two might have screened out a good many candidates. Clearly, this requirement is less than the seven- and nine-year citizenship requirements for U.S. representatives and senators, respectively.

Only in 1991 did a question involving this provision arise. The attorney general issued an opinion that a legislator elected to complete an unexpired term was required to meet the one-year residency requirement, just as if the candidate were running to represent the district for a full term (1991 Op. Atty. Gen. No. 91-15). This interpretation of the requirement of residency is consistent with expectations about the representativeness of the legislators.

The section was amended in 1984 to make technical corrections in the wording, consistent with *Reynolds v. Sims* (1964) regarding representation in "districts" rather than political subdivisions like "counties." The amendment also made this provision consistent with the new amendments to Article IV, sections 2 and 6 by removing all references to counties as a unit of representation.

SECTION 8

Legislative Immunity; Exceptions. Senators and Representatives, in all cases except treason, felony, and breach of the peace, shall be privileged from arrest, during the session of the General Assembly, and in going to and returning from the same; and shall not be subject to any civil process, during the session of the General Assembly, nor during the fifteen days next before the commencement thereof. For any speech or debate in either House, a member shall not be questioned in any other place.

This section closely parallels the Speech or Debate Clause and the immunity from prosecution clause of the U.S. Constitution (U.S. Const. Article, I, section 6, Cl. 1). It indicates that the members of the General Assembly are to enjoy freedom from interference with the performance of their official duties. These protections from civil process include travel to and from the meeting of the legislature. (This is specified to be a fifteen-day period before the start of the session.) Through interpretation, Indiana legislators enjoy much the same protection as U.S. Senators and Representatives do under the Speech or Debate Clause of the U.S. Constitution. The state provision protects legislators from being questioned about their speech or debate in any other place than in the legislature. They are still subject to breach of peace claims while they are in attendance of a session of the state legislature. This provision has not been changed by judicial interpretation of governmental immunity, since this set of protections is individual and specific to the performance of legislative functions (*Bd. of Comm'rs of Delaware County v. Briggs,* 1975). This provision of the constitution has been interpreted to prevent the garnishment of the legislator's salary while in session, even though there is nothing in this section relating to pay (1939 Op. Atty. Gen. p. 19).

SECTION 9

Sessions of General Assembly. The sessions of the General Assembly shall be held at the capitol of the State, commencing on the Tuesday next after the second Monday in January of each year in which the General Assembly meets unless a different day or place shall have been appointed by law. But if, in the opinion of the Governor, the public welfare shall require it, he may, at any time by proclamation, call a special session. The length and frequency of the sessions of the General Assembly shall be fixed by law. (Amended November 3, 1970) (The schedule adopted with the 1970 amendments to Sections 9 and 29 of Article 4 was stricken out by the November 6, 1984 amendment.)

Under this provision regular legislative sessions begin on the Tuesday in January after the second Monday. A 1970 amendment called for annual sessions to replace the original provision for biennial sessions. By legislative enactment, the legislature has specified the length and frequency of legislative sessions (IC 2-2.1-1-1). The Indiana legislature provides for a biennial "term." However, at the start of a biennium, the length of the session is 61 days (IC 2-2.1-1-2), while on the second year of the biennium, the "short session" can be no more than 30 session days (IC 2-2.1-1-1-3).

The governor has the authority to call special sessions of the legislature. Such a session can deal with more than a single issue (1935 Op. Atty. Gen. p. 75). However, the length of a special session is limited, by the statute, to no more than 30 session days or 40 calendar days (IC 2-2.1-1-4).

SECTION 10

Selection of Officers; Rules of Proceedings; Adjournment. Each House, when assembled, shall choose its own officers, the President of the Senate excepted; judge the elections, qualifications, and returns of its own members; determine its rules of proceeding, and sit upon its own adjournment. But neither House shall, without the consent of the other, adjourn for more than three days, nor to any place other than that in which it may be sitting.

This section contains a variety of provisions focusing on the power of each house to meet, organize, conduct business. and then adjourn. Each house is to elect its own leaders, except for the president of the Senate, who is designated by Article V, section 21 of the constitution to be the lieutenant governor. Each house can determine its own rules for proceeding with its business and within the specified limitations adjourn itself.

The organizing duties of each house include determining who has been elected to the house and whether they are constitutionally qualified to serve in the house. Each house is the sole judge of the qualifications of its members. That judging of elections and qualifications is beyond the authority of either the judiciary or the executive branches of state government (1947 Op. Atty. Gen. No. 142; *State ex rel. Batchelet v. Dekalb Circuit Court,* 1967).

The few interpretations of these provisions have elaborated the particular wording and operation of this section. Each house can remove a presiding officer who refuses to sign legislation that the house has passed (1977 Op. Atty. Gen. No. 29). After such a removal, the body can appoint a replacement who will carry out those duties.

SECTION 11

Quorum. Two-thirds of each House shall constitute a quorum to do business; but a smaller number may meet, adjourn from day to day, and compel the attendance of absent members. A quorum being in attendance, if either House fail to effect an organization within the first five days thereafter, the members of the House so failing, shall be entitled to no compensation, from the end of the said five days until an organization shall have been effected.

This subdivision of the constitution specifies that two-thirds of either house constitutes the quorum required to conduct the business of the house. The remainder of the section focuses on insuring that a house will organize itself and begin its session by permitting a "smaller" number of members to meet and adjourn and compel the attendance of the absent members. Originally, this provision accommodated travel difficulties and delays. The incentive to begin the session includes withholding compensation after the fifth day, absent the organization of the session and a quorum.

After the organization of each house, a quorum must be present in order for that body to conduct business. The only interpretation of this section was a 1982 Attorney General's Opinion which specified that less than a quorum of either house could adopt legislation as long as a quorum had been present for a rollcall earlier in the day, and no division or count had been called (i.e., no quorum call) before the passage of the specific legislation in question (1982 Op. Atty. Gen. No. 8).

SECTION 12

Journal; Entry of Yeas and Nays. Each House shall keep a journal of its proceedings, and publish the same. The yeas and nays, on any question, shall, at the request of any two members, be entered, together with the names of the members demanding the same, on the journal; *Provided,* that on a motion to adjourn, it shall require one-tenth of the members present to order the yeas and nays.

This provision of the constitution specifies that each house will keep a journal, in which the votes, when properly requested, will be recorded. The journal is to record the proceedings of the house and the journal is to be published. This part is a formal requirement to insure that the business of the General Assembly will be a matter of public record and available to the population of the state, permitting the voters of the state to hold the legislators responsible for their actions. The provision has been interpreted to require that the governor's action with regard to legislation submitted for signature be recorded in the journal, thereby becoming part of the public record (*State ex rel. Holt v. Denny*, 1888).

This section permits the journals to be examined as any other record by a court when the court is considering a right or defense emerging from an action of the legislature (*Coleman v. Dobbins*, 1856). These journals can be used by courts to help determine the legislature's intent regarding a vague or ambiguous statutory provision (*Roeschlein v. Thomas*, 1972). However, these legislative journals cannot be impeached (i.e., questioned or challenged) except in the General Assembly itself (*McCulloch v. State*, 1859).

SECTION 13

Open Session and Committee Meetings. The doors of each House, and of Committees of the Whole, shall be kept open, except in such cases, as, in the opinion of either House, may require secrecy.

This section indicates the expectation is that the legislative sessions will be open and public, although each house may determine that a session requires secrecy. This requirement does not explicitly apply to committee hearings or other meetings that are not the business of the entire house, but the presumption is that the legislature will conduct its business in open, public sessions.

In 1970, this section was substantially enhanced or expanded by the enactment of the Open Door Law (IC 5-14-1.5 et seq.). The provisions of this statute reach public agencies, including state and local governing bodies and administrative agencies. The emphasis or focus of the law is to require open meetings and votes, the posting of agendas and minutes of meetings, and public notices of meetings. There are exceptions to these requirements including specified matters for executive sessions (IC 5-14-1.5-6) and portions of collective bargaining processes involving a governing body as an employer (IC 5-14-1.5-7). However, the presumption of these statutory provisions reflects this section of the constitution in favor of open and public meetings for all governing body deliberations (IC 5-14-1.5-1).

SECTION 14

Discipline of Members. Either House may punish its members for disorderly behavior, and may, with the concurrence of two-thirds, expel a member; but not a second time for the same cause.

This section provides that members of either house can be punished for disorderly behavior. Each house can expel the offending member with the concurrence of two-thirds of the body's members. It is not clear whether punishment short of expulsion requires a two-thirds concurrence of the house. There are no other sanctions (punishments) specified in the section. This extreme sanction—expulsion—specifies disciplinary action in extreme cases, but it leaves "lesser" disorderly behavior to be tolerated by the General Assembly.

Expulsion can only occur once for a specific offense. This may indicate that the sanction of expulsion was expected to be temporary rather than permanent, but there are no case law or examples of the imposition of this segment of the constitutional provision that answer this question. It has been determined that a presiding officer can be expelled and replaced if that officer refuses to sign legislation that has been properly adopted by one house of the General Assembly (1977 Op. Atty. Gen. No. 29; see also, Article, IV, section 10).

SECTION 15

Contempt by Non-Members; Punishment. Either House, during its session, may punish, by imprisonment, any person not a member, who shall have been quilty of disrespect to the House, by disorderly or contemptuous behavior, in its presence; but such punishment shall not, at any one time, exceed twenty-four hours.

This provision gives to each house of the General Assembly the power to control the behavior of nonmembers of the chamber. Although "disrespect" and "disorderly or contemptuous behavior" are not defined in the section and never have been defined, behavior which disrupts the conduct of business or shows disrespect for the assembly or a member of the house would probably be included. The provision also sets a limited, maximum punishment for this kind of behavior of imprisonment for no more than 24 hours. Although it is not specified in the section and there is no case law on the subject, it is probably necessary that some kind of proceeding to determine the guilt of the accused would precede any imposition of a sanction, by the house.

SECTION 16

Legislative Powers. Each House shall have all powers necessary for a branch of the Legislative department of a free and independent State.

This section indicates that each house of the legislature possesses all the powers that a legislature must have in order to maintain a free and independent state. This is an element of state's rights, which ran through the Union in the 1850s. However, it also may serve to grant to the legislature plenary authority or "any other powers" that were not specified in the constitution, which later emerge as essential for a legislature to possess. This may be a counterpart to the "Necessary and Proper" clause of the U.S. Constitution (Article I, section 8, Cl. 18).

This section has been used to insure the separation of powers between the judiciary and the legislature. A 1920 court decision emphasized that all the legislative (i.e., lawmaking) power resides solely in the legislature (*Central Union Telephone Co. v. Indianapolis Telephone Co.*, 1920). The legislature has the sole power of taxation, both in terms of the imposition of taxes and allocating the revenue from the taxes it imposes (*Lutz v. Arnold*, 1935; *South Bend Transportation Corp. v. South Bend*, 1981). Generally, this segment of the Indiana Constitution has been the basis for the development and specification of the features of legislative power when the legislative action has been challenged on the grounds of an absence of specific authority to act in a particular area. These powers include a general police power to protect the health, safety, morals, and welfare of the public (*Edwards v. Housing Authority of City of Muncie*, 1939).

The state courts have not, however, granted the General Assembly plenary or complete authority to enact statutes. Judicial interpretations of this provision focus on arguable limitations (by other constitutional provisions) on the enactment of legislation. Thus, the Due Process protections of the constitution do not prevent the legislature from enacting statutes that modify property rights, repeal statutes, or modify and expand or contract existing legislation (*Dague v. Piper Aircraft Corp.*, 1981). Yet, this power has been interpreted broadly and positively rather than as a limitation on the grant of legislative power. The courts of Indiana have repeatedly held, under this provision, that any legislative enactment is presumed constitutional and the challenger has the burden of rebutting this presumption (*Ruge v. Kovach*, 1984; *Lawrence v. State*, 1972).

SECTION 17

Bills; Raising Revenue. Bills may originate in either House, but may be amended or rejected in the other; except that bills for raising revenue shall originate in the House of Representatives.

This section provides that revenue bills, as in the U.S. Constitution (Article I, section 7, Cl. 1), must originate in the lower house of the General Assembly. The philosophy of this provision was undoubtedly the desire to insure that revenue would be raised only if the "popular representatives of the People" (i.e., the lower house) began the process. However, either house can modify or adjust proposed legislation, as well as reject proposed legislation, so each house is equally involved in the legislative process except for the initiation of revenue bills. Interpretations of the revenue limitations have focused on how narrowly "revenue" is to be interpreted. That definition includes bills which strictly levy taxes, but the section does not limit other kinds of legislation (*Stith Petroleum Co. v. Dept. of Audit and*

Control of Indiana,1937). It is possible for a bill that "incidentally" raises revenue to originate in the Senate and still comply with the Indiana Constitution.

SECTION 18

Reading and Passage of Bills. Every bill shall be read, by title, on three several days, in each House; unless, in case of emergency, two-thirds of the House where such bill may be pending shall, by a vote of yeas and nays, deem it expedient to dispense with this rule; but the reading of a bill, by title, on its final passage, shall, in no case, be dispensed with; and the vote on the passage of every bill or joint resolution shall be taken by yeas and nays. (Amended November 6, 1984)

This section requires three separate readings of a bill in each house, unless two-thirds of the house dispenses with the requirement because of an emergency. The requirement of a reading for final passage, however, is absolute.

The necessary proof that a bill was enacted is that the presiding officer in each house attests to that fact (*Lewis v. State*, 1897). However, the judiciary can legitimately inquire into facts relating to the legislative process (i.e., the passage of an act) (*Coleman v. Dobbins*, 1856).

The 1984 amendment involved technical wording changes that did not affect the substance of this requirement. The difference is that "title" was substituted for "by sections" which means now the third reading need only involve the title of the bill rather than each section. This change speeds up the reading process somewhat and may be important in the last days of the legislative session when a large number of bills reach the floor for final consideration.

SECTION 19

One Subject Acts; Exceptions. An act, except an act for the codification, revision or rearrangement of laws, shall be confined to one subject and matters properly connected therewith. (Amended November 6, 1960; November 5, 1974)

This provision deals with the requirement that any bill (act) must pertain to only one subject, unless the bill involves the codification or systematic revision of the laws of the state. This serves to prevent legislators from coupling unpopular proposals with popular ones in order to get the bill that is not favored adopted, as part of the popular proposed law. Thus, the practice in Congress of attaching riders to bills cannot occur in the Indiana legislature (*Dortch v. Lugar*, 1971; *Lutz v. Arnold*, 1935). This requirement of separation does not prevent some linkage of component parts, as long as there is a reasonable basis for grouping the provisions (*Stith Petroleum Co. v. Dept. of Audit and Control on Indiana*, 1937). How closely the parts of a bill must fit is unclear, but the general view is that the subjects of various legislation should be interpreted liberally or broadly (*Ule v.*

State, 1935; *Dague v. Piper Aircraft Corp.*, 1981). A statute can include both a provision and the repeal of the former law it is replacing (*Gabbert v. Jeffersonville R. Co.*, 1858). One statute can include a great many unrelated provisions if it condifies or oreorganizes the laws of the state.

This provision does not apply to resolutions proposing constitutional amendments (1966 Op. Atty. Gen. No. 49). That means more than one proposed amendment to the constitution could be contained in a single legislative resolution, even though Article XVI, section 2 requires the separate submission of amendments for voter approval. Yet, this requirement of separation does apply to statutory amendments (*State ex rel. Blieden v. Gleason*, 1946).

The 1960 amendment was a technical change requiring that any proposed bills amending existing statutes be clearly identified and the existing statute be referenced. This complicated change was simplified in the 1974 amendment, which also removed the requirement that a citation to the Indiana statutory provision under consideration for amendment be specified in the bill. Thus, the current version of this section is much less rigorous than either the 1851 original or the 1960 replacement.

SECTION 20

Acts and Resolutions; Plain Language. Every act and joint resolution shall be plainly worded, avoiding, as far as practicable, the use of technical terms.

This section requires that statutes enacted by the state be written in clear and understandable language in order to increase the accessibility of the state law to the people of Indiana. Obviously, as legislation has evolved over time, the style and the complexity of statutory wording has changed a good deal, and interpreting courts must decide what is "plainly worded" law and what violates this provision of the constitution. Statutory language may be difficult to understand but still comply with this requirement as long as the statute is plainly worded (*Welch v. Sells*, 1963). The statute need not be "crystal clear." Furthermore, if the meaning of a statute can be aided or reasonably understood as the result of a judicial interpretation of the original wording, that complies with the clarity requirements of the section (*Mogilner v. Metropolitan Planning Commission of Marion County*, 1957).

SECTION 21

Repealed. (Repealed November 8, 1960)

This provision, repealed in 1960 in conjunction with the amendment to Article IV, section 19, involved a requirement in the 1851 Constitution that revisions or amendments of statutes must be done explicitly, by quoting the original, not by implication or by mere reference to the title. Repeal of this provision made statutory repeals by reference possible, thus, it is less complicated to make revisions or changes in existing statutes.

SECTION 22

Local and Special Laws; Restrictions. The General Assembly shall not pass local or special laws:

    Providing for the punishment of crimes and misdemeanors;
    Regulating the practice in courts of justice;
    Providing for changing the venue in civil or criminal cases;
    Granting divorces;
    Changing the names of persons;
    Providing for laying out, opening, and working on highways, and for the election or appointment of supervisors;
    Vacating roads, town plats, streets, alleys, and public squares;
    Summoning and empaneling grand and petit juries, and providing for their compensation;
    Regulating county and township business;
    Regulating the election of county and township officers and their compensation;
    Providing for the assessment and collection of taxes for State, county, township, or road purposes;
    Providing for the support of common schools, or the preservation of schools funds;
    Relating to fees or salaries, except that the laws may be so made as to grade the compensation of officers in porportion to the population and the necessary services required;
    Relating to interest on money;
    Providing for opening and conducting elections of State, county, or township officers, and designating the places of voting;
    Providing for the sale of real estate belonging to minors or other persons laboring under legal disabilities, by executors, administrators, guardians, or trustees.
(Amended March 14, 1881; November 6, 1984)

This provision of the constitution was included in the organic act of 1851 to prevent the state legislature from devoting its time and attention to matters of local or special, idiosyncratic concern. Much of the work of the legislature, before the 1851 Constitution, had focused on local bills, and the constitutional convention fashioned this section in order to eliminate the possibility that the legislature would be asked to override the immediate, narrow decisions of local government. The itemized list of local matters that are not subject to legislative attention indicates something of the nearsighted vision of the early (pre-1851) state legislature, and the concern of the drafters of the 1851 Constitution about that parochial perspective. It is part of the judicial function to determine what kinds of legislation fall within this prohibition (*Rosencranz v. Evansville*, 1924).

Questions have inevitably arisen about how narrow a statute must be to fall within this prohibition. The courts have interpreted these restrictions on legislative enactments narrowly (*State ex rel. City of Terre Haute v. Kolsem*, 1891). Thus, some laws may be applicable to a portion of the state, to some local governments, even to a single county, or a single class of cases. However, such classification schemes or narrowing efforts of statutory provisions do not mean the statute violates this constitutional provision (*Sarlls v. State*, 1929). Moreover, classifications under this requirement of generality need not be categorizations that are based on logic or science, and they need not be exact or consistent (*Graves v. City of Muncie*, 1970).

One particular exception to the categorization issue is population. Indiana courts have repeatedly allowed nearly any kind of classification that is based on proportionality or population. Reasonable classifications, even if they are somewhat arbitrary, do not violate this ban on special legislation (e.g., *Lyons v. Bd. of Comm'rs of Perry County*, 1905; *Evansville-Vanderburgh Levee Authority Dist. v. Kamp*, 1960). The operation of a statute need not be uniform under this requirement either, as long as it operates the same in all parts of the state (*Martin v. State*, 1976). Thus, despite the provisions in this section, courts have permitted and validated a variety of classifications that deal with local subject matter, such as a state statute requiring a licensed pilot for boats "at the falls of the Ohio river." Since a falls is local, it was inevitable that such state regulation was "local," but it did not violate the constitution (*Cash v. Auditor of Clark County*, 1855).

This section has been amended twice. The first amendment, in 1881, permitted the grading and compensating of officers in proportion to population. This was to permit paying identical officers in different locations different amounts. It also reinforces the element of proportionality. That aspect of fees and salaries had been precluded from legislative attention under the original version of the section. The 1984 amendment involved technical revisions or refinements to the section focusing on grammar and wording, but do not affect the substance.

SECTION 23

General and Uniform Laws. In all cases enumerated in the preceding section, and in all other cases where a general law can be made applicable, all laws shall be general, and of uniform operation throughout the State.

This provision indicates the opposite side of the coin covered in the previous section (Article IV, section 22). This requires the legislature to enact laws of general applicability wherever possible. This section also indicates that the previous laundry list of local subject matter may be a legitimate subject of general legislation. Thus, a statewide or comprehensive divorce law would be constitutional while one that granted a divorce to specific, named individuals would not be constitutional. This section has often been treated in conjunction with section 22, as indicated in the wording here. The interpretation of the two has simultaneously allowed various classifications. In fact, section 22 is a set of itemized categories of legislation that must be general. The legislature, beyond section 22 limits, is given a good deal of discretion in the application of statutes and the accompanying classifications (*Schneck v. City of Jeffersonville*, 1898).

Legislation can meet these constitutional requirements even if it is not uniform, as long as its operation is similar, in like circumstances. In *State ex rel. Todd v. Hatcher* (1973) the Indiana court of appeals permitted a statutory classification of firemen based on population categories, because any city could qualify for this categorization if it reached the appropriate size, regardless of the fact that only two Indiana cities met the requirement at the time of the litigation. A great many legal questions deal with the issue of whether legislative classification schemes make the statute "local" and thus violative of section 22. For the most part, Indiana courts have given the legislature wide latitude in choosing categories or schemes for classifying people (population), cities, corporations, taxation, and circumstances for purposes of legislating. This view of these provisions is the most workable and, given modern modes of legislating, it is probably the only practicable view of these requirements which permit the legislature to function.

SECTION 24

Right to Sue the State. Provisions may be made, by general law, for bringing suit against the State; but no special law authorizing such suit to be brought, or making compensation to any person claiming damages against the State, shall be passed. (Amended November 6, 1984)

This section authorizes the General Assembly to provide for suits against the State of Indiana, by general legislation, but forbids special laws authorizing particular suits. Furthermore, it prohibits private bills compensating individual persons for damages. This provision is a complement to the previous two sections (Article IV, sections 22 and 23) in that it permits enactments of a general law relating to suing the state.

The bar on suing the state for damages (sovereign immunity) was not implicitly waived by this segment of the constitution (*Burr v. Duckworth*, 1982). That means the existence of a provision permitting the legislature to provide for suits against the state was not a waiver of the Sovereign Immunity doctrine. This section of the constitution has largely been the focus of arguments that it waives this immunity. However, that is certainly not the case. The provision precludes suits except where and when the legislature explicitly waives Sovereign Immunity (*Ford Motor Co. v. Dept. of Treasury of the State of Indiana*, 1945).

The 1984 amendment involved a technical revision of the wording that did not alter the substantive features of the section at all. It removed the phrase "as to all liabilities originating after the adoption of this Constitution." This qualification was obsolete, given the expiration of any old, pre-1851 claims, extinguished by the statutes of limitations.

SECTION 25

Passage of Bills and Resolutions; Signing. A majority of all the members elected to each House, shall be necessary to pass every bill or joint resolution; and all bills and joint resolutions so passed, shall be signed by the Presiding Officer of the respective Houses.

This section requires passage of legislation by an absolute majority of legislators in each house (*McCulloch v. State*, 1859). This majority is more than a plurality of approval, and it requires more than a majority of those present and voting at the time of passage. This provision insures a consistent, though extreme, decision rule for adoption. While it might be commonly expected that such a majority vote requirement would operate, this explication eliminates questions about this aspect of the legislative process. It should be noted that a bill is considered passed without the signature of the presiding office of each house, since the provision indicates that a bill, passed by the required majority, "shall" be signed rather than requiring the signature in order to achieve passage (1977 Op. Atty. Gen. No. 29). There is no discretion regarding the signature. However, the signature of each of the presiding officers, the Speaker of the House, and the president of the Senate, is conclusive proof of the passage of the legislation (*Stout v. Bd. of Comm'r of Grant County*, 1886).

If a bill is voted down in the final reading, that is, does not receive a majority of votes, then it is dead for the session and cannot be resurrected for reconsideration (*McCulloch v. State*, 1859). The journal record of the vote cannot be examined unless allegations of fraud are raised in a court, once the presiding officers have signed the bill (*Mogliner v. Metropolitan Planning Comm. of Marion County*, 1957). Furthermore, the question of the presence of a quorum cannot be raised if there was a quorum present on the same day as the vote (1982 Op. Atty. Gen. No. 8).

This provision clearly implies bicameralism. That is, "each House" must pass the bill by a majority. This bicameral requirement has not been challenged. It is only implicit here.

SECTION 26

Protest by members; Entry of Dissent on Journal. Any member of either House shall have the right to protest, and to have his protest, with his reasons for dissent, entered on the journal.

This provision guarantees that legislators who oppose legislation can "protest" and have that protest, along with reasons for it, entered into the journal of the appropriate house of the General Assembly. Although "protest" is not defined and has never been treated by an Indiana court, it likely included spoken debate in opposition to enactment of a bill. While today there can be little discussion or surprise at this right, in the 1850s the right to disagree with a legislative outcome may not have been so widely accepted, and so was included in the 1851 Constitution.

SECTION 27

Public Laws. Every statute shall be a public law, unless otherwise declared in the statute itself.

This section indicates that unless there is some exception, all statutes enacted by the General Assembly and signed by the governor will be considered public laws. This provision implies that there is a distinction between public and private laws but it does not differentiate between them. The section provides that the residual category of legislation is "public." Unless the legislature specifies and act to be private, it will be considered public, by definition. That applies even when the statute provides for the reimbursement of a single public official after the failure of a bank (*McClelland v. State ex rel. Speer*, 1894).

SECTION 28

Effective Dates of Acts. No act shall take effect, until the same shall have been published and circulated in the several counties of the State, by authority, except in cases of emergency, which emergency shall be declared in the preamble, or in the body, of the law.

This segment of the constitution was intended to insure that laws would not take effect until they had been made public by requiring "notice" of a new law to the people (through publication and circulation) in the counties. This provides local officials, as well as private citizens, with the chance to prepare for the implementation of any legislation enacted by the General Assembly. It also provides an effective way that jurisdications within the state (executive officers, law enforcement officials, and other administrators at the local level) receive notice of changes in the existing laws or the *status quo*. Any amendments or changes in statutory law must also be published prior to implementation (*Herrick v. Sayler*, 1957). Furthermore, until the publication of amendments or changes, the original or existing statute remains in effect (1933 Op. Atty. Gen. p. 133). The notification must reach all counties before the implementation of the statute can be effective (*State v. Williams*, 1910). The only exception to the publication requirement is "Cemergency" legislation that is clearly and explicitly indicated as such.

"Published" and "circulated" have been interpreted to mean the same thing (*Jones v. Cains*, 1853). The effective date of a statute, which can be specified in the legislation, must occur after the publication and circulation of the new enactment in order for it to comply with this section of the constitution (*Lohm v. State*, 1978). The secretary of state has no discretion to withhold the publishing of a newly enacted statute (1921-22 Op. Atty. Gen. p. 105). Furthermore, legislation can only have a prospective application, and the legislation cannot specify a retroactive date for implementation, absent language in the statute that imperatively requires retrospective application (*City of Connersville v. Connersville Hydraulic Co.*, 1882).

If a statute declares an emergency and thereby avoids the restrictions of this section, the enactment becomes operative law without publication or circulation, at all (*Lohm v. State*, 1978). The legislature can declare a specific date upon which the emergency law will become effective, but it does not have to specify such a date. In the latter case, the law becomes effective upon filing with the secretary of state by the governor, or without the governor's signature, when permitted (1915-16 Op. Atty. Gen. p. 607). The legislature must explicity declare the existence of the emergency in the preamble or the body of the law (not in the title) (*Hendrickson v. Hendrickson*, 1855; 1949 Op. Atty. Gen. No. 179).

SECTION 29

Compensation of Members; Conditions. The members of the General Assembly shall receive for their services a compensation to be fixed by law; but no increase of compensation shall take effect during the sessison in which such increase may be made. (Amended November 3, 1970) (The schedule adopted with the 1970 amendments to sections 9 and 29 of Article 4 was stricken out by the November 6, 1984 amendment)

This provision specifies that legislators can receive compensation for their services. It is comparable to Article I, section 6, Cl. I of the U.S. Constitution and Amendment 27. The legislature is to set the amount of compensation by enacting a statute—in 1995 $15,400 (IC 2-3-1-1). No increases in compensation can take effect until the next session of the legislature. Thus, legislators cannot vote themselves a pay increase. This limitation on increases does not apply if it is determined that all legislators need some item for the maintenance of their offices (1943 Op. Atty. Gen. p. 10). That permits such administrative increases to be available immediately. They are not considered "compensation" for purposes of this constitutional requirement. This limit now parallels the recent Twenty-seventh Amendment to the U.S. Constitution, which prevents any compenstation increase for U.S. Senators and Representatives from becoming effective until an election has occurred.

The 1970 amendment of the section specified the length of sessions (60 days maximum) and special sessions (40 days). These limitations were removed by the 1984 amendment. The lengths of legislative sessions are now set by statute. (See the discussion accompanying Article IV, section 9.)

SECTION 30

Holding of Public Office; Eligibility. No Senator or Representative shall, during the term for which he may have been elected, be eligible to any office, the election to which is vested in the General Assembly; nor shall he be appointed to any civil office of profit, which shall have been created, or the emoluments of which shall have been increased during such term; but this latter provision shall not be construed to apply to any office elective by the People.

This section prohibits a legislator from holding any office that depends on election (i.e., selection) by the General Assembly. Legislators cannot be appointed to any office or paid for any office that was created during that legislator's service in the General Assembly. This section prevents legislators from profiting from their own legislative actions. These requirements also prevent someone from holding a second office or being compensated for a second position while serving in the General Assembly.

After a legislator has left office, that former legislator can hold an administrative office and receive compensation for it (1962 Op. Atty. Gen. No.60). This means he cannot resign his legislative position and fill that second remunerative office before his elected term expires. Potential conflicts of interest were a focal point of this section when it was drafted, and where such conflicts have emerged, the provision bars holding the second office or it bars receiving compensation for the second office (1937 Op. Atty. Gen. p. 123).

Article V

Executive

SECTION 1

Governor; Term of Office. The executive power of the State shall be vested in a Governor. He shall hold his office during four years, and shall not be eligible more than eight years in any period of twelve years. (Amended November 7, 1972)

This section creates the office of the chief executive of the state, the governor. The separation of powers is inherent in the function of each branch of government (*Carlson v. State ex rel. Stodola*, 1966). The executive power is vested solely in the governor, as a coequal branch of government under the Separation of Powers provisions of Article III rather than in the Executive Branch (*State ex rel. Sendak v. Marion County Superior Ct, No. 2*, 1978). This executive power includes the power to appoint and remove other officers. This power to appoint is an executive function, without a legislative role even if the legislature provides for appointment (*City of Evansville v. State*, 1889). The removal power permits action by the governor without notice, charges or reasons, which means the appointees serve at the pleasure of the governor (1944 Op. Atty. Gen. No. 81).

The 1972 amendment eliminated the previous limit of one four-year term in any period of eight years and permitted a governor to serve two terms in succession. This earlier term limitation dated from the original 1851 Constitution.

SECTION 2

Lieutenant Governor; Term of Office. There shall be a Lieutenant Governor who shall hold his office during four years.

The office of lieutenant governor is created by this section. The term of office is four years, understood as official years rather than calendar years (*Kirkpatrick v. King*, 1950). This section does not specify the powers of this office or limit the number of four-year terms an individual can serve as lieutenant governor.

SECTION 3

Election of Governor and Lieutenant Governor. The Governor and Lieutenant Governor shall be elected at the times and places of choosing members of the General Assembly.

This section indicates that the two top executive officers of the state are to be elected at the same time as the General Assembly members are chosen. The gubernatorial candidates are determined by party primary election. The candidates for lieutenant governor are nominated at state party conventions (IC 3-1-10-3).

SECTION 4

Method of Voting. Each candidate for Lieutenant Governor shall run jointly in the general election with a candidate for Governor, and his name shall appear jointly on the ballot with the candidate for Governor. Each vote cast for a candidate for Governor shall be considered cast for the candidate for Lieutenant Governor as well. The candidate for Lieutenant Governor whose name appears on the ballot jointly with that of the successful candidate for Governor shall be elected Lieutenant Governor. (Amended November 5, 1974)

This section, as amended in 1974, provides that the two executive officers are to run for office and be elected to office jointly, just as the president and vice president do at the federal level. Prior to 1974, voters voted separately for governor and lieutenant governor, raising the possibility that the two elected officials would *not* be of the same political party or share the same policy mandates. The original version of this provision, that operated until 1974, allowed voters to "designate, for whom they vote as Governor, and for whom as Lieutenant Governor."

SECTION 5

Tie Vote. In the event of a tie vote, the Governor and Lieutenant Governor shall be elected from the candidates having received the tie vote, by the affirmative vote in joint session of a majority of the combined membership of both Houses as the first order of business after their organization. (Amended November 5, 1974)

This section provides for the resolution of a tie vote between the candidates for the executive offices. The tie is to be resolved by an affirmative vote of a joint session of the General Assembly as the first order of business after its organization as the legislature. The 1974 amendment reworded the provision, but did not change its substance. It is obviously highly unlikely that the popular vote for either of these two offices would end in a tie, and it never has. However, this provision addresses this contingency.

SECTION 6

Contested Elections of Governor and Lieutenant Governor. Contested elections for Governor or Lieutenant Governor, shall be determined by the General Assembly, in such manner as may be prescribed by law.

If there is any challenge to the election of a governor or lieutenant governor, that contest is to be resolved by the General Assembly (*Robertson v. State*, 1886). The legislature has provided by statute how to deal with such contests or challenges, by means of a State Recount Commission, composed of the secretary of state and the designees of the state chairman of each major political party (IC 3-12-10-1 *et seq.*).

SECTION 7

Qualifications of Governor and Lieutenant Governor. No person shall be eligible to the office of Governor or Lieutenant Governor, who shall not have been five years a citizen of the United States, and also a resident of the State of Indiana during the five years next preceding his election; nor shall any person be eligible to either of the said offices, who shall not have attained the age of thirty years.

This constitutional provision indicates the minimum age (30 years), citizenship (five years a U.S. citizen), and residency (five years preceding "his election") requirements for the offices of governor and lieutenant governor. This provision has not generated much legal dispute. However, the state supreme court has interpreted residency to mean "domicile" rather than strict "residency" (*State Election Bd. v. Bayh*, 1988). That permits an individual to live outside the state, but remain eligible to run for either of these offices if he has maintained domicile in the state, even while living outside the state.

SECTION 8

Ineligible Persons. No member of Congress, or person holding any office under the United States or under this State, shall fill the office of Governor or Lieutenant Governor.

This section specifically prohibits any member of Congress or other official of the United States from holding the office of governor or lieutenant governor. While this wording does not prevent someone who previously held such an office from occupying the executive offices of the state, they cannot hold both offices simultaneously. This also precludes the occupant of another state office from simultaneously holding either of these two highest state executive offices.

SECTION 9

Term of Office; Commencement. The official term of the Governor and Lieutenant Governor shall commence on the second Monday of January in the year one thousand eight hundred fifty-three; and on the same day every fourth year thereafter.

This section specifies that the terms of office for the governor and lieutenant governor begin on the second Monday in January after the election to office (1933 Op. Atty. Gen. p. 14). The election of officials to these offices occurs in presidential election years, and since the term is for four years, their terms coincide with the U.S. president's term. The "year" specified here is considered to be more or less 365 days long (*Kirkpatrick v. King*, 1950).

SECTION 10

Vacancies and Disabilities; Succession.

(a) In case the Governor-elect fails to assume office, or in case of the death or resignation of the Governor or his removal from office, the Lieutenant Governor shall become Governor and hold office for the unexpired term of the person whom he succeeds. In case the Governor is unable to discharge the powers and duties of his office, the Lieutenant Governor shall discharge the powers and duties of the office as Acting Governor.

(b) Whenever there is a vacancy in the office of Lieutenant Governor, the Governor shall nominate a Lieutenant Governor who shall take office upon confirmation by a majority vote in each house of the general assembly and hold office for the unexpired term of the person whom he succeeds. If the general assembly is not in session, the Governor shall call it into special session to receive and act upon the Governor's nomination. In the event of the inability of the Lieutenant Governor to discharge the powers and duties of his office, the General Assembly may provide by law for the manner in which a person shall be selected to act in his place and declare which powers and duties of the office such person shall discharge.

(c) Whenever the Governor transmits to the President pro tempore of the Senate and the Speaker of the House of Representatives his written declaration that he is unable to discharge the powers and duties of his office, and until he transits them a written declaration to the contrary, such powers and duties shall be discharged by the

Lieutenant Governor as Acting Governor. Thereafter, when the Governor transmits to the President pro tempore of the Senate and the Speaker of the House of Representatives his written declaration that no inability exists, he shall resume the powers and duties of his office.

(d) Whenever the President pro tempore of the Senate and the Speaker of the House of Representatives file with the Supreme Court a written statement suggesting that the Governor is unable to discharge the powers and duties of his office, the Supreme Court shall meet within forty-eight hours to decide the question and such decision shall be final. Thereafter, whenever the Governor files with the Supreme Court his written declaration that no inability exists, the Supreme Court shall meet within forty-eight hours to decide whether such be the case and such decision shall be final. Upon a decision that no inability exists, the Governor shall resume the powers and duties of his office.

(e) Whenever there is a vacancy in both the office of Governor and Lieutenant Governor, the general assembly shall convene in joint session forty-eight hours after such occurrence and elect a Governor from and of the same political party as the immediately past Governor by a majority vote in each house. (Amended November 7, 1978)

This section provides for the succession of officers if a vacancy occurs in either the office of governor or lieutenant governor. In addition, an inability on the part of the governor permits the lieutenant governor to exercise the powers of governor as the acting governor. If a vacancy occurs, then the lieutenant governor becomes governor for the remainder of the term. This elaborate provision was the result of the 1978 amendment which completely replaced the original 1851 language in order to provide for various contingencies in this regard. The original wording that permitted the lieutenant governor to succeed the governor in cases of "death, resignation, or inability to discharge the duties of office" was not sufficient to accommodate incapacity on the part of one of the officers.

The incapacity of the governor can be voluntarily declared by him in a written declaration to the Speaker of the House and the president pro tempore of the Senate. This voluntary acknowledgment leaves the lieutenant governor to act until the governor indicates that the inability no longer exists, again by written declaration to the leaders of the two houses of the General Assembly.

If there is no clear statement of disability by the governor, then the General Assembly and the supreme court can become involved in the elaborate and delicate process of determining the capacity of the governor to perform the duties of office. The actual determination is made by the supreme court at the request of legislative leaders. If such a determination is made by the court, then the court must respond to any subsequent filing by the governor that he is not unable to govern.

If a vacancy occurs in the office of the lieutenant governor, the governor is to nominate a replacement, and the General Assembly is to confirm the nominee by majority vote of both houses. The replacement serves out the unexpired term of the lieutenant governor (1948 Op. Atty. Gen. No. 153). The General Assembly is to provide the means by which someone shall be selected to act in place of the lieutenant governor when the lieutenant governor is disabled.

Should both executive officers be unable to perform their duties, the General Assembly shall provide removal and replacement of both officers. Clearly, the 1978 revision was intended to make the process of succession more definite and airtight, given the concerns about possible loopholes or the development of unforeseen contingencies. These provisions have not been invoked since their adoption.

SECTION 11

President of the Senate. Whenever the Lieutenant Governor shall act as Governor, or shall be unable to attend as President of the Senate, the Senate shall elect one of its own members as President for the occasion.

The lieutenant governor serves as the president of the Senate, but the Senate elects one of its own members to serve as president when the lieutenant governor is not able to serve. The election of such a president is done at the beginning of each legislative term, based on strict party lines. The president *pro tempore* of the Senate has long been the leader of the majority political party in the Senate.

SECTION 12

Commander-in-Chief. The Governor shall be commander-in-chief of the armed forces, and may call out such forces, to execute the laws, or to suppress insurrection, or repel invasion. (Amended November 6, 1984)

This grant of power to the governor was perhaps more important in the nineteenth century than it is today. However, the governor is still the commander-in-chief of the militia. In addition to defending the state from invasion or suppressing insurrection, the governor is to execute the laws of the state and may use the armed forces for that purpose. Thus, the chief executive can enforce the law by commanding the armed forces to carry it out. While that has not generally been necessary for the governor to do, the power as commander-in-chief is an inherent power which he possesses in order to carry out his executive functions (1948 Op. Atty. Gen. No. 377). It is clear that this power as commander-in-chief gives the governor a great deal of discretion in determining when and how that power will be exercised (*Cox v. McNutt*, 1935).

At an operational level, this power gives the governor the authority to make rules and regulations for the governance of the militia (1944 Op. Atty. Gen. No. 362). Thus, the governor can order payment to members of the state militia who are engaged in training and instruction (1915-1916 Op. Atty. Gen. p. 415). However, as commander-in-chief, the governor cannot sell or dispose of worn-out property used by the National Guard (1909-1910 Op. Atty. Gen. p. 160).

The 1984 amendment involved a technical correction or modernization by replacing the terms "military and naval" with "armed forces."

SECTION 13

Messages by Governor to General Assembly. The Governor shall, from time to time, give to the General Assembly information touching the condition of the State, and recommend such measures as he shall judge to be expedient. (Amended November 6, 1984)

This constitutional requirement gives the governor the obligation and authority to deliver a State of the State message to the General Assembly. The content of this message may include measures that the governor recommends the legislature enact at the next opportunity. This permits the governor to seek to set the public policy agenda for the state in a formal way. This provision has been viewed as a positive grant of power to the governor rather than a limitation (*Tucker v. State*, 1941).

The 1984 amendment removed the gender specific pronoun "he" and replaced it with "The Governor." This amendment did leave the masculine pronoun in the section, as well. It is interesting to note that this was not consistently done in this article in 1984, because there are other provisions of Article V, such as section 10, dealing with vacancies and disabilities of the governor and lieutenant governor, which was dramatically modified in 1978 but still contain the masculine pronoun.

SECTION 14

Presentment of Bills for Signature; Veto Power.

(a) Every bill which shall have passed the General Assembly shall be presented to the Governor. The Governor shall have seven days after the day of presentment to act upon such bill as follows:

(1) He may sign it, in which event it shall become a law.

(2) He may veto it:

(A) In the event of a veto while the General Assembly is in session, he shall return such bill, with his objections, within seven day of presentment, to the House in which it originated. If the Governor does not return the bill within seven days of presentment, the bill becomes law notwithstanding the veto.

(B) If the Governor returns the bill under clause (A), the House in which the bill originated shall enter the Governor's objections at large upon its journals and proceed to reconsider and vote upon whether to approve the bill. The bill must be reconsidered and voted upon within the time set out in clause (C). If, after such reconsideration and vote, a majority of all the members elected to that House shall approve the bill, it shall be sent, with the Governor's objections, to the other House, by which it shall likewise be reconsidered and voted upon, and, if approved by a majority of all the members elected to that House, it shall be a law.

(C) If the Governor returns the bill under clause (A), the General Assembly shall reconsider and vote upon the approval of the bill before the final adjournment of the next regular session of the General Assembly that follows the regular or special session in which the bill was originally passed. If the House in which the bill originated does not approve the bill under clause (B), the other House is not required to reconsider and vote upon the Approval of the bill. If, after voting, either House fails to approve the bill within this time, the veto is sustained.

(D) In the event of a veto after final adjournment of a session of the General Assembly, such bill shall be returned by the Governor to the House in which it originated on the first day that the General Assembly is in session after such adjournment, which House shall proceed in the same manner as with a bill vetoed before adjournment. The bill must be reconsidered and voted upon within the time set out in clause (C). If such bill is not so returned, it shall be a law notwithstanding such veto.

(3) He may refuse to sign or veto such bill in which event it shall become a law without his signature on the eighth day after presentment to the Governor.

(b) Every bill presented to the Governor which is signed by him or on which he fails to act within said seven days after presentment shall be filed with the Secretary of State within ten days of presentment. The failure to so file shall not prevent such a bill from becoming a law.

(c) In the event a bill is passed over the Governor's veto, such bill shall be filed with the Secretary of State without further presentment to the Governor: Provided, that in the event of such passage over the Governor's veto in the next succeeding General Assembly, the passage shall be deemed to have been the action of the General Assembly which initially passed such bill. (Amended November 7, 1972, and November 6, 1990)

This provision details how legislation is considered by the governor. Under the presentment requirement, legislation adopted by both houses is presented to the governor, and the governor can veto the legislation, sign it into law, or not sign it and let it become law without his signature after it sits on his desk for eight days. A gubernatorial veto can be overridden by simple, absolute majorities in both houses of the General Assembly. There is no pocket veto provision in this section (*State ex rel. Mass Transp. Auth. of Greater Indianapolis v. Indiana Revenue Bd.*, 1968). A veto by the governor after the General Assembly adjourns will result in the presentation of that veto to the next General Assembly "on the first day that the General Assembly is in session after such adjournment." This scheme clearly makes a legislative override of the governor's veto easier to achieve than in the case of the president of the United States and Congress. There is a presumption in this section of enactment of a law, absent an explicit, overt veto by the governor (*Harvey v. State ex rel. Carson*, 1889).

This veto and presentment process is considered to be essential to the separation of powers and as limits on the power of the General Assembly (*Hendricks v. Northwest Indiana Crime Comm., Inc.*, 1964). But since the provision inhibits the smooth operation of government, this section should be strictly construed.

The 1972 amendments to this provision involved technical changes in the wording of the section, but no significant, substantive changes in the procedure or the powers of either the General Assembly or the governor in connection with the veto powers. For example, at all times since the adoption of the constitution in 1851, only a majority of each house has been required to override the governor's veto. There has never been a pocket veto available to the governor. The earlier provision gave the governor less time to return a vetoed bill, and previously, the governor did not have any time limit in which to sign or veto the proposed law.

The 1990 amendment to this section largely involved a set of technical corrections that were overlooked in the 1972 revisions. These involved the addition of sections (a)(2)(B) and (a)(2)(C) to clarify the operation of these override provisions, but they do not change any of the relative power of the governor or the General Assembly in case of a veto.

SECTION 15

Administrative Officers and Departments. The Governor shall transact all necessary business with the officers of government, and may require information in writing from the officers of the administrative department, upon any subject relating to the duties of their respective offices.

This section provides the governor with the authority to conduct state business with executive officials. Furthermore, the governor can require information from these officers. The only limitation on this provision is that the requested information must relate to the officer's duties. Thus, the chief executive has the authority to require information as the governor feels is necessary.

SECTION 16

Laws Faithfully Executed. The Governor shall take care that the laws are faithfully executed. (Amended November 6, 1984)

The section, which parallels the U.S. Constitution "take care" provision of Article II, section 3, imposes on the governor the obligation to faithfully take care to execute the laws. Although this was amended in 1984 to replace the masculine pronoun "he" with "The Governor," there have been no changes or interpretations of this provision. It is clearly a constitutional obligation, and perhaps the most fundamental duty of the chief executive.

Under this provision of the constitution, the governor has authority to issue executive orders that govern the administration of the laws of Indiana (1969 Op. Atty. Gen. No. 6). These orders continue to operate until they are rescinded or changed by subsequent statutory enactments or later executive orders. The section serves as the basis for the governor to specify the effective date for the census to insure uniform and effective application of the census throughout the state (*Cato v. Chaddock*, 1978).

SECTION 17

Pardons and Reprieves; Exceptions. The Governor may grant reprieves, commutations, and pardons, after conviction, for all offenses except treason and cases of impeachment, subject to such regulations as may be provided by law. Upon conviction for treason, the Governor may suspend the execution of the sentence, until the case has been reported to the General Assembly, at its next meeting, when the General Assembly shall either grant a pardon, commute, direct the execution of the sentence, or grant further reprieve. The Governor may remit fines or forfeitures, under such regulations as may be provided by law; and shall report to the General Assembly, at its next meeting, each case of reprieve, commutation, or pardon granted, and also the names of all persons in whose favor remission of fines and forfeitures were made, and the several amounts remitted; provided, however, the General Assembly may, by law, constitute a council composed of officers of the State, without whose advice and consent the Governor may not grant pardons, in any case, except those left to his sole power by law. (Amended November 6, 1984)

This section gives the governor the power to grant pardons and reprieves. The exercise of this power by the governor is subject to regulations provided by law, but the legislature cannot restrict the exercise of this power by the governor (1874 Op. Atty. Gen. p. 38). The judiciary likewise cannot interfere with the governor's exercise of this power (*Misenheimer v. State*, 1978). The General Assembly has provided for an application procedure (IC 11-9-2-1) and created the Parole Board to make recommendations to the governor on these matters (IC 11-9-2-2). The Parole Board is an instrument for advising the governor on these matters, and this section does authorize the legislature to require the "council's" "advice and consent" for the governor to act.

The governor is prohibited from granting pardons in cases of treason or impeachment. With regard to treason, the General Assembly is to be informed by the governor and the legislature can pardon, commute, reprieve, or impose the sentence in these cases. Given the seriousness of the crime of treason, the drafters clearly felt the General Assembly should be given the responsibility to consider the possibility of alterations of the penalties for treason on a case-by-case basis.

The governor is also required to report all remissions, reprieves, commutations, and pardons to the General Assembly, identifying the individual beneficiaries of the actions. There is no authority of the legislature to rescind such actions by the governor, but the actions must be made public by informing the General Assembly.

The 1984 amendment replaced the masculine pronoun in this section. The other changes in 1984 were minor technical changes in wording.

SECTION 18

Vacancies; Filling during Recess. When, during a recess of the General Assembly, a vacancy shall happen in any office, the appointment to which is vested in the General Assembly; or when, at any time, a vacancy shall have occurred in any other State office, or in the office of Judge of any Court; the Governor shall fill such vacancy, by appointment, which shall expire, when a successor shall have been elected or qualified.

This section authorizes the governor to make interim appointments to fill vacancies in judicial offices, state offices (including a vacancy in the lieutenant governor's office) (1948 Op. Atty. Gen. No. 153), or offices where appointment is given to the General Assembly (*Tucker v. State*, 1941). The interim appointment will end when a successor is elected or qualified, as provided by law. This provision applies to offices created after the adoption of the 1851 Constitution as well as those in existence at the time of the adoption of the constitution (1945 Op. Atty. Gen. No. 28).

A vacancy occurs when an officer dies or submits a resignation (*Roberts v. State ex rel. Jackson County Bd. of Comm'rs*, 1972; *State v. Hauss*, 1873). There is no requirement for a formal recognition or declaration of the existence of the vacancy before the governor can act (*Wells v. State*, 1911). There is no need for either the General Assembly or the Judiciary to determine or declare that a vacancy exists (*Youngblood v. Marr*, 1970; *State ex rel. Kopsinski v. Grzesko-wiak*, 1945). The vacancy depends on the facts and circumstances of each case (*State v. Allen*, 1863). The interim appointment by the governor only operates until the next general election if the office is created in the constitution. If the office has been created by statute, then the interim officer can hold the office until the expiration of the specified term of office, even if that term extends beyond the next general election (1927–1928 Op. Atty. Gen. p. 145).

SECTION 19

Repealed. (Repealed November 6, 1984)

This repealed provision authorized the General Assembly to fill vacancies occurring in the General Assembly. This provision became Article IV, section 4.

SECTION 20

Meeting Place of General Assembly. Should the seat of government become dangerous from disease or a common enemy, the Governor may convene the General Assembly at any other place. (Amended November 6, 1984)

This provision, now probably antiquated, authorizes the governor to convene the General Assembly in another place than the state capital, when there is danger from the enemy or disease. The drafters had a concern about the possibility that state business could not be conducted under either of these two contingencies. So the constitution authorizes the relocation of government so that it could continue, during emergencies. The 1984 change replaced the masculine pronoun with "The Governor."

SECTION 21

Functions and Duties of Lieutenant Governor. The Lieutenant Governor shall, by virtue of his office, be President of the Senate; have a right, when in committee of the whole, to join in debate, and to vote on all subjects; and whenever the Senate shall be equally divided, he shall give the casting vote.

The duties of the lieutenant governor are to serve as president of the Senate, with certain powers in that context, including breaking a tie vote by casting his own vote. The lieutenant governor has the authority to vote and speak in the Senate when it is in committee of the whole. This office is considered an exception to the strict separation of powers doctrine, since it blends duties and powers of both the executive and the legislative branches (*Tucker v. State*, 1941).

SECTION 22

Compensation of Governor. The Governor shall, at stated times, receive for his services a compensation, which shall neither be increased nor diminished during the term for which he shall have been elected.

This authorizes the governor to be paid for his services, and ensures that the governor's compensation cannot be increased or reduced during the term for which he is elected.

In 1995, the salary of the governor was $77,000, as it has been since 1978 (IC 4-2-1-1).

SECTION 23

Compensation of Lieutenant Governor. The Lieutenant Governor, while he shall act as President of the Senate, shall receive, for his services, the same compensation as the Speaker of the House of Representatives; and any person, acting as Lieutenant Governor, shall receive the compensation attached to that office of Governor.

This authorizes the lieutenant governor to be paid for his services. However, contrary to the governor's salary, the lieutenant governor receives a salary as a member of the executive, and another, identical to the Speaker of the House, for serving as president of the Senate. The lieutenant governor is also entitled to the same expense account that is paid to legislators (1966 Op. Atty. Gen. No. 15). This service as president of the Senate is to be compensated as long as the lieutenant governor has been clearly elected and is qualified, despite the Senate's forcible barring of the lieutenant governor from performing his Senate duties (1888 Op. Atty. Gen. p. 134).

The salary of the lieutenant governor, provided by statute, was $72,000 in 1995, consisting of $64,000 compensation as lieutenant governor and $8,000 as president of the Senate (IC 4-2-1-1; IC 2-3-1-1).

SECTION 24

Dual Holding of Office. Neither the Governor nor Lieutenant Governor shall be eligible to any other office, during the term for which he shall have been elected.

Despite the blending of executive and legislative functions that attaches to the position of lieutenant governor, neither of the two people at the head of the executive branch can hold any other office during their terms in these offices. This does not prohibit a governor, while serving as the governor, from seeking another office, such as U.S. Senator (*State ex rel. Handley v. Superior Ct of Marion County*, 1958). Obviously, the governor could not serve in both capacities simultaneously; the governor must resign the governorship before holding the office of U.S. Senator (1958 Op. Atty. Gen. No. 7) (see Article II, section 9).

This bar covers any public position or employment that is created by law. It also encompasses appointed or elected office involving the exercise of any sovereign state functions. These positions may include offices where compensation is usual, even if not an essential part of the office (*Book v. State Office Bldg. Comm.*, 1958).

Article VI

Administrative

SECTION 1

State Officers; Secretary; Auditor and Treasurer; Election. There shall be elected, by the voters of the state, a Secretary, and Auditor and a Treasurer of State, who shall, severally, hold their offices for four years. They shall perform such duties as may be enjoined by law; and no person shall be eligible to either of said offices, more than eight years in any period of twelve years. (Amended November 3, 1970)

This section of the constitution specifies the state offices, in addition to the governor and lieutenant governor, that are to be elected in general elections throughout the state. These are the secretary of state, the state auditor, and the state treasurer. Their terms of office are four years, increased from two years by a 1970 amendment. These officers may not hold office for more than two terms out of any three. The duties and functions of these constitutional offices are to be specified by law, that is, by the General Assembly (Secretary of State: IC 4-5-1-1 *et seq.*; Auditor: IC 4-7-1-1 *et seq.*; Treasurer: IC 4-8, 1-2-1 (*et seq.*).

Interstingly, these officers do not have the power to appoint the administrators or assistants, as this would violate the executive powers of the governor (*Tucker v. State*, 1941) (see Article V, section 18). The governor retains the power to make these subsidiary appointments within these three constitutional offices.

That derives from the constitutional grant of power to the governor and the "take care" duties attached to the office of the governor in Article V, section 16.

SECTION 2

County Officers; Clerk of Circuit Court; Auditor, Treasurer, Sheriff, Coroner and Surveyor; Election. There shall be elected, in each county by the voters thereof, at the time of holding general elections, a Clerk of the Circuit Court, Auditor, Recorder, Treasurer, Sheriff, Coroner, and Surveyor, who shall, severally, hold their offices for four years; and no person shall be eligible to the office of Clerk, Auditor, Recorder, Treasurer, Sheriff, or Coroner more than eight years in any period of twelve years. (Amended November 4, 1952; November 6, 1984)

This provision identifies the offices within each county which will be elected by the qualified voters in the county. These offices are:

- Clerk of the Circuit Court
- Auditor
- Recorder
- Treasurer
- Sheriff
- Coroner
- Surveyor

These officers hold office for four-year terms (changed from two years in 1984). Furthermore, while the surveyor can hold office indefinitely, the rest of these county officers—clerk, auditor, recorder, treasurer, sheriff, and coroner—can hold their offices for no more than two out of any three terms. The exception for surveyor may be because that office is not considered particularly political and there is no need to insure turnover among holders of that office (1952 Op. Atty. Gen. No. 72). Even if an officeholder has not served two full terms out of three, he cannot occupy the office for more than the maximum number of years allowed (1970 Op. Atty. Gen. No. 5). The term limit has been interpreted to require a vacancy in the office of clerk of the circuit court at the expiration of the term, even if there is no successor selected (1967 Op. Atty. Gen. No. 40; *Gosman v. State*, 1886).

These offices are constitutional even though they are not statewide, but rather selected by the electors in a county or other jurisdiction (1934 Op. Atty. Gen. p. 140; *Dortch v. Lugar*, 1971). However, the duties and responsibilities of these offices have been specified by state statute as the constitution is silent on these matters. (Auditor: IC 36-2-9-1 *et seq.*; Recorder: IC 36-2-11-1 *et seq.*; Sheriff: IC 36-2-13-1 *et seq.*; & 36-8-10-1 *et seq.*; Surveyor: IC 36-2-12-1 *et seq.*; Treasurer: IC 36-2-10-1 *et seq.*) The clerk's position is a circuit rather than a county position so interim vacancies are to be filled by gubernatorial appointment, rather than by a board of county commissioners (*State ex rel. McClure v. Marion Superior Court*, 1959). The clerk's duties are judicial and ministerial and they can be outlined by court authority as well as by statute (1951 Op. Atty. Gen. No. 312).

SECTION 3

Election or Appointment of Other County and Township Officers. Such other county and township officers as may be necessary, shall be elected, or appointed, in such manner as may be prescribed by law.

This provision permits the General Assembly to create additional county offices. These offices are obviously statutory rather than constitutional in nature and that makes some difference in the duties assigned to these offices, and their operation. The terms of such offices are dependent upon statutory enactment. Furthermore, the legislature is authorized to provide for the filling of such offices either by election or by appointment. The primary focus of. this provision has dealt with the organization of township government (IC 36-6-1-1 *et seq.*). In addition, there are a large number of statutory provisions relating to county government, including the creation of other county offices, executive, budgetary, and legislative (IC 36-2-1-1 *et seq.*).

SECTION 4

County Officers; Qualifications. No person shall be elected, or appointed, as a county officer, who is not an elector of the county and who has not been an inhabitant of the county one year next preceding his election or appointment. (Amended November 6, 1984)

This is a residency requirement for county officers. No one can be selected to occupy a county office unless he is a voter in that county and has been a resident of the county for a year, prior to the election. The interpretation of this provision focuses on defining which officers are governed by this requirement. A county superintendent of schools is not required to comply with this provision (*State ex rel. Ocborn v. Eddington*, 1935; 1929-1930 Op. Atty. Gen. p. 242). Neither must a notary public be a county resident (*U.S. v. Bixby*, 1881). Deputies or employees of county offices need not be county residents (1970 Op. Atty. Gen. No. 2). However, a deputy county treasurer is a county officer within the meaning of this provision (1931-1932 Op. Atty. Gen. p. 275).

The 1984 amendment was a technical change in the section to modernize the wording. These changes did not alter the meaning of the provision.

SECTION 5

State Officers; Residence. The Governor, and the Secretary, Auditor, and Treasurer of State, shall, severally, reside and keep the public records, books, and papers, in any manner relating to their respective offices, as the seat of government.

These four state officers are required to reside and maintain records at the seat of government. In addition, this section requires that they keep all records open to the public, for the obvious reason that public access to state records is an essential element of representative government. The seat of government or the capital of the state is clearly specified and the residency requirement is an effective means of insuring that state business (and the records of it) will be maintained at the place of government.

SECTION 6

Local Officers; Residence. All county, township, and town officers, shall reside within their respective counties, townships, and towns; and shall keep their respective offices at such places therein, and perform such duties, as may be directed by law.

This section indicates that local officials must reside in the jurisdiction they serve during their term of office. This is comparable to the preceding requirement for state officers. In addition, these officials are to maintain their offices as directed by statute. This ensures that local officials are within the "reach" of their constituents and their performance of duties is to be governed by law.

Most of the questions about this provision have focused on the residency requirement. Thus, whether a township office is constitutional or statutory, the incumbent was to reside within the township (*Willsey v. Newlon*, 1974). Any officer leaving the township loses the right to serve as a township trustee (1944 Op. Atty. Gen. No. 58). County commissioners must reside in the county while in office (*Relender v. State*, 1898).

The last section of this provision indicates that statutes can provide direction for the performance of duties as well as the places for performance. However, this does not permit the legislature to expand or change the qualifications for a constitutional office (*Petition of the Justice of the Peace Ass'n of Indiana*, 1958).

SECTION 7

State Officers; Removal Methods; Impeachment. All State officers shall, for crime, incapacity, or negligence, be liable to be removed from office, either by impeachment by the House of Representatives, to be tried by the Senate, or by a joint resolution of the General Assembly; two-thirds of the members elected to each branch voting, in either case, therefor.

This section specifies the manner in which a state officer can be removed from office, and the grounds for removal. The officer is to be impeached by the House and tried by the Senate or two-thirds of both houses voting for a joint resolution may remove the officer.

This provision has specifically not been applied to prosecuting attorneys (*State v. Patterson*, 1914) or circuit court judges (*State v. Dearth*, 1939). Since this provision specifies state officers, the exclusion of these categories is not particularly surprising. However, the following section (Article VI, section 8) can clearly be interpreted as relating to these particular kinds of offices, although Indiana courts seem to have blended or mixed these two provisions for some purposes (*McComas v. Krug*, 1882). The exclusion of these offices from coverage by this section relates to the fact that they are judicial offices that are not merely administrative or subject to the usual legislative controls. These officers, by statute, can be removed by impeachment. The General Assembly has provided for the procedures for impeachment by statute (IC 5-8-1-1 *et seq.*).

SECTION 8

State, County, Township and Town Officers; Impeachment and Removal. All State, county, township, and town officers, may be impeached, or removed from office, in such manner as may be prescribed by law.

This section provides for the removal of county and other local officers, and it parallels the preceding provision (section 7) for state officers. It allows a variety of methods, including impeachment *or* another form of removal if the General Assembly sets an alternative out in a statute (IC 5-8-1-24 *et seq.*). The provision relates to offices that are not state offices.

These removal provisions are limited in that the power does not extend to public employees who express their political beliefs or feelings (*Garrett v. Barnes*, 1992; *Selch v. Letts*, 1992). Such actions are protected by the Free Speech provisions of the federal and state constitutions. However, a policy making employee can be removed from office for political reasons or any other consideration. The issue is whether political beliefs or party affiliation can be an appropriate requirement for satisfactory performance of the public office (*McDermott v. Bicanic*, 1990). The court of appeals reasoned that the policy making nature of the office (the Hammond City Parks and Recreation Administrator) means political affiliation can be a valid criterion for removal, regardless of the First Amendment protections.

SECTION 9

County, Township and Town Offices; Vacancies. Vacancies in county, township, and town offices, shall be filled in such manner as may be prescribed by law.

Vacancies in county, township, or town offices are to be filled according to procedures set forth in state statutes. This provision has required very little interpretation to operate. A "Town" has consistently been broadly applied to mean cities, as well (1959 Op. Atty. Gen. No. 65). A tie election outcome does not create a vacancy that is to be filled using the provisions based on this section (*Youngblood v. Marr*, 1970). Rather, the incumbent continues to occupy the office until a replacement is designated in the appropriate fashion.

SECTION 10

Powers of County Boards. The General Assembly may confer upon the boards doing county business in the several counties, powers of a local, administrative character.

This section authorizes the General Assembly to outline administrative and local duties for various county boards to perform. It thus resembles other constitutional provisions which authorize the legislature to specify duties, procedures, or functions that various constitutionally created offices are to perform. Thus, this provision allows the state legislature to fill in a variety of administrative gaps at the county level of government. This legislative power is not limited to providing duties to boards of county commissioners (*Mogilner v. Metropolitan County Planning Commission*, 1957) but rather allows the legislature to allocate administrative duties to other county offices as well. The county board possesses those powers specified by statutes, as well as those implied from them (*Tomlinson v. Marion County Planning Commission*, 1955). Thus, the source of power for these governing bodies is statutory, and all powers must be derived from statutes.

SECTION 11

Repealed. (Repealed November 6, 1984)

This provision related to the election of county sheriffs when the term of the sheriffs's office changed from two to four years, in 1950. It specified that sheriffs would be elected at the general election in 1950 and every four years afterward.

Article VII

Judicial

Article VII of the constitution originally provided for the judicial branch of the state government and it still does that. However, it was completely revised by a set of amendments in 1970. These revisions completely restructured the article and the judicial system of the state. The discussion of individual sections which follows reflects the current form of the article and the current authority of the judicial branch.

SECTION 1

Judicial Power. The judicial power of the State shall be vested in one Supreme Court of Appeals, Circuit Courts, and such other courts as the General Assembly may establish. (Amended March 14, 1881; November 3, 1970)

This section specifies the state's judicial power is lodged in a single supreme court, one court of appeals, circuit courts, and any other courts created by the General Assembly. Thus, the general grant of the state's judicial power is to a three-tiered system with an intermediate appellate court, similar to that of many other states. The General Assembly has the authority to create courts of limited jurisdiction by statute (*Lake County Council v. Arredondo*, 1977).

Although they are constitutional courts, the courts of appeals do not have general appellate jurisdiction over trial proceedings, but rather must rely on the supreme court to afford them judicial competence over various kinds of issues as they emerge or as the high court feels need attention (*State v. Pease*, 1988). Thus, the courts of appeals are used to alleviate episodic workload problems as determined by the supreme court, and their jurisdiction is prescribed by the supreme court.

The trial court of general jurisdiction is the circuit court. The circuits are geographical but do *not* coincide with county lines. The circuit courts are staffed by circuit judges elected by partisan ballot at the general election. Their powers cannot be diminished by the legislature, because of the circuit court's constitutional status, but they have been affected by the creation of a number of other trial courts over the years (*Youngblood v. Warrick Circuit Court of Carwick Co.*, 1935). For example, much of the growing workload of Indiana trial courts has been allocated to superior courts, created idiosyncratically in a number of counties by the state legislature. These are statutory courts subject to the same limitations as all statutory courts (*Gary Taxpayers Ass'n v. Lake Superior Court*, 1948). They can be abolished, their work and authority can be changed, and their membership can be modified in ways that a constitution protects against. The creation of these statutory courts is sensitive to local and state politics, rather than judicial, workload or needs for the efficient or prompt administration of justice.

As noted, the legislature may create additional courts as necessary, and it has used this power largely to create individual courts of limited or idiosyncratic jurisdiction. This ad hoc development of the lower parts of the judiciary, as political forces align and realign, makes marginal adjustments in the structure of the judicial branch possible. This may not yield a coherent judicial system, although it also provides remedies for idiosyncratic problems as they arise in the processing of cases and judicial workload.

The supreme court has interpreted its judicial power broadly. Recently, it held that the constitution does not restrict its jurisdiction to cases or controversies, as the U.S. Constitution requires of federal courts in Article III. For example, the state court has held that it can decide cases that are moot (*Matter of Lawrence*, 1991). That would suggest that other, preliminary features of a case or controversy are not necessarily required in the state judiciary. Perhaps this would allow the supreme court to render advisory opinions. The court gave little indication in *Lawrence* of what considerations it would weigh in choosing whether to decide or decline to decide such moot issues, and it is likely that the court will not rush into a number of these kinds of issues. The holding indicates that the court may decide such issues, if it chooses to do so.

The supreme court is the supreme judicial authority in the state, reigning supreme over the other two departments—the executive and legislative—including the bureaucracy, as well as the lower courts in connection with judicial matters (*Ex Parte France*, 1911). The legislature cannot deprive it of the powers granted it by the constitution (*Branson v. Studebaker*, 1892; *Ex Parte France*, 1911). While this statement may be self-evident, it has explicitly been asserted and established by the state courts and recognized by the other branches of state government.

SECTION 2

Supreme Court. The Supreme Court shall consist of the Chief Justice of the State and not less than four nor more than eight associate justices; a majority of whom shall form a quorum. The court may appoint such personnel as may be necessary. (Amended November 3, 1970)

This provision specifies that the supreme court will consist of a chief and from four to eight associate justices, along with the chief justice, as mandated by the legislature (IC 33-2.1-2-1). The number has been set at four associate justices and the chief justice, for a total of five justices for a number of years. The original provision in the 1851 Constitution specified the court could have three to five members. In fact the court has always had five justices.

A quorum of the justices, in 1995 three of the five, can decide cases. That quorum requirement allows a case to be decided by a two-to-one vote, even though two justices do not constitute a majority of the five-member court (*Davidson v. State*, 1966).

SECTION 3

Chief Justice. The Chief Justice of the State shall be selected by the judicial nominating commission from the members of the Supreme Court and he shall retain that office for a period of five years, subject to reappointment in the same manner, except that a member of the Court may resign the office of Chief Justice without resigning from the Court. During a vacancy in the office of Chief Justice caused by absence, illness, incapacity or resignation all powers and duties of that office shall devolve upon the member of the Supreme Court who is senior in length of service and if equal in length of service the determination shall be by lot until such time as the cause of the vacancy is terminated or the vacancy is filled.

The Chief Justice of the State shall appoint such persons as the General Assembly by law may provide for the administration of his office. The Chief Justice shall have prepared and submit to the General Assembly regular reports on the condition of the courts and such other reports condition of the courts and such other reports as may be requested. (Amended November 3, 1970)

This section provides for the selection of the chief justice of Indiana by the judicial nominating commission, from among the sitting justices. That designee serves as chief justice for five years, and can be reappointed to the chief justiceship. The chief justice can resign that office without leaving the supreme court during the five-year term as chief justice.

The specific duties of the chief justice are to be performed by the ranking associate justice if the chief justice is unable to perform them during his tenure in office. As outlined in the constitution, those duties include the appointment of administrative personnel, as authorized by the General Assembly, to administer the office of chief justice. In addition, the chief justice is to prepare and submit regular reports on the state of the judiciary to the General Assembly. These have evolved into an annual report to the legislature.

SECTION 4

Jurisdiction of Supreme Court. The Supreme Court shall have no original jurisdiction except in admission to the practice of law; discipline or disbarment of those admitted; the unauthorized practice of law; discipline, removal and retirement of justices and judges; supervision of the exercise of jurisdiction by the other courts of the State; and issuance of writs necessary or appropriate in aid of its jurisdiction. The Supreme Court shall exercise appellate jurisdiction under such terms and conditions as specified by rules except that appeals from a judgment imposing a sentence of death, life imprisonment or imprisonment for a term greater than fifty years shall be taken directly to the Supreme Court. The Supreme Court shall have, in all appeals of criminal cases, the power to review all questions of law and to review and review the sentence imposed. (Amended November 3, 1970; amended November 8, 1988)

The jurisdiction of the supreme court is spelled out in this section. There is some original jurisdiction, focusing on the practice of law in Indiana, and the operation of the state judiciary where jurisdiction may be necessary to take formal action. The court can specify its rules for proceeding with its appellate jurisdiction, and it is the judge of its constitutional jurisdiction (*In re Marriage of Lopp*, 1978). In other words, the bulk of the court's business derives from its appellate jurisdiction, and the court is given significant control over its exercise of that jurisdiction. There are some categories in which appeal from criminal convictions is directly to the supreme court, and appellate review appears to be mandatory. These cases include the imposition of the death penalty or a prison sentence of fifty or more years. This section also indicates that the court's appellate jurisdiction over criminal cases involves all questions of law and permits the supreme court to review and revise the sentence imposed by the trial court. This jurisdiction is also under the control of the legislature. In fact, it appears that the legislature's control is comparable to that of the U.S. Congress over the appellate jurisdiction of the U.S. Supreme Court (*Montgomery v. State*, 1944). However, as the wording and discussion of Article VII, section 6 below indicate, the supreme court can specify, by rule, the appellate jurisdiction of the court of appeals in order to siphon off some of the supreme court's business as needed.

The legislature's power is to grant appellate jurisdiction to the supreme court and to "regulate and restrict" appeals to the supreme court, but only as to the manner in which the court's jurisdiction is to be invoked (*Gardner v. Lohmann Const. Co.*, 1945). On the one hand, the legislature has the authority to grant the right to appeal since that right is not constitutionally based (*Curless v. Watson*, 1913; *In re Petition to Transfer Appeals*, 1931). On the other hand, the court itself may allocate some of this jurisdiction to the lower appellate court. The legislature does not have absolute power to deprive the supreme court of appellate jurisdiction in all cases or confer the ultimate jurisdiction in cases for recovery of money to another court of the legislature's creation (*Ex parte France*, 1911). The General Assembly may enlarge that jurisdiction within reasonable limits, as public policy requires, but not remove it completely (*Lake Erie W.R. Co. v. Watkins*, 1902). This is an explicit difference with the U.S. Congress's control over U.S. Supreme Court appellate jurisdiction.

The 1988 amendment to this provision makes supreme court review available for prison sentences of fifty years or more. The prior provision, the 1970 version, specified ten or more years' imprisonment would be subject to direct appellate review by the court. Apparently, too many appeals forced on the supreme court's docket by the ten-year minimum led to the change.

SECTION 5

Court of Appeals. The Court of Appeals shall consist of as many geographic districts and sit in such locations as the General Assembly shall determine to be necessary. Each geographic district of the Court shall consist of three judges. The judges of each geographic district shall appoint such personnel as the General Assembly may provide by law. (Amended November 3, 1970)

The intermediate court of appeals for Indiana is divided into five geographic districts, each of which is set along county lines, as determined by the General Assembly. Since there are three judges on each court of appeals, the current number of court of appeals judges is fifteen (IC 36-2.1-2-2). The authority of this court is general, in the sense that jurisdiction does not reside with a particular geographic region, but rather with the court of appeals as a whole (*Shortbridge v. Court of Appeals*, 1984).

This section also allows court of appeals judges of each district to appoint such personnel as the General Assembly authorizes by statute. The legislature has given this discretion back to the courts, indicating that the judges appoint "such personnel" as the court thinks "necessary." The statute does specify law clerks and secretaries (IC 36-2.1-2-7).

SECTION 6

Jurisdiction of Court of Appeals. The Court shall have no original jurisdiction, except that it may be authorized by rules of the Supreme Court to review directly decisions of administrative agencies. In all other cases, it shall exercise appellate jurisdiction under such terms and conditions as the Supreme Court shall specify by rules which shall, however, provide in all cases an absolute right to one appeal and to the extent provided by rule, review and revision of sentences for defendants in all criminal cases. (Amended November 3, 1970)

The supreme court's control over the jurisdiction of the court of appeals is a product of the 1970 revisions of this article and the constitutionalization of the intermediate court of appeals (*Tyson v. State*, 1992). This control extends to the original jurisdiction of the court of appeals (*State v. Pease*, 1988).

A major purpose of the court of appeals is to provide criminal defendants with one appeal after conviction. That appeal insures that the criminal trial is free from legal error or is reviewed in that connection. It also permits review of the sentence that was imposed in the criminal prosecution. This appellate jurisdiction in criminal cases siphons off a great many of the routine appeals that would otherwise fall to the supreme court.

SECTION 7

Judicial Circuits. The State shall, from time to time, be divided into judicial circuits; and a Judge for each circuit shall be elected by the voters thereof. He shall reside within the circuit and shall have been duly admitted to practice law by the Supreme Court of Indiana; he shall hold his office for the term of six years, if he so long behaves well. (Amended November 3, 1970)

The basic trial court in Indiana is the circuit court which involves the geographic division of the state into circuits. For the most part, these circuits are the creature of the General Assembly (*Stocking v. State*, 1855), and these courts number 88, in 1995 (IC 33-4-1-1). Most of these circuits are drawn precisely along county lines, but there are some counties that contain more than one circuit or one circuit may combine more than one county because of population. The judges and the jurisdiction of the circuit courts are set by statute, and can be amended or changed by the legislature. However, the legislature cannot remove a judge by abolishing or changing a circuit (*State ex rel. Wardsworth v. Wright*, 1937).

The judges of the circuit courts are elected by partisan ballot for six-year terms (or they serve during good behavior), and they must reside in the circuit in which they are serving. They are considered to be judicial officers (1917–1920 Op. Atty. Gen. p. 658) rather than state, county, or township officers (*State ex rel. Pitman v. Tucker*, 1874). The judges who serve in circuit courts, as well as those serving on superior and county courts are *not* county officers, but rather are members of the state judiciary.

The selection, tenure, and authority of circuit judges are based on the state judicial system, rather than the county system provided in the constitution. This applies even when the judge clearly is serving within the geographic reach of only one county. Thus, they are not subject to the tenure and term limits specified for county officers in Article VI, section 2.

SECTION 8

Circuit Courts. The Circuit Courts shall have such civil and criminal jurisdiction as may be prescribed by law. (Amended November 3, 1970)

This section provides that these general trial courts have jurisdiction conferred by statute. That includes originals jurisdiction in civil and criminal cases except where exclusive jurisdiction has been conferred on another court (IC 33-4-4-3). This court possesses the residual and bulk of original trial court jurisdiction in the State of Indiana. Although the law (statutory and case) on this court's jurisdiction is voluminous, the core of jurisdiction is well established within statutory parameters and the constitution's inherent powers to conduct its business (*Knox County Council v. State ex rel. McCormick*, 1940).

SECTION 9

Judicial Nominating Commission. There shall be one judicial nominating commission for the Supreme Court and Court of Appeals. This commission shall, in addition, be the commission on judicial qualifications for the Supreme Court and Court of Appeals.

The judicial nominating commission shall consist of seven members, a majority of whom shall form a quorum, one of whom shall be the Chief Justice of the State or a Justice of the Supreme Court whom he may designate, who shall act as chairman. Those admitted to the practice of law shall elect three of their number to serve as members of said commission. All elections shall be in such manner as the General Assembly may provide. The Governor shall appoint to the commission three citizens, not admitted to the practice of law. The terms of office and compensation for members of a judicial nominating commission shall be fixed by the General Assembly. No member of a judicial nominating commission other than the Chief Justice or his designee shall hold any other salaried public office. No member shall hold an office in a political party or organization. No member of the judicial nominating commission shall be eligible for appointment to a judicial office so long as he is a member of the commission and for a period of three years thereafter. (Amended November 3, 1970)

This section establishes a judicial nominating commission to provide the governor with lists of three qualified people when a vacancy occurs at either the supreme court or court of appeals level. The commission is composed of seven members, with the chief justice (or his designee from the state supreme court) as chair. The governor appoints three citizens who are not members of the practicing bar in Indiana to serve on the commission. The remaining three members of the commission are selected as the General Assembly provides (IC 33-2.1-4-1), from among those admitted to practice law in the state. No member of the commission, except the chief justice, can hold public office. Furthermore, no members of the commission are eligible for appointment to a judicial office while serving on the commission or for three years after their service ends. They cannot hold office in a political party. This section does not outline the commission's powers or procedures, but rather the composition of the commission and the procedures of the commission are outlined in the next section of the constitution.

SECTION 10

Selection of Justices of the Supreme Court and Judges of the Court of Appeals. A vacancy in a judicial office in the Supreme Court or Court of Appeals shall be filled by the Governor, without regard to political affiliation, from a list of three nominees presented to him by the judicial nominating commission. If the Governor shall fail to make an appointment from the list within sixty days from the day it is presented to him, the appointment shall be made by the Chief Justice of the acting Chief Justice from the same list.

To be eligible for nomination as a justice of the Supreme Court or Judge of the Court of Appeals, a person must be domiciled within the geographic district, a citizen of the United States, admitted to the practice of law in the courts of the State for a period of not less than ten (10) years or must have served as a judge of a circuit, superior or criminal court of the State of Indiana for a period of not less than five (5) years. (Amended November 3, 1970)

This section focuses on the selection of members of the Indiana Supreme Court and the court of appeals. The nominating commission (Article VII, section 9) is to provide the governor with a list of three nominees. The governor has sixty days to select one of the nominees, and if that does not happen, then the chief justice shall appoint one of the three from the list. This procedure operates for the initial selection of all appellate judges in Indiana, even when a vacancy coincides with a general election. That is, the governor makes all of the initial appointments to the appellate courts from the lists supplied by the nominating commission.

This section of the constitution also specifies the eligibility requirements for supreme court justices and court of appeals judges. The requirements are identical for both levels of court. The nominee must be a citizen of the United States, reside in the judicial district (if the court of appeals is involved), be admitted to practice law in the state for ten years, or have five years' experience as a judge of the circuit, superior, or criminal courts of the state.

SECTION 11

Tenure of Justices of the Supreme Court and Judges of the Court of Appeals. A justice of the Supreme Court or Judge of the Court of Appeals shall serve until the next general election following the expiration of two years from the date of appointment, and subject to approval or rejection by the electorate, shall continue to serve for terms of ten years, so long as he retains his office. In the case of a justice of the Supreme Court, the electorate of the entire state shall vote on the question of approval or rejection. In the case of judges of the Court of Appeals the electorate of the geographic district in which he serves shall vote on the question of approval or rejection.

Every such justice and judge shall retire at the age specified by statute in effect at the commencement of his current term.

Every such justice and judge is disqualified from acting as a judicial officer, without loss of salary, while there is pending (1) an indictment or information charging him in any court in the United States with a crime punishable as a felony under the laws of Indiana or the United States, or (2) a recommendation to the Supreme Court by the commission on judicial qualifications for his removal or retirement.

On recommendation of the commission on judicial qualifications or on its own motion, the Supreme Court may suspend such justice or judge from office without salary when in any court in the United States he pleads guilty or no contest or is found guilty of a crime punishable as a felony under the laws of Indiana or the United States, or of any other crime that involves moral turpitude under that law. If his conviction is reversed, suspension terminates and he shall be paid his salary for the period of suspension. If he is suspended and his conviction becomes final the Supreme Court shall remove him from office.

On recommendation of the commission of judicial qualifications the Supreme Court may (1) retire such justice or judge for disability that seriously interferes with the performance of his duties and is or is likely to become permanent, and (2) censure or remove such justice or judge, for action occurring not more than six years prior to the commencement of his current term, when such action constitutes willful misconduct in office, willful and persistent failure to perform his duties, habitual interperance, or conduct prejudicial to the administration of justice that brings the judicial office into disrepute.

A justice or judge so retired by the Supreme Court shall be considered to have retired voluntarily. A justice or judge so removed by the Supreme Court is ineligible for judicial office and pending further order of the Court he is suspended from practicing law in this State.

Upon receipt by the Supreme Court of any such recommendation, the Court shall hold a hearing, at which such justice or judge is entitled to be present, and make such determinations as shall be required. No justice shall participate in the determination of such hearing when it concerns himself.

The Supreme Court shall make rules implementing this section and provide for convening of hearings. Hearings and proceedings shall be public upon request of the justice or judge whom it concerns.

No such justice or judge shall, during his term of office, engage in the practice of law, run for elective office other than a judicial office, directly or indirectly make any contribution to, or hold any office in, a political party or organization or take part in any political campaign. (Amended November 4, 1952; November 3, 1970)

Judges appointed by the governor to serve on the supreme court or the court of appeals serve for a period of at least two years, after the next general election after the appointment. Then, they are subject to a retention election in which they run unopposed. If they receive majority approval from the electorate, they serve for a ten-year period, after which they are subject to another retention election. The electorate approves the supreme court justices in the entire state, while the court of appeals judge must be approved only by a majority of those voters in the appropriate geographic district of the court of appeals.

Retirement age for Indiana appellate judges is specified by the General Assembly, in 1995, at 75 years of age (IC 33-2.1-5-1). The bulk of this section of the constitution is devoted to dealing with the disqualification of sitting judges under various circumstances. These considerations include a pending indictment or information relating to a felony charge against the judge, or the recommendation of the commission on judicial qualifications. While this is a narrow, specifically worded portion of the constitution, it clearly reflects general concern for the treatment of such sitting judges and the possible contingencies that might develop regarding the performance of judicial duties.

SECTION 12

Substitution of Judges. The General Assembly may provide, by law, that the Judge of one circuit may hold the Courts of another circuit, in cases of necessity or convenience; and in case of temporary inability of any Judge, from sickness or other cause, to hold the Courts in his circuit, provision may be made by law, for holding such courts. (Amended November 3, 1970)

This section authorizes circuit judges to perform duties in other circuits, when necessity or convenience call for that. The General Assembly has the authority to provide for such adjustments and also to appoint special judges who have the same judicial power as a regular judge to preside over cases in a circuit (*Perkins v. Hayward*, 1890).

SECTION 13

Removal of Circuit Court Judges and Prosecuting Attorneys. Any Judge of the Circuit Court or Prosecuting Attorney, who shall have been convicted of corruption or other high crime, may, on information in the name of the State, be removed from office by the Supreme Court, or in such other manner as may be prescribed by law. (Amended November 3, 1970)

The supreme court has the authority to remove a prosecuting attorney or a circuit court judge who has been convicted of "corruption or other high crime." This removal power does not allow the legislature to remove these officials at will, but rather provides that they may be removed, by the supreme court, and only after conviction for various serious crimes (*State v. Bear*, 1893).

This section of the constitution provides the only basis and procedure for removal of judicial personnel. That is, circuit court judges and prosecuting attorneys are considered judicial officers and are not subject to other impeachment provisions that operate with regard to county officials (Article VI, sections 7 and 8; *State v. Dearth*, 1939).

SECTION 14

Repealed. (Repealed November 6, 1984)

This repealed provision dealt with the office of justice of the peace. This township office had a four-year term, and was abolished with the repeal of this section in 1984.

SECTION 15

No Limitation on Term of Office. The provisions of Article 15, Section 2, prohibiting terms of office longer than four years, shall not apply to justices and judges. (Amended November 3, 1970)

This section exempts judicial officers from the term limitations imposed by Article XV, section 2. This later provision indicates that when no term of office is specified, the term will be at the pleasure of the appointing official. The term may be specified by the General Assembly, but may not exceed four years. This exception permits judges, if retained or reelected by their constituents, and subject to good behavior requirements, to serve until reaching the mandatory retirement age.

SECTION 16

Prosecuting Attorneys. There shall be elected in each judicial circuit by the voters thereof a prosecuting attorney, who shall have been admitted to the practice of law in the State before his election, who shall hold his office for four years, and whose term of office shall begin on the first day of January next succeeding his election. The election of prosecuting attorneys under this section shall be held at the time of holding the general election in this year 1974 and each four years thereafter. (Amended November 3, 1970)

Each judicial circuit is to have an elected prosecuting attorney. This office is a constitutional one, whereas the office of attorney general is a statutory office, which can be changed by legislative enactment (*State ex rel. Steers v. Holovachka*, 1957; *State v. Market*, 1973). The prosecuting attorney serves for a four-year term, and has authority to prosecute criminal cases within the circuit. This officer must be a resident of the circuit at the time of election(*State v. Johnston*, 1885). The General Assembly has the authority to specify the duties and authority of this office, since only the office is created by the constitution (1947 Op. Atty. Gen. No. 327; IC 33-14-1-3; IC 33-14-1-4).

SECTION 17

Grand Jury. The General Assembly may modify, or abolish, the grand jury system. (Amended November 3, 1970)

This provision authorizes the General Assembly to change or abolish the Grand Jury as it wishes. The system has not been abolished, but statutes govern the conduct of Grand Jury inquiries (IC 35-34-2-1 *et seq.*). There is no right of accused persons to be charged by an indictment of a Grand Jury rather than by information (*Rhoton v. State*, 1991).

SECTION 18

Criminal Prosecutions. All criminal prosecutions shall be carried on in the name, and by the authority of the state; and the style of all process shall be: "The State of Indiana." (Amended November 3, 1970)

This provision outlines the form criminal prosecutions will follow in Indiana. The obvious point is that the prosecution of persons accused of crimes in Indiana is done in the name of and by authority of the people of the state.

SECTION 19

Pay. The Justices of Supreme Court and Judges of the Court of Appeals and of the Circuit Court shall at stated times receive a compensation which shall not be diminished during their continuance in office. (Amended November 3, 1970)

The judges in the Indiana court system are to be compensated, at a rate set by the legislature. The rate was last set in 1991, and provided that the supreme court justice received $81,000 per year, plus a $3,000 to $5,500 annual subsistence allowance. Judges on the court of appeals are paid $76,500 per year, plus the same subsistence allowance. Circuit court judges receive $61,700 per year, but they reside in the circuit they preside over so they receive no subsistence allowance (IC 33-13-12-7; IC 33-13-12-9).

The protection against the reduction in judicial salaries during tenure on an Indiana court is explicitly provided for in this section. The level of state funding for the judicial system as a whole is specified by statute.

SECTION 20

Repealed. (Repealed November 6, 1984)

This section authorized a commission to codify the statutes of Indiana, after the adoption of the constitution in 1851. By 1995, however, condification of statutory enactments is done automatically.

SECTION 21

Repealed. (Repealed November 8, 1932)

This provision, repealed in 1932, specified that every person who was of good moral character and a voter, was entitled to admission to practice law in Indiana. The repeal of this provision was a matter of increasing controversy during the first third of this century. The original inclusion of this section and the repeated efforts at repealing it is discussed in Part I on the History of the Indiana Constitution.

Article VIII

Education

SECTION 1

Common Schools System. Knowledge and learning, generally diffused throughout a community, being essential to the preservation of a free government; it shall be the duty of the General Assembly to encourage, by all suitable means, moral, intellectual, scientific, and agricultural improvement; and to provide, by law, for a general and uniform system of Common Schools, wherein tuition shall be without charge, and equally open to all.

This section charges the General Assembly with encouraging intellectual, scientific, and agricultural improvement by establishing a general and uniform system of free, public common schools. The emphasis in this 1851 provision was one primary education without detailed attention to secondary or postsecondary education in the state. This might have been a reaction to the inability of the state to establish a more developed educational system earlier, including higher education, as required by the 1816 Constitution. Thus, Indiana University is *not* a common school within the meaning of this provision of the constitution (1948 Op. Atty. Gen. No. 35).

The General Assembly's obligation under this section makes the legislature superior to any local school board (*Bright v. Isenbarger*, 1970), and gives it direct control and comprehensive supervision over the school system that is established (*Stone v. Fritts*, 1907; *U.S. v. Bd. of School Comm'rs, City of Indianapolis*, 1973).

This effectively means that the legislature's authority in this regard is comprehensive and superior to that of any other institutions that are created to provide or govern education in the state.

This includes extensive power to equalize school systems in a variety of ways in order to achieve the fundamental directive of a general and uniform system. (*State ex rel. Snoke v. Blue*, 1889). However, this uniformity requirement permits differences in expenditure at the local level, for a specific project (*Lafayette v. Jenner*, 1858; *Robinson v. Schenck*, 1885). Furthermore, this provision does not require the legislature to levy all school taxes for each locality, but rather allows the legislature to provide for school boards that will implement the policy in various localities. This section has been used to create a strong public policy favoring the establishment of both a general and a uniform system of public schools in the state (*Phillips v. Stern*, 1969). The uniformity requirement of the section does not mean that each school system has to be identical, although a similar course of study and equal qualifications for admission are established by the constitution (*School, City of Gary v. State ex rel. Gary Artists' League, Inc.*, 1970; *Cory v. Carter*, 1874). For example, the state can classify people in terms of their qualifications to attend.

SECTION 2

Common School Fund. The Common School fund shall consist of the Congressional Township fund, and the lands belonging thereto:

The Surplus Revenue fund;

The Saline fund and the lands belonging thereto;

The Bank Tax fund, and the fund arising from the one hundred and fourteenth section of the Charter of the State Bank of Indiana; The fund to be derived from the sale of County Seminaries; and the moneys and property heretofore held for such seminaries; from the fines assessed for breaches of the penal laws of the State; and from all forfeitures which may accrue;

All lands and other estates which shall escheat to the State, for want of heirs or kindred entitled to the inheritance;

All lands that have been, or may hereafter be, granted to the State, where no special purpose is expressed in the grant, and the proceeds of the sales thereof; including the proceeds of the sales of the Swamp Lands, granted to the State of Indiana by the act of Congress of the twenty-eighth of September, eighteen hundred and fifty, after deducting the expense of selecting and draining the same;

Taxes on the property of corporations, that may be assessed by the General Assembly for Common School purposes.

The section identifies the Common School fund and its component parts. In part, this is the result of the prior experience with the 1816 Constitution's education requirement, for which no clear funding was provided, and none ever developed. The 1851 framers relied on their experience and the failure of the earlier education requirement to provide for a very explicit and detailed set of sources for education funding. This section also authorizes the General Assembly to impose various taxes to generate revenue that would go into the school fund.

There are a variety of funds specified as components of the School Fund. Some do not appear to be significant today, but they each contribute something to the fund. Over time, additional minor sources of public moneys have been added to those specified in the section. These include fines derived from contempt of court citations, money and valuables found on dead bodies, and the estate of prisoners with no heirs. These funds are to be distributed throughout the state in order to promote equality and uniformity in the education system (*Quick v. White Water Township*, 1856).

The permanent endowment fund created to support the state university (Indiana University) is to enjoy all the protections afforded school funds under this section (*Fisher v. Brower*, 1902). The expenditure from this fund does not extend to functions beyond the common school enterprise, however (1917–1920 Op. Atty. Gen. p. 188; 1917–1920 Op. Atty. Gen. p. 582).

SECTION 3

Principal and Income of Fund. The principal of the Common School fund shall remain a perpetual fund, which may be increased, but shall never be diminished; and the income thereof shall be inviolably appropriated to the support of Common Schools, and to no other purpose whatever.

This section provides that state expenditures for meeting its Article VIII, section 1 obligation will be composed of the income from the Common School Fund. This income will be the moneys that must be spent on common schools, while leaving untouched and unreduced the principal from which that income derives. That means that the income from interest on the fund can be (and is expected to be) spent for achieving the constitutional objectives (*Bd. of Comm'rs of Hamilton County v. State ex rel. Michner*, 1890). The legislature is given the sole authority to determine the exact purpose of the expenditures, but the money must be spent on common schools (1917–1920 Op. Atty. Gen. p. 582). Some distribution of common school funds to counties can take place, but there is a debtor/creditor relationship established between the county recipients and the state with regard to these funds. As a result, counties are obligated to make good any losses that occur with regard to the funds they have received. Furthermore, counties are obligated to use the money for education or support of schools, just as if they were functioning as school boards.

SECTION 4

Investment and Distribution of Fund Interest. The General Assembly shall invest, in some safe and profitable manner, all such portions of the Common School fund, as have not heretofore been entrusted to the several counties; and shall make provision, by law, for the distribution, among the several counties, of the interest thereof.

This section makes the General Assembly responsible for the investment of new moneys for the Common School Fund in "safe and profitable" investments. Furthermore, the legislature is required to enact statutes that distribute the interest or the income from these additional investments among the counties in order to provide for the schools. The only indication of what constitutes a safe and profitable investment of the Common School Fund is an attorney general's opinion indicating that an investment in long-term U.S. government bonds satisfied the requirements of this section (1957 Op. Atty. Gen. No. 3). The fund is a "trust" but not in the legal sense of that word. That means the state both administers and holds title to the funds, as well as receives the benefit of the school fund. In addition, the school children of the state are the beneficiaries of the school fund (*School City of Terre Haute, of Vigo County v. Honey Creek School Tp. of Vigo County*, 1916). In this sense, the "trust" is viewed as a public, constitutional, and moral obligation on the state's part to use the income for the intended purpose.

SECTION 5

Reinvestment of Unused Interest. If any county shall fail to demand its proportion of such interest, for Common School purposes, the same shall be re-invested, for the benefit of such county.

This provision interestingly permits the reinvestment of any interest that is not claimed by a county for the operation of its schools. In other words, excess income can be banked "for the benefit of such county." So if a county does not expend all of its allotted school funds, those funds are not lost to other counties or to the state, but rather held for future expenditure by that particular county.

SECTION 6

Preservation of Fund by Counties; Liability. The several counties shall be held liable for the preservation of so much of the said fund as may be entrusted to them, and for the payment of the annual interest thereon.

Counties are obligated, by this section, to preserve any of the Common School Fund that is entrusted to them. Thus, if a county receives any of the principal of the fund, it must preserve those moneys and the county is also responsible for the annual interest that is earned by that part of the fund. The drafters of the constitution insured that the fund for the schools could not be violated by the legislature distributing the fund to counties, or by recipient counties which are not under the same constitutional obligation that is contained in Article VIII, section 1 (*Mitsch v. City of Hammond*, 1955).

Judicial interpretations of this section have limited counties' use of the income from the funds. While a county can make loans using the money (*Shoemaker v. Smith*, 1871), the county cannot pay mortgages (*Bd. of Comm'rs, Hamilton County v. State ex rel Michner*, 1890) or attorney's fees (*Bd. of Comm'rs, Bartholomew County v. State ex rel Baldwin*, 1888) using income from the fund that it has received. Thus, this provision forces the counties to use the Common School Fund money in a carefully controlled and limited set of ways.

This section, and the preceding ones, show how carefully the framers of the 1851 Constitution wanted the school funds controlled, and how distrustful they were of local school and governmental officials. That may have been based on their experience or their view that the size of the fund would pose a temptation to misuse.

SECTION 7

State Trust Funds Inviolate. All trust funds, held by the State, shall remain inviolate, and be faithfully and exclusively applied to the purposes for which the trust was created.

This provision is a general statement that reinforces the specific provisions about the Common School Fund that have been outlined above. That is, any trust fund which the state holds must be inviolate and can only be used for the purpose(s) that have been specified. This reflects the framers' concerns about the long-term commitment of the state to projects which the General Assembly adopted and committed funds to complete. There can be little disagreement with the spirit or meaning of this provision, and it has generated little litigation or interpretation.

SECTION 8

State Superintendent of Public Instruction. There shall be a State Superintendent of Public instruction, whose method of selection, tenure, duties, and compensation shall be prescribed by law. (Amended November 7, 1972)

This section creates an office of state superintendent of public instruction, but leaves the specifics of selection and the term of office to the legislature. Thus, while the office is constitutional, the functions and characteristics of the office are left entirely to the General Assembly. This has the advantage of permitting the legislature to modify or adjust the nature of the office as it deems necessary or as tasks and duties evolve and change. Another consequence is that the office could be effectively eliminated by legislative action, except in name. The superintendent is considered to have no constitutional status under the 1972 amendment, and this section of the constitution, because the selection and tenure of the superintendent are entirely subject to legislative act (1972 Op. Atty. Gen. No. 33). Prior to the 1972 amendment, this section provided that the superintendent would be elected as the General Assembly provided. The 1972 wording removes the requirement for election of this office and thus the constitutional status of the office.

While this office is created by the constitution, the constitutional duty to provide for the public school system remains with the legislature. It cannot be allocated to the superintendent by statute. That means that while the superintendent can execute and administer the public school system, as provided for by state statute, the General Assembly is still the authority responsible for the development and operation of the system statewide (*Blue v. State ex rel. Brown*, 1934).

Article IX

State Institutions

SECTION 1

Institutions for the Deaf, Mute, Blind, and Insane. It shall be the duty of the General Assembly to provide, by law, for the support of institutions for the education of the deaf, the mute, and the blind; and for the treatment of the insane. (Amended November 6, 1984)

This section of the constitution requires that the state (through the General Assembly) establish a facility for the care of people who are deaf, mute, blind, and/or insane. The 1984 amendment involved a technical correction of the wording to remove the phrase "Deaf and Dumb" and replace it with "deaf, mute."

This provision has been interpreted to constitute an express grant of authority to the legislature to provide for the selection of officials or administrators to accomplish the objectives or duties provided for in this section (*Hovey v. State ex rel. Carson*, 1889). The actual selection or appointment of such officers can be done by the legislature or by its designate, such as the governor. But, the selection of state officers to operate and manage these facilities is part of the power granted the legislature by this section of the constitution. The actual implementation of this policy is left to the legislature, with a wide grant of authority to accomplish the objective of providing care or assistance to these categories of people.

The constitutional provision, as well as others in this article, suggest that the legislature's power is not plenary (or not considered plenary by the supreme court).

Rather, there are explicit grants of such authority in various constitutional provisions. However, there are clearly mixed dimensions to this proposition and some allusion to the plenary nature of some legislative power.

SECTION 2

Institutions for Juvenile Offenders. The General Assembly shall provide institutions for the correction and reformation of juvenile offenders. (Amended November 6, 1984)

This provision of the constitution obligates the General Assembly to provide institutions for the correction and reform of juvenile offenders. The 1984 amendment modernized the language by replacing "houses of refuge" with "institutions." The core authority that derives from this provision is the power to prescribe measures for committing "boys" to a reformatory if they are entering on a career of vice (*Jarrard v. State*, 1888). This section has also been treated in connection with the authority of the state to terminate the rights of parents in certain cases. Such termination by the state can only be done if there is clear and convincing evidence that such termination is in the best interests of the child (*In the Matter of J.H.*, 1984). This section seems to have developed as a plenary or at least a mandatory power of the legislature.

SECTION 3

County Asylum Farms. The counties may provide farms, as an asylum for those persons who, by reason of age, infirmity, or other misfortune, have claims upon the sympathies and aid of society. (Amended November 6, 1984)

This provision permits counties to establish facilities for needy people. This is an optional authority; no county is required by this wording to provide such "farms." This may indicate that counties are to be concerned with and respond to the needs of poor and destitute people in the state, but there has been little case law that clarifies this provision since the constitution was adopted in 1851. The 1984 amendment, by changing the language from "shall have the power" to "may" in the first line of the section, did not change the meaning or the nature of this discretionary county authority, and if anything it only emphasizes the discretionary nature of this provision.

It appears that the county could contract with a private party to provide for the facilities that are specified in this section. Such a private contract is not against public policy, and it would permit the county to discontinue its own operation of an asylum (*Bd. of Comm'rs of Pulaski County v. Shields*, 1891). The precise procedures by which the county meets the obligation of this provision are left to the county's discretion, with little direct or explicit judicial guidance (*Platter v. Bd. of Comm'rs of Elkhart County*, 1885).

Article X

Public Finance

SECTION 1

Property Assessment and Taxation. (a) The General Assembly shall provide, by law, for a uniform and equal rate of property assessment and taxation and shall prescribe regulations to secure a just valuation for taxation of all property, both real and personal. The General Assembly may exempt from property taxation any property in any of the following classes: (1) Property being used for municipal, educational, literacy, scientific, religious or charitable purposes; (2) Tangible personal property other than property being held for sale in the ordinary course of a trade or business, property being held, used or consumed in connection with the production of income, or property being held as an investment; (3) Intangible personal property.
(b) The General Assembly may exempt any motor vehicles, mobile homes, airplanes, boats, trailers or similar property, provided that an excise tax in lieu of the property tax is substituted therefor. (Amended November 8, 1966)

This section is the core of the legislature's authority to assess property and tax it. The taxing authority is general, and there are no limits on the number of excise taxes that can be imposed by the legislature if it chooses(*Welsh v. Sells*, 1963). This power is considered to be an inherent aspect of sovereignty that is an attribute of all independent governments, subject only to limitations imposed by the state or federal constitution (*County of Monroe v. Harrell*, 1896). Taxing property, no matter what the impact, is not a "taking" of property governed by the just compensation provisions of the Due Process of Law clause (*Forsythe v. City of Hammond*, 1895). Limitations on this power depend on constitutional or statutory provisions, since the power is an indispensable attribute of sovereignty (*Washington Nat' Bank v. Daily*, 1906). Furthermore, this power can be granted to cities by the General Assembly and then modified or revoked as the legislature chooses (*Zoercher v. Agler*, 1930).

This power to tax is the power to raise revenue, and it is not to have a primary purpose of regulation. That regulatory purpose involves the police power of the state, which differs from the power to tax or to generate public revenue. It is not clear where the line or difference between these two powers and their effects falls, but the court has explicitly dealt with the two sets of sovereign powers (*Dept. of Treasury v. Midwest Liquor Dealers*, 1943; *State Bd. of Tax Comm'rs v. Pioneer Hi-Bred International, Inc.*, 1985). The court decisions seem to imply that a "primary purpose" of regulation is impermissible where a primary purpose of raising revenue is a legitimate exercise of this taxing power by the state (*Besozzi v. Indiana Employment Sec. Bd.*, 1958).

Any property assessment and tax must be uniform and the rate of taxation must be equal. However, some variation is allowed throughout the state, as long as the tax is uniform and equal in the locality in which the tax is imposed (*Bright v. McCullough*, 1866). The actual assessments and the rate of taxation are questions for legislative judgment (*Smith v. Stephens*, 1910). The Equal Protection provisions of the United States and Indiana Constitutions do not require rigorous equality in taxing properties (*Indiana Aeronautics Comm. v. Ambassadair, Inc.*, 1977).

Three subsections designate categories of property that the General Assembly can choose to exempt from taxation, and the legislature has granted a variety of these exemptions. For example, those exempted in subsection (a)(1) are clearly and legitimately granted such an exemption for public policy reasons. These categories of property all provide some public benefit that might be diminished if property taxes were imposed (*State Bd. of Tax Comm'rs v. Wright*, 1966). The words of this first exemption are to be considered in their broadest constitutional sense (*Indianapolis Elks Bldg. v. State Bd. of Tax Comm'rs*, 1969). However, the general meaning of this category does not include an exemption for a medical office building that is owned by a nonprofit hospital, because private medical practice is not reasonably necessary in order for the hospital to provide its services (*St. Mary's Medical Center of Evansville, Inc. v. State Bd. of Tax Comm'rs*, 1991). The justification for such a tax exemption is the public benefit that the undertaking provides (*State Bd. of Tax Comm'rs v. Wright*, 1966).

The second exemption category allows the state to exempt tangible personal property that is not being held for commercial sale. The purpose of this category of exemption to the state's property tax is to allow the exemption of personal property (*State Bd. of Tax Comm'rs v. Carrier Corp.*, 1977). But household furnishings cannot be exempted even though the wording of the section would seem to allow that (1954 Op. Atty. Gen. No. 18). The state cannot exempt stock of a building and loan association, and by implication any other common stock, under this provision (*State ex rel. Morgan v. Workingmen's Bldg. Loan Fund and Savings Ass'n*, 1895).

The last category of exemption (3) allows the state to exempt intangible personal property from property tax assessments. In fact, all the exemptions to this property tax have dealt with tangible property, used for some public benefit, rather than intangible property.

The amendment of this provision in 1966 dramatically changed it from earlier wording. The change included adding subsections (2) and (3), the last two categories of exemptions, and it added section (b). These revisions changed the range of authority of the General Assembly both in terms of taxation and in terms of granting exemptions.

SECTION 2

Public Debt; Payment. All the revenues derived from the sale of any of the public works belonging to the State, and from the net annual income thereof, and any surplus that may, at any time, remain in the Treasury, derived from taxation for general State purposes, after the payment of the ordinary expenses of the government, and of the interest on bonds of the State, other than Bank bonds; shall be annually applied, under the direction of the General Assembly, to the payment of the principal of the Public Debt.

This provision directs that any revenue remaining in public coffers, after the payment of "ordinary expenses" derived from whatever source, is to be used to pay the public debt. The General Assembly is given the authority to direct this payment, so that a payment priority could be established, if that is necessary. However, the overall direction of this segment of the constitution is that any public debt is to be retired as soon as practicable after immediate expenses are covered. It is necessary that all public revenues that are to be paid against the public debt must first be deposited in the state treasury, and then dispersed as prescribed by law to pay the debt (*Ristine v. State*, 1863).

The ordinary expenses that precede this public debt payment are characterized as being appropriate. Those can be budgeted and statutorily appropriated (1942 Op. Atty. Gen. p. 74). However, an appropriation can be "implied" by the wording of the statute, rather than be explicit (*Carr v. State ex rel. Du Coet-losquet*, 1891).

SECTION 3

Appropriations Made by Law. No money shall be drawn from the Treasury, but in pursuance of appropriations made by law.

This portion of the constitution requires that any money spent from the treasury requires an appropriation. Thus, unless the General Assembly appropriates the money, and specifies the purpose for the appropriation, no money can be drawn from the treasury. (Note the discussion of this point relating to section 2 of this article, above.) The appropriation process is intended to permit the state to raise and expend public funds to exercise its police powers in order to protect the public health, safety, and morals. (*Carr v. State ex rel. Du Coetlosquet*, 1891). There is no particular form that the appropriation must take, as long as it is an appropriation (*Orbison v. Welsh*, 1962; 1948 Op. Atty. Gen. No. 141). The legislature must indicate either the sum or a method for determining the maximum sum that is appropriated. The courts cannot determine whether an appropriation should be made. That is a policy determination for legislative judgment or decision (*Carr v. State ex rel. Du Coetlosquet*, 1891).

SECTION 4

Receipts and Expenditures; Publication. An accurate statement of the receipts and expenditures of the public money, shall be published with the laws of each regular session of the General Assembly.

This provision of the constitution requires that a public accounting of the receipts and expenditures of public funds be made at each regular session of the legislature. This straightforward requirement insures that a public accounting of these funds is made. This accounting does not have to be a detailed and complex accounting. A brief, but accurate accounting will satisfy this requirement (1900–1902 Op. Atty. Gen. p. 108).

SECTION 5

State Debt; Requirements. No law shall authorize any debt to be contracted, on behalf of the State, except in the following cases: to meet casual deficits in the revenue; to pay the interest on the State Debt; to repel invasion, suppress insurrection, or, if hostilities be threatened, provide for the public defense.

This section prohibits the state from contracting any debt except to fund a casual debt (for immediate but temporary purposes), such as paying interest on the state debt, repelling invasion, suppressing insurrection, or providing for the public defense. Such acceptable debt is not carefully or consciously brought about by legislative consideration and deliberation, but rather it involves occasional discrepancies or differences between revenues and debts that are not anticipated. The legislature's judgment about the existence of these conditions is generally final, but the court reserves the role of determining if the contingencies were "plainly apparent" (*Hovey v. Foster*, 1889).

This section does not prevent a municipality from contracting for services for an extended period of time, as long as the installment payment for these services follows the actual furnishing of the services (*Teperich v. North Judson-San Pierre High School Bldg. Corp.*, 1971). The state is not generally obligated to pay interest on its debts unless it has specifically contracted to pay such interest.

SECTION 6

Corporation Stock and Subscription by Counties; State Assumption of County Debts. No county shall subscribe for stock in any incorporated company, unless the same be paid for at the time of such subscription; nor shall any county loan its credit to any incorporated company, nor borrow money for the purpose of taking stock in any such company; nor shall the General Assembly ever, on behalf of the State, assume the debts of any county, city, town, or township; nor of any corporation whatever.

This section is designed to insure that counties do not assume the debt of incorporated companies and that the state does not assume the debts of a municipal government. Furthermore, a county cannot pledge its future credit to underwrite the stock of an incorporated company. Such companies have been defined to include companies for public benefit, such as turnpike, bridge, canal, and railroad companies (*Lafayette, M. & B. R. Co. v. Geiger*, 1870). This concern of the framers resulted from the fiscal disasters that emerged from the state's Improvement Plan of the 1840s. This financial crisis is discussed in Part I, and focused on a large debt incurred by the state to underwrite the cost of road construction and other kinds of municipal and civic improvements. A municipal government can purchase stock in a company but the money must be paid in cash at the time of the purchase (*State ex rel. Scobey v. Wheadon*, 1872). A municipal government is also prohibited from borrowing the money in order to have the cash to pay for this kind of purchase. The prohibition against local governments assuming such debt was intended to eliminate the likelihood of debt imposing and limiting the functioning of any local governments in Indiana.

The additional prohibition of this section against the state assuming the debts of any local or municipal government was the result of the fiscal experience of the state prior to 1851 when the state did assume some local debt, with disastrous fiscal results. The state was unable to conduct its normal affairs or make expected policy decisions because of its inability to pay for those functions. This bar on assumption of debt applies to all governmental levels even though it may have been based on the experience of the state.

SECTION 7

Wabash and Erie Canal. No law or resolution shall ever be passed by the General Assembly of the State of Indiana, that shall recognize any liability of this State to pay or redeem any certificate of stocks issued in pursuance of an act entitled "An Act to provide for the funded debt of the State of Indiana, and for the completion of the Wabash and Erie canal to Evansville," passed January 19th, 1846; and an act supplemental to said act, passed January 29th, 1847, which, by the provisions of the said acts, or either of them, shall be payable exclusively from the proceeds of the canal lands, and the tolls and revenues of the canal, in said acts mentioned, and no such certificate or stock shall ever be paid by this State. (Added February 18, 1873)

This section is a specific prohibition against the state assuming any liability for the completion of the Wabash and Erie Canal. This undertaking was a point of major public cost and concern for people in the first half of the nineteenth century in Indiana. This kind of specific attention is probably not needed any more, but it has not been cleared out of the constitution, and, in fact, it was added in 1873 to prevent the assumption of this specific debt.

The general concern for this kind of governmental commitment surfaced most specifically in connection with the effort to build the canal as an internal improvement in the mid-nineteenth century. The opposition to it was sufficient to result in the adoption of this provision as an addition to the constitution in 1873. This constitutional change was the first amendment made to the 1851 Constitution.

SECTION 8

Income Tax; Levy and Collection Authorized. The general assembly may levy and collect a tax upon income, from whatever source derived, as such rates, in such manner, and with such exemptions as may be prescribed by law. (Added November 8, 1932).

This grant of authority to tax incomes expanded the power of the legislature in 1932. This power parallels, with a delay of over a decade, the federal government's power to impose a progressive income tax reflected in the Sixteenth Amendment to the U.S. Constitution. Clearly, this was a substantial addition to the power of the General Assembly to generate revenue. It was added to permit the state to raise revenue from sources alternative to the property tax outlined in section 1 of this article. The interpretation of this recent constitutional addition has not been expansive. The state supreme court has indicated that the addition of the power to impose an income tax did not support questionable taxes intended to support "greedy and overindulgent, benevolent government" (*Gross Income Tax Division of Ind. v. Surface Combustion Corp.*, 1953), however that may be defined.

This taxing power, as the property taxing power, is to be exercised to raise revenue, not to exercise police powers involving regulation. Here again, the difference between regulating and raising revenue is operative, although that difference is not at all clear. The state can set the rate and nature of the income tax, with public policy considerations governing classifications for these purposes (*Miles v. Department of Treasury*, 1936). Only the legislature can define what constitutes income for purposes of this tax.

Article XI

Corporations

SECTION 1

Banks; Banking Companies and Moneyed Institutions; Incorporation. The General Assembly shall not have power to establish, or incorporate, any bank or banking company, or moneyed institution, for the purpose of issuing bills of credit, or bills payable to order or bearer, except under the conditions prescribed in the Constitution.

This provision of the constitution prevents the creation of individual or idiosyncratic financial institutions by specifically prohibiting the establishment of banks by the General Assembly, unless they meet the conditions and requirements spelled out in the constitution (IC 28-1-1-1 *et seq.*). This section reinforces earlier prohibitions against specific or particular legislation (Article IV, sections 22 and 23), but here it relates specifically to banking legislation. The reason for this is that banks are expected to serve the public in a reliable manner that instills confidence. The framers of the constitution thought that should mean these institutions should be regulated in order to protect the public interest (*Bud-nick v. Citizens Trust and Savings Bank of South Bend*, 1942). *Budnick* specifies that banking is affected with the public interest and that permits state regulation under the police power (*State v. Richcreek*, 1906). Special legislation in this regard might allow for differential regulation and differentiate among creditors and debtors, and this provision guards against that.

The power of the legislature to create corporations is considered unlimited (*City of Aurora v. West*, 1857). However, this section of the constitution does channel the legislative power in connection with banking. These limits include the other sections of this article which prohibit the state from establishing banks for the specified purposes.

SECTION 2

General Banking Laws; Exception. No banks shall be established otherwise than under a general banking law, except as provided in the fourth section of this article.

This section is the reverse side of the previous section. Here, any bank that is not established consistent with general or universal requirements that are applicable to all banks. There are a variety of state statutory requirements that have been established regarding the general structure and nature of banks. The legislature has implemented this provision of the constitution with extensive regulations governing the number and nature of shareholders in banks, the election of a board of directors, and the filing of articles of incorporation (IC 28-1-1-1 *et seq.*). The statutes also create a state Department of Financial Institutions which regulates and monitors the operation of banks in Indiana.

SECTION 3

Registry by State of Votes. If the General Assembly shall enact a general banking law, such law shall provide for the registry and countersigning, by an officer of the State, of all paper credit designed to be circulated as money; and ample collateral security, readily convertible into specie, for the redemption of the same in gold or silver, shall be required; which collateral security shall be under the control of the proper officer or officers of the State.

This section is a specific feature the drafters of the constitution wanted contained in any general banking regulations adopted by the state. It requires the identification of a state officer with whom sufficient collateral is to be posted to insure that banks doing business in the state can pay their debts. The collateral to cover any paper credit issued by a bank is to be under the control of that state officer. Clearly, the financial responsibility of banking corporations was a point of great concern among the drafters. They felt a visible state official should hold collateral security for any paper credit designed to function as money. That would provide the public with confidence in any bank so governed, and it would provide creditors with insurance against default by the banks.

SECTION 4

Banks and Branches of Banks; Charter. The General Assembly may also charter a bank with branches, without collateral security as required by the preceding section.

This provision (referred to in Article XI, section 2) permits the state to charter branch banks. However, banks that establish such branches are not required to post collateral security for each branch. This provision, in conjunction with the next section (Article XI, section 5), directs that while each branch of a bank need not have collateral posted, each branch is mutually dependent on and responsible for all the branches chartered to operate in the state (IC 28-1-17-1 *et seq.*).

SECTION 5

Bank Branches Mutually Liable. If the General Assembly shall establish a bank with branches, the branches shall be mutually responsible for each other's liabilities upon all paper credit issued as money.

This provision specifies that each branch of a bank is financially responsible for the debts and obligations of the other branches if the bank is chartered by the state. This is also related to the absence of a specific requirement (Article XI, section 4) that each branch have independent security established for it. Thus, while no branch bank need establish its financial security, each branch is equally secured by the collateral posted by the general bank.

SECTION 6

Repealed. (Repealed November 5, 1940)

This section, repealed in 1940, provided that individual stockholders of banks would be individually responsible for all debts and liabilities of the bank they owned stock in. The repeal absolved stockholders from such personal liability.

SECTION 7

Redemption of Bills and Notes. All bills or notes issued as money shall be, at all times, redeemable in gold or silver; and no law shall be passed, sanctioning, directly or indirectly, the suspension, by any bank or banking company, of specie payments.

This provision requires all bills and notes to be redeemable in gold or silver, and it prohibits any modification or suspension of this requirement to pay debts in specie by a bank. The legal tender of money has replaced this requirement through the policies and practices of the federal government. That means this specie requirement is suspended by federal supercession (*Reynolds v. Bank of*

Indiana, 1862). State banks can redeem any debts in treasury notes without being subject to forfeiture.

SECTION 8

Holders of Bank Notes. Holders of bank notes shall be entitled, in case of insolvency, to preference or payment over all other creditors.

This provision specifies a priority of bank note holders if the bank involved reaches insolvency. The note holders hold first priority among bank creditors in such a case. This was intended to encourage and then protect private investment in such banks. This subordination of some creditors does not violate the Due Process Clause of the constitution (*Todd v. Davidson*, 1939).

SECTION 9

Interest Rates. No bank shall receive, directly or indirectly, a greater rate of interest than shall be allowed, by law, to individuals loaning money.

This constitutional limitation requires that the rate of interest which banks can charge shall not exceed the rate set by statute. For example, consumer credit sales, not relating to revolving credit, can have a maximum interest rate no greater than (IC 24-4.5-2-201):

—36% per year for unpaid balances of $300 or less.
—21% per year for unpaid balances from $300.01 to $1,000.
—15% per year for unpaid balances greater than $1,000.
—18% per year on the unpaid balances of the amount financed.

The legislature has also sought to define certain bank services as *not* being "interest" and therefore not subject to any of the limitations that would arise from this section (IC 28-1-11-13).

It appears as if this constitutional provision was designed to insure that private, individual investors and debtors would not be disadvantaged by the interest that banks could pay. In that sense, the constitution prohibits this particular competitive advantage which banks may be able to enjoy vis-à-vis individual lenders.

SECTION 10

Repealed. (Repealed November 5, 1940)

This repealed provision required that banks and banking companies must cease all banking operations within twenty years of their creation. This limitation was originally meant to insure that banks would deal with only short-term transactions and thereby be accountable and controllable. However, it clearly became a significant hurdle (and perhaps an unnecessary one) as banking practices became regulated and controlled more extensively in the 1930s. This original provision also was inconsistent with federal banking laws and deposit insurance, as well as other federal regulatory protection.

SECTION 11

Trust Funds; Investment in Banks with Branches. The General Assembly is not prohibited from investing the Trust Funds in a bank with branches; but in case of such investment, the safety of the same shall be guaranteed by unquestionable security.

This section indicates that the General Assembly can invest trust funds in banks or bank branches, as long as the investment is guaranteed by "unquestionable security." There is no specification in the constitution, and no statutory or case law, on how unquestionable securities could be identified. This provision may have been designed to discourage, to the point of a bar on, such investment. However, the use of "is not prohibited" seems to indicate a positive permission to make such investments. Thus, the only concern is the level of protection or guarantee for those investments, and the "unquestionable" expectation indicates an extreme level of expected security.

SECTION 12

State as Stockholder in Banks; Prohibition. The state shall not be a stockholder in any bank; nor shall the credit of the State ever be given, or loaned, in aid of any person, association or corporation; nor shall the State become a stockholder in any corporation or association. (Amended November 6, 1984)

This section prohibits the state from holding stock in any bank, any corporation, or any association, or giving its credit to any bank or corporation. This provision is intended to insure that the state does not risk state money or credit in corporate stocks (*Bd. of Public Trustees of Public Employees' Retirement Fund of Indiana v. Pearson*, 1985). The state is not to speculate or take investment risks using public funds in risky transactions. The state is permitted, however, to invest public funds in savings associations because they are not hazardous in nature, and because the deposits would be protected by deposit insurance (*Northern Indiana Bank & Trust Co. v. State Bd. of Finance*, 1983).

The credit of the state cannot be given or loaned in order to assist anyone—individual, association, or corporation. However, the state can invest in another state agency (*Orbison v. Welsh*, 1962). A state employees' retirement fund is governed by this interpretation of this provision because it is a state agency (1962 Op. Atty. Gen. No. 37). Furthermore, the trustees of a state university can hold stock in a private corporation only if that stock was a gift to the university (i.e., not purchased by the university) (1978 Op. Atty. Gen. No. 8).

The 1984 amendments to this section were technical corrections that made this section consistent with the repeal of section 10 of this article.

SECTION 13

Corporations Other Than Banking; Creation. Corporations, other than banks, shall not be created by special act, but may be formed under general laws.

This section resembles Article XI, section 1, but applies to all corporations other than banks. It requires that any (all) corporations other than banks must be created under general laws, rather than specific or individual statutes that govern only a single corporation. This is an absolute bar on idiosyncratic corporations. There are no limitations or exceptions recognized for this provision (*City of Aurora v. West*, 1857). There can be no special or unique corporations created by the General Assembly. This provision is intended to insure that the formation of any corporation is done by general laws that operate uniformly in like situations (*Central Trust Co. of New York v. Citizen's St. R. Co. of Indianapolis*, 1897).

This provision, however, does not apply to the creation of public corporations which may serve specific, unique, or idiosyncratic functions within the state (*Orbison v. Welsh*, 1962). Furthermore, the legislature can modify the laws of incorporation without violating any constitutional rights possessed by corporations or their stockholders (*Denny v. Brady*, 1928; *Orbison v. Welsh*, 1962).

SECTION 14

Liability of Stockholders. Dues from corporations shall be secured by such individual liability or the stockholders, or other means, as may be prescribed by law. (Amended November 5, 1940)

This provision of the constitution requires that the individual stockholders of a corporation are liable for the corporation's dues to the state. State statute can provide for the dues and how they are to be paid and regulated (IC 23-1-2-6). This section is not self-executing and requires the enactment of appropriate legislation (*Williams, v. Citizen's Enterprise Co.*, 1899).

Article XII
Militia

SECTION 1

Membership. A militia shall be provided and shall consist of all persons over the age of seventeen (17) years, except those persons who may be exempted by the laws of the United States or of this state. The militia may be divided into active and inactive classes and consist of such military organizations as may be provided by law. (Amended November 3, 1936; November 5, 1974)

This section establishes that the Indiana militia is composed of all persons over the age of seventeen years, unless the person is exempt as a result of state or federal law. In addition to this exemption, people are exempt from service for ministerial duties (*U.S. v. Norris*, 1965). (Note Article XII, section 4 for the exemption relating to conscientious objection.) The governor has the authority to assemble and organize the militia and to replace the active militia when it has been called into federal service (1940 Op. Atty. Gen. p. 239). The governor's authority over the militia includes the power to revoke the commission of an officer in the National Guard for negligence of duty, loss of interest, dilatoriness in reporting, failure to comply with instructions, or frequent unauthorized absences (1936 Op. Atty. Gen. p. 17).

The 1936 amendment to this section replaced "white" with "able bodied" in the first sentence of the provision in order to remove the racial component of the original. The 1974 amendment replaced "able bodied males" with "all" in the first sentence, this time to remove the sexual differentiation among the militia.

SECTION 2

Commander-in-Chief. The Governor is Commander-in-Chief of the militia and other military forces of this state. (Amended November 5, 1974)

This provision confirms that the governor is the commander-in-chief of the militia. The governor can establish such rules and regulations as are necessary for the governance of the militia, and these regulations are binding with all branches of the state government. The governor possesses implied or inherent powers as commander-in-chief (1948 Op. Atty. Gen. No. 377). Those inherent powers are the result of the nature of military command that operates in the position of commander-in-chief at the federal level of government as well. These include power to remove officers of the militia for a variety of reasons (1936 Op. Atty. Gen. p. 17).

SECTION 3

Adjutant General. There shall be an Adjutant General who shall be appointed by the Governor. (Amended November 5, 1974)

This provision indicates that an adjutant general of the militia is to be appointed by the governor. There are no case law or other interpretations of this provision, although the 1974 amendment was a technical change of the earlier provision.

SECTION 4

Conscientious Objectors. No person, conscientiously opposed to bearing arms, shall be compelled to do so in the militia. (Amended November 5, 1974)

This provision indicates there is a moral basis for exempting individuals from service in the state militia. There seem to be a variety of moral, ethical, and religious grounds that would serve as adequate bases for conscientious objector status. These grounds include "reading, family and religious influence"(*U.S. v. Garvin*, 1971). A deeply held moral or ethical value system is sufficient to support this claim of conscientious objection (*U.S. ex rel. Conrad v. Hoffman*, 1970). However, conduct punishable under the criminal law cannot be excused by a religious belief (*U.S. v. Kime*, 1951).

SECTION 5

Repealed. (Repealed November 5, 1974)

This section, repealed in 1974, specified there would be different classes of the militia, as provided by the General Assembly. This was not considered important in the late twentieth century, given the role that state militia plays and the current regulation of the military.

SECTION 6

Repealed. (Repealed November 5, 1974)

This section provided for what is now contained in Article XII, section 4, regarding conscientious objectors. Originally, this provision required that the individual pay an equivalent for the conscientious objection exemption, as prescribed by law.

Article XIII

Municipal Debt

This article of the Indiana Constitution originally dealt with slavery, "Negroes and Mullatos," and other dimensions of this issue that were explicitly dealt with by the Reconstruction Amendments to the U.S. Constitution (U.S. Constitution Amendments XIII, XIV, and XV). As a result of those amendments, this article of the state constitution was declared null and void by the supreme court in 1866 (*Smith v. Moody*, 1866). This article was completely replaced with the single section of Article XIII that deals with municipal debt in 1881.

SECTION 1

Limitations on Debt; Excess; Exceptions. No political or municipal corporation in this State shall ever become indebted, in any manner or for any purpose, to an amount, in the aggregate, exceeding two per centum on the value of the taxable property within such corporation, to be ascertained by the last assessment for State and county taxes, previous to the incurring of such indebtedness, and all bond or obligations in excess of such amount given by such corporation shall be void: *Provided*, That in time of war, foreign invasion, or other great public calamity, on petition of a majority of the property owners, in number and value, within the limits of such corporation, the public authorities, in their discretion, may incur obligations necessary for the public protection and defense to such amount as may be requested in such petition. (Amended March 14, 1881)

This section prohibits any county, municipal, or local government from incurring debt greater than two percent of the assessed valuation of real property in the jurisdiction, except in times of war or public calamity. This is clearly intended to insure very limited public indebtedness that can be repaid from likely tax revenue (*Hawkins v. City of Greenfield*, 1967). The state can use current state revenues to pay for local government expenses, without violating this provision of the constitution (*Bennett v. Spencer County Bridge Comm.*, 1938).

The exception to this level of indebtedness is the extreme emergencies of war or public calamity. However, the limit can be exceeded only upon a petition by a majority of the property owners involved. This requires an extreme level of support for such indebtedness, no matter how great the emergency.

This limit does not prevent localities from contracting for service with a long-term contract, even if the debt limit is exceeded by the contract. Such contractual commitments are not long-term indebtedness (*Becker v. Jefferson-Craig Consolidated School Corp.*, 1952). Neither does a long-term lease or rental create an indebtedness within the meaning of this provision (*Kees v. Smith*, 1956). Construction bonds do not constitute indebtedness for purposes of this section either (*Hutton v. Boze*, 1910).

In short, this debt limit is clear, but the courts have allowed a variety of long-term financial commitments to be made by a government, without holding to the constitutional two percent limit. In addition, where a school board would exceed the two percent limit with a construction contract, the board may create a separate entity to issue the bonds, contract for the construction, own the school building, and then lease it back to the school corporation, without violating this provision of the constitution (*Garius v. Stern*, 1970).

SECTION 2

Repealed. (Repealed March 14, 1881)

As noted at the beginning of the discussion of Article XIII, this section was repealed in 1881 as a result of the Fourteenth Amendment to the U.S. Constitution. Originally, this section voided all contracts made with "any negro or mulatto coming into the State." Furthermore, it provided for a fine of $10 to $500 for anyone who employed or encouraged a "negro or mulatto" to remain in the state.

SECTION 3

Repealed. (Repealed March 14, 1881)

This repealed section provided that all fines generated by section 2 above "shall be set apart and appropriated for the colonization of such negroes and mulattoes, and their descendants . . ., [as] may be willing to emigrate."

SECTION 4

Repealed. (Repealed March 14, 1881)

This provision empowered the General Assembly to enact laws in order to carry out the provisions of this original Article XIII.

Article XIV

Boundaries

SECTION 1

Boundaries of State Established. In order that the boundaries of the State may be known and established, it is hereby ordained and declared, that the State of Indiana is bounded, on the East, by the meridian line, which forms the western boundary of the State of Ohio; on the South, by the Ohio River, from the mouth of the Great Miami river to the mouth of the Wabash river, on the West, by a line drawn along the middle of the Wabash river, from its mouth to a point where a due north line, drawn from the town of Vin-cennes, would last touch the north-western shore of said Wabash river, and then, by a due north line, until the same shall intersect an east and west line, drawn through a point two miles north of the southern extreme of Lake Michigan; and on the North, by said east and west line, until the same shall intersect the first mentioned meridian line, which forms the western boundary of the State of Ohio.

This article of the Indiana Constitution specifies the boundaries of the state. Clearly, the eastern, western, and most of the northern state lines are very nearly straight lines, certainly artificial and distinct from any natural features in the region. The eastern boundary was largely the result of Ohio's grant of land, at the time it became a state. The western edge of the state is largely the result of the concentration of population along the Ohio River at the time of Indiana statehood. The northern boundary includes a bit of the southern shore of Lake Michigan in the northwest corner of the state. Since the western line of the state extends ten miles into the lake, the northern boundary follows a precise east-west line to the Ohio/Indiana border, except for the uneven segment of Lake Michigan shore that is included in the northwestern corner.

The southern boundary, the Ohio River, has generated some difficulties or questions, largely because of changes in the flow of the river, and because of questions regarding the overlap of this boundary with Kentucky. In fact, the north side of the Ohio River at low water marks the southern boundary of the state. This line has led to some jurisdictional disputes regarding the reach of the two states' criminal laws. However, these disputes have been resolved amicably, with both states willing to cooperate with the other for purposes of the apprehension of suspects and the trial of persons accused of crimes (*Welch v. State*, 1890).

SECTION 2

Jurisdiction and Sovereignty. The State of Indiana shall possess jurisdiction and sovereignty co-extensive with the boundaries declared in the preceding section; and shall have concurrent jurisdiction in civil and criminal cases, with the State of Kentucky on the Ohio River, and with the State of Illinois on the Wabash River, so far as said rivers form the common boundary between this State and said States respectively.

This section of the constitution indicates the state's jurisdiction in relation to its boundaries. This jurisdiction is shared by the federal government and is subservient to federal law under the Supremacy Clause of the U.S. Constitution (*Freeman v. Robinson*, 1935). Otherwise, within the state's borders its jurisdiction and control are considered to be supreme. In relation to the river boundaries of the state, the adjacent states share concurrent jurisdiction. There have been some disputes in this regard. With Illinois, the jurisdiction is concurrent on the Wabash River in the southwestern portion of the state. The jurisdiction on the Ohio River is shared with Kentucky.

Article XV

Miscellaneous

SECTION 1

Nonconstitutional Officers; Appointment. All officers, whose appointment is not otherwise provided for in this Constitution, shall be chosen in such manner as now is, or hereafter may be, prescribed by law.

The first section of Article XV indicates that the legislature can specify by statute what process is to be used for the selection of all officers other than those provided for in this constitution. The purpose of this provision is to provide an explicit grant of authority to the legislature to create, select, compensate, and remove any officers not otherwise provided for elsewhere in the constitution. This provision does not apply to the selection of judges or their terms of office (*State ex rel. Taylor v. Mount*, 1898), because they are judicial officers subject to Article VII control. Nor does this section apply to other offices specified in the constitution because those positions are governed by the appropriate segments of the constitution (*State ex rel. Collet v. Gorby*, 1890). Furthermore, when the constitution creates an office and specifies the qualifications for that office, this section does not authorize the government to attach additional qualifications to the office. This grant of power specifically deals with the possibility that challenges to the government's creation of offices or the selection of occupants would be clouded if the office were not initially specified in the constitution, and it indicates that the selection of additional officers, when created, is subject to statutory provision.

This provision grants significant power to the state government over the offices of government not outlined in the constitution. The legislature can specify terms, salaries, and duties, but need not outline the duties and emoluments. The state can increase and reduce income for an office covered by this section, during a term. That is somewhat surprising given the widespread interest in preventing political institutions and actors of the moment from seeking to influence the policies and choices of officials by reducing or threatening to reduce their salaries. However, that has been the supreme court's interpretation (*Bd. of Comm'rs of Perry County v. Lindeman*, 1905; *Rogers v. Calumet National Bank of Hammond*, 1938). The legislature may not abolish a statutory office by reducing the salary or the jurisdiction of the office. Abolition requires a positive enactment by the legislature (*State ex rel. Wadsworth v. Wright*, 1937).

SECTION 2

Term of Office. When the duration of any office is not provided for by this Constitution, it may be declared by law; and, if not so declared, such office shall be held during the pleasure of the authority making the appointment. But the General Assembly shall not create any office, the tenure of which shall be longer than four years.

This section indicates that the term of an office can be determined by the legislature, when it is not specified in the constitution. However, that power is limited so that no term of office set by the legislature can exceed four years. If no term is specified by the legislature, then the office is held at the pleasure of the appointing authority (*Manlove v. Curtis*, 1913).

This constitutional authority has been interpreted to permit the legislature to shorten or abolish an office during the term originally specified (*Rogers v. Calumet Nat'l Bank of Hammond*, 1938; *Corn v. Oakland City*, 1981). However, this authority to change terms clearly does not extend to constitutional offices (*Russell v. State*, 1909).

SECTION 3

Holding Over of Office Pending Successor. Whenever it is provided in this Constitution, or in any law which may be hereafter passed, that any officer, other than a member of the General Assembly, shall hold his office for any given term, the same shall be construed to mean, that such officer shall hold his office for such term, and until his successor shall have been elected and qualified.

This provision permits an officer (other than a state legislator) to continue in office after the expiration of their term, if a successor has not been designated. This prevents a vacancy in office due to the expiration of the term (*State ex rel. Fares v. Karger*, 1948), and the functions of the office continue to be performed even if there is some delay in the selection of the successor (*Swank v. Tyndall*, 1948). This applies whether the office is constitutional or statutory in origin. Vacancies can still occur due to death in office or resignation or removal from office.

SECTION 4

Oath of Affirmation of Office. Every person elected or appointed to any office under this Constitution, shall, before entering on the duties thereof, take an oath or affirmation, to support the Constitution of this State, and of the United States, and also an oath of office.

This provision requires that any constitutional officer must take an oath or affirmation to support the constitutions of both the state and the United States. This provision has been used to define the point at which a new officer replaces the outgoing incumbent (1967 Op. Atty. Gen. No 1). Despite the guarantees of jury trial in the constitution, the members of a jury are not considered constitutional officers, required to take the oath or affirmation required by this section, even though other judicial officers are so required (*Swain v. State*, 1931; *Adams v. State*, 1938).

SECTION 5

Seal of State. There shall be a Seal of State, kept by the Governor for official purposes, which shall be called the Seal of the State of Indiana.

This section specifies there will be a seal of the state and that it will be kept by the governor. It is to be used only for official purposes. The seal is described by statute (IC 1-2-4-1).

SECTION 6

Commission Issued by State. All commissions shall issue in the name of the State, shall be signed by the Governor, sealed with the State Seal, and attested by the Secretary of State.

This section indicates one of the official purposes for which the state seal is to be used. The governor is to sign commissions issued by the state, the secretary of state to attest them, and the seal to be affixed to those commissions.

SECTION 7

Areas of Counties. No county shall be reduced to an area less than four hundred square miles; nor shall any county, under that area, be further reduced.

This section of the constitution guarantees a minimum geographic size for counties at 400 square miles. If a county is smaller than that, then it cannot not be reduced to a smaller size than it was at the time this provision was adopted (1851). This provision not only prevents the creation of counties of less than the minimum size specified here, but also prevents (small) portions of existing counties from splitting off from existing counties for policy or political disagreements.

SECTION 8

Repealed. (Repealed, November 8, 1988)

This provision of the constitution prohibited lotteries or the sale of lottery tickets in the state. Since its 1988 repeal, the state has instituted a variety of lotteries to generate public revenues.

SECTION 9

State Grounds in Indianapolis. The following grounds owned by the State in Indianapolis, namely: the State House Square, the Governor's Circle, and so much of out-lot numbered one hundred and forty-seven, as lies north of the arm of the Central Canal, shall not be sold or leased.

This section provides that the state will retain ownership of the grounds on which the state buildings were placed in Indianapolis. Certainly, there are additional state office buildings located nearby today, or other leased property occupied by state offices, but the constitutional provision freezes the specified property from sale or lease by the state.

SECTION 10

Tippecanoe Battle Ground. It shall be the duty of the General Assembly, to provide for the permanent enclosure and preservation of the Tippecanoe Battle Ground.

This section indicates that the legislature is to provide for the preservation of the battlefield where the Battle of Tippecanoe was fought. In addition, there was to be a permanent enclosure of that area. It is now designated as a memorial to the battle and the victims of that battle.

Article XVI

Amendments

SECTION 1

Constitutional Amendments; Procedure. Any amendment or amendments to this Constitution, may be proposed in either branch of the General Assembly; and, if the same shall be agreed to by a majority of the members elected to each of the two houses, such proposed amendment or amendments shall, with the yeas and nays thereon, be entered in their journals, and referred to the General Assembly to be chosen at the next general election; and if, in that General Assembly so next chosen, such proposed amendment or amendments shall be agreed to by a majority of all the members elected to each House, then it shall be the duty of the General Assembly to submit such amendment or amendments to the electors of the State; and if a majority of said electors shall ratify the same, such amendment or amendments shall become a part of this Constitution.

This section of the constitution, which provides for the amendment of the constitution, has generated considerable controversy (discussed in Part I). It has most recently been interpreted to require approval by a majority of those voting on the proposed agreement in the General Election to adopt it (*In re Todd*, 1935). However, historically, earlier interpretations of "electors of the state" meant all persons eligible to vote, whether voting in the election or not. That severely inhibited amendments to the constitution. Since the interpretation changed in 1935, it has been easier to make both fundamental and technical corrections or changes to the constitution. In addition, there is, by implication, the constitutional convention as a means of changing the state constitution. Although advocated and proposed widely in earlier days, no convention has been called or held since the Convention of 1851 created the current constitution.

Amendments have been recognized as largely comparable to the original provision. Thus, an amendment has the same status as the initial or the original constitution (*Pommerehn v. Sauley*, 1954). If an amendment to the constitution is inconsistent with an existing provision of the constitution, then the amendment is deemed to repeal the original portion of the constitution, since the amendment supersedes the original (*Fesler v. Brayton*, 1896).

SECTION 2

Multiple Amendments; Separate Vote. If two or more amendments shall be submitted at the same time, they shall be submitted in such manner that the electors shall vote for or against each of such amendments separately.

Section 2 of the Article XVI indicates that if there are multiple, proposed amendments on the ballot, the voters must be given the opportunity to vote on each proposal separately. This procedure prevents an unpopular amendment from being tied to a popular one and thus adopted by the voters because of the popularity of the one. It prevents riders to amendments being used in the amending process. The popular vote on the amendment should therefore clearly indicate whether the voters have approved or rejected each proposed amendment.

■ TABLE OF CASES

A

Adams v. State, 214 Ind. 603, 17 N.E.2d 84 (1938), **169**
Allen v. State, 428 N.E.2d 1237 (Ind. 1981), **52**
Andrews v. State, 505 N.E.2d 815 (Ind. App. 1987), **75**
Appelby v. State, 221 Ind. 544, 48 N.E.2d 646 (1943), **52**
Argersinger v. Hamlin, 407 U.S. 25 (1972), **50**

B

Bailey v. State, 397 N.E.2d 1024 (Ind. 1979), **49**
Baker v. Gordon, 23 Ind. 204 (1864), **58**
Baker v. State, 109 Ind. 47, 9 N.E. 711 (1887), **60**
Barnes v. State 435 N.E.2d 235 (Ind. 1982), **52**
Barrick Realty v. City of Gary, 354 F.Supp. 126 (N.D.Ind. 1973),
    aff m'd, 491 F.2d 161 (7th Cir. 1974), **39, 46**
Bates v. State Bar of Arizona, 433 U.S. 350 (1977), **46**
Beavers v. State, 236 Ind. 549, 141 N.E.2d 118 (1957), **57**
Becker v. Jefferson-Craig Consolidated School Corp., 231 Ind. 527, 109 N.E.2d 889 (1952), **162**
Bennett v. Jackson, 186 Ind. 533, 116 N.E. 921 (1917), **27, 81**
Bennett v. Spencer County Bridge Comm., 213 Ind. 520, 13 N.E. 2d 597 (1938), **162**
Besozzi v. Indiana Employment Sec. Bd., 237 Ind. 341, 146 N.E.2d 100 (1958), **144**
Bigelow v. Valentine, 421 U.S. 809 (1976), **46**
Bissell Carpet Sweeper Co. v. Shane, 237 Ind. 188, 143 N.E.2d 415 (1957), **82**
Blalock v. State, 483 N.E.2d 439 (Ind. 1985), **47**
Blue v. State ex rel. Brown, 206 Ind. 96, 188 N.E. 583 (1934), **69, 140**
Bd. of Comm'rs, Bartholomew County v. State ex rel. Baldwin, 116 Ind. 329,
    19 N.E. 173 (1888), **139**
Bd. of Comm'rs of Delaware County v. Briggs, 167 Ind. App. 96,
    337 N.E.2d 852 (1975), **86**
Bd. of Comm'rs of Hamilton County v. Blue Ribbon Ice Cream & Milk Corp., 231 Ind. 436, 109
    N.E.2d 88 (1952), **59**
Bd. of Comm'rs, Hamilton County v. State ex rel. Michner, 122 Ind. 333, 24 N.E. 347 (1890),
    137, 137
Bd. of Comm'rs of Marion County v. Jewett, 184 Ind. 63, 110 N.E. 553 (1915), **84**
Bd. of Comm'rs of Perry County v. Lindeman, 165 Ind. 186, 73 N.E. 912 (1905), **168**
Bd. of Comm'rs of Pulaski County v. Shields, 130 Ind. 6, 29 N.E. 385 (1891), **142**
Bd. of Public Trustees of Public Employees' Retirement Fund of Indiana v. Pearson,
    459 N.E.2d 715 (Ind. 1985), **155**
Bonahoon v. State, 203 Ind. 51, 178 N.E. 570 (1931), **53**
Book v. State Office Bldg. Comm., 238 Ind. 120, 149 N.E.2d 273 (11958), **113** In re Boswell, 179
    Ind. 292, 100 N.E. 833 (1913), **25**
Branigin v. Morgan Superior Court, 516 Ind. 220, 231 N.E.2d 516 (1967), **78**

Bright v. Isenbarger, 314 F. Supp. 1382 (D.C.Ind. 1970), affi m'd, 445 F.2d 412 (7th Cir. 1970), **135**
Bright v. McCullough, 27 Ind. 223 (1866), **144**
Brooks v. State, 162 Ind. 568, 70 N.E. 980 (1904), **84**
Brown v. Goben, 122 Ind. 113, 23 N.E. 519 (1890), **74**
Brown v. State, 147 Ind. 28, 46 N.E. 34 (1897), **54, 55**
Bruck v. State ex rel. Money, 228 Ind. 189, 91 N.E.2d 349 (1950), **39**
Brunson v. State, 182 Ind. App. 146, 394 N.E.2d 229 (1979), **50**
Bryant v. Lake County Trust Co., 152 Ind. App. 628, 284 N.E.2d 537 (1972), **82**
Buchman v. State, 59 Ind. 1 (1877), **59**
Budnick v. Citizens Trust and Savings Bank of South Bend, 220 Ind. 410,
    44 N.E.2d 298 (1942), **151**
Burr v. Duckworth, 547 F.Supp. 192 (N.D. Ind. 1982), **96**

C

Cain v. Allen 168 Ind. 8, 79 N.E. 201 (1906), **62**
Candler v. State, 266 Ind. 440, 363 N.E.2d 1233 (1977), **57**
Carlson v. State ex rel. Stodola, 247 Ind. 631, 220 N.E.2d 532 (1966), **78, 101**
Carmichael v. Adams, 91 Ind. 526 (1883), **58**
Carr v. State ex rel. Du Coetlosquet, 127 Ind. 204, 26 N.E. 78 (1891), **145, 146**
Carson v. McPhetridge, 15 Ind. 327 (1860), **74**
Carter v. State, 471 N.E.2d 1111 (Ind. 1984), **54**
Cash v. Auditor of Clark County, 7 Ind. 227 (1855), **95**
Cato v. Chaddock, 175 Ind. App. 514, 373 N.E.2d 172 (1978), **110**
Central Trust Co. of New York v. Citizen's St. R. Co. of Indianapolis,
    82 F. 1 (Ind. Cir. 1897), **456**
Central Union Telephone Co. v. Indianapolis Telephone Co., 189 Ind. 210,
    126 N.E. 628 (1920), **62, 94**
Church of Christ of Indianapolis v. Metro Bd. of Zoning Appeals of Marion County, 175 Ind.
    App. 346, 371 N.E.2d 1331 (1978), **41**
City of Aurora v. West, 9 Ind. 74 (1857), **152, 156**
City of Connersville v. Connersville Hydraulic Co., 86 Ind. 184 (1882), **99**
City of Evansville v. State, 118 Ind. 426, 21 N.E. 267 (1889), **101**
City of Mishawaka v. Mohney, 156 Ind. App. 668, 297 N.E.2d 858 (1973), **78**
Clemons v. State, 162 Ind. App. 50, 317 N.E.2d 859 (1974), **78**
Coleman v. Dobbins, 8 Ind. 156 (1856), **89, 92**
Communist Party of Indiana v. Whitcomb, 414 U.S. 441 (1974), **94**
Corley v. State, 455 N.E.2d 965 (Ind. 1983), **51**
Corn v. Oakland City, 415 N.E.2d 126 (Ind. App. 1981), **168**
Cory v. Carter, 48 Ind. 327 (1874), **136**
County of Monroe v. Harrell, 147 Ind. 500, 46 N.E. 124 (1896), **143**
Cox v. McNutt, 12 F.Supp. 355 (D.C.Ind. 1935), **106**
Craig v. State, 177 Ind. App. 278, 379 N.E.2d 490 (1978), **54**
Critchlow v. State, 264 Ind. 458, 346 N.E.2d 591 (1976), **54**
Curless v. Watson, 180 Ind. 86, 102 N.E. 497 (1913), **125**

D

Dague v. Piper Aircraft Corp., 275 Ind. 520, 418 N.E.2d 207 (1981), **91, 93**
Davidson v. State, 248 Ind. 26, 221 N.E.2d 814 (1966), **123**

Davis v. Bandemer, 478 U.S. 109 (1986), **85** In re Denny, 156 Ind. 104, 59 N.E. 359 (1900), **25**
Denny v. Brady, 201 Ind. 59, 163 N.E. 489 (1928), **156**
Dept. of Treasury v. Midwest Liquor Dealers, 113 Ind. 569, 48 N.E.2d 71 (1943), **144**
Dobbyn v. Rogers, 225 Ind. 525, 76 N.E.2d 570 (1948), **69**
Dolan v. City of Tigard, 114 S.Ct. 2309 (1994), **59**
Dortch v. Lugar, 255 Ind. 480, 266 N.E.2d 25 (1971), **116**
Driskill v. State, 7 Ind. 338 (1855), **56**
Dunn v. Jenkins, 268 Ind. 478, 377 N.E.2d 868 (1978), **48**

E

Edwards v. California, 314 U.S. 160 (1941), **66**
Edwards v. Housing Authority of City of Muncie, 215 Ind. 330, 19 N.E.2d 741 (1939), **91**
Ellingham v. Dye, 178 Ind. 336, 99 N.E. 1 (1912), **26, 82**
Evansville-Vanderburgh Levee Authority Dist. v. Kamp, 240 Ind. 659,
    168 N.E.2d 208 (1960), **95**
Everson v. Board of Education, 330 U.S. 1 (1947), **44**

F

Ferry v. State, 255 Ind. 27, 262 N.E.2d 523 (1970), **47**
Fesler v. Brayton, 145 Ind. 71, 44 N.E. 37 (1896), **172**
Fisher v. Brower, 159 Ind. 139, 64 N.E. 614 (1902), **137**
Ford Motor Co. v. Dept. of Treasury of the State of Indiana, 323 U.S. 459 (1945), **96**
Forsythe v. City of Hammond, 68 F. 774 (D.C.Ind. 1895), **144**
Ex Parte France, 176 Ind. 72, 95 N.E. 515 (1911), **122, 125**
Frazier v. State, 181 Ind. App. 421, 391 N.E.2d 1192 (1979), **50**
Freeman v. Robinson, 75 F.2d 913 (7th Cir. 1935), **166**
Fryback v. State, 272 Ind. 660, 400 N.E.2d 1128 (1980), **49**

G

Gabbert v. Jeffersonville R. Co., 11 Ind. 365 (1858), **93**
Gardner v. Lohmann Const. Co., 116 Ind. App. 132, 62 N.E.2d 867 (1945), **125**
Garius v. Stern, 254 Ind. 563, 261 N.E.2d 578 (1970), **162**
Garrett v. Barnes, 961 F.2d 629 (7th Cir. 1992), **119**
Gary Taxpayers Ass'n v. Lake Superior Court, 225 Ind. 478, 76 N.E.2d 254 (1948), **122**
Gibson v. Kincaid, 140 Ind. App. 186, 221 N.E.2d 834 (1966), **45**
Gosman v. State, 106 Ind. 203, 6 N.E. 349 (1886), **116**
Gougar v. Timberlake, 148 Ind. 38, 46 N.E. 339 (1897), **69, 70**
Graves v. City of Muncie, 255 Ind. 360, 262 N.E.2d 607 (1970), **95**
Gray v. Seitz, 162 Ind. 1, 69 N.E. 456 (1904), **72**
Green v. Aker, 11 Ind. 223 (1858), **60**
Greencastle Township v. Black, 5 Ind. 557 (1854), **19**
Greencastle Turnpike Co. v. State, 28 Ind. 382 (1867), **19**
Griffin v. State, 275 Ind. 107, 415 N.E.2d 60 (1981), **52**
Griffin v. Wilcox, 21 Ind. 370 (1863), **63**
Gross Income Tax Division of Ind. v. Surface Combustion Corp., 232 Ind. 100, 111 N.E.2d 50
    (1953), cert. den'd, 346 U.S. 829 (1953), **148**
Gross v. State, 186 Ind. 581, 117 N.E. 562 (1917), **75**

H

Hackett v. State, 266 Ind. 103, 360 N.E.2d 1000 (1977), **50**
Hall v. State, 199 Ind. 592, 159 N.E. 420 (1928), **53**
Hardenbrook v. Town of Ligonier, 95 Ind. 70 (1883), **60**
Harrell v. State, 614 N.E.2d 959 (Ind. 1993), **49**
Hart v. State, 220 Ind. 469, 44 N.E.2d 346 (1942), **56**
Harvey v. State ex rel. Carson, 119 Ind. 395, 21 N.E. 21 (1889), **109**
Haskell v. State, 255 Ind. 206, 263 N.E.2d 529 (1970), **53**
Hawkins v. City of Greenfield, 248 Ind. 593, 230 N.E.2d 396 (1967), **162**
Hendricks v. Northwest Indiana Crime Comm., Inc., 245 Ind. 43, 196 N.E.2d 66 (1964), **109**
Hendrickson v. Hendrickson, 7 Ind. 13 (1855), **99**
Herrick v. Sayler, 245 F.2d 171 (7th Cir. 1957), **98**
Hewell v. State, 411 N.E.2d 1235 (Ind. App. 1984), **47**
Highland Sales Corp. v. Vance, 244 Ind. 20, 186 N.E.2d 682 (1962), **62**
Hoey v. McCarthy, 124 Ind. 464, 24 N.E. 1038 (1890), **59**
Hogue v. State ex rel. Bd. of Comm'rs, 28 Ind. App. 285, 62 N.E. 656 (1902), **74**
Holland v. State, 454 N.E.2d 409 (Ind. 1983), **52**
Hollenbauch v. State, 11 Ind. 556 (1859), **82**
Home Building & Loan Ass'n. v. Blaisdell, 290 U.S. 398 (1934), **62**
Hovey v. Foster, 118 Ind. 502, 21 N.E. 39 (1889), **147**
Hovey v. State ex rel. Carson, 119 Ind. 395, 21 N.E. 21 (1889), **141**
Hudgins v. McAtee, 596 N.E.2d 286 (Ind. App. 1992), **48**
Hughes v. Sheriff of Vigo County, 268 Ind. 21, 373 N.E.2d 144 (1978), **55**
Hutton v. Boze, 173 Ind. 719, 90 N.E. 893 (1910), **162**
Hyde v. Bd. of Comm'rs of Wells County, 209 Ind. 245, 198 N.E. 333 (1935), **82**

I

Indiana Aeronautics Comm. v. Ambassadair, Inc., 267 Ind. 137, 368 N.E.2d 1340 (1977), cert. den'd, 436 U.S. 905 (1977), **144**
Indianapolis Elks Bldg. v. State Bd. of Tax Comm'rs, 145 Ind. 182, 251 N.E.2d 673 (1969), **144**
Indianapolis Northern Traction Co. v. Brennan, 174 Ind. 1, 90 N.E. 65 (1909), **58**
Ingram v. State, 421 N.E.2d 1103 (Ind. 1981), **51**
Irvin v. Doud, 366 U.S. 717 (1961), **50**

J

Jarrard v. State, 116 Ind. 98, 17 N.E. 912 (1888), **142**
Johnson v. Burke, 238 Ind. 1, 148 N.E.2d 413 (1958), **63**
Johnson v. St. Vincent Hospital, Inc., 273 Ind. 374, 404 N.E.2d 585 (1980), **61**
Johnson v. State, 299 N.E.2d 194 (Ind. App. 1973), **47**
Johnson v. State, 265 Ind. 689, 359 N.E.2d 525 (1977), **42**
Jones v. Cains, 4 Ind. 305 (1853), **99**
Jones v. State, 240 Ind. 230, 163 N.E.2d 605 (1960), **62**

K

Karcher v. Daggett, 462 U.S. 725 (1983), **70**
Kees v. Smith, 235 Ind. 687, 137 N.E.2d 541 (1956), **162**
Kirkpatrick v. King, 228 Ind. 236, 91 N.E.2d 785 (1950), **102, 104**

Knox County Council v. State ex rel. McCormick, 111 Ind. 493, 29 N.E.2d 405 (1940), **127**
Kokenes v. State, 213 Ind. 476, 13 N.E.2d 524 (1938), **53**
Kompier v. Thegza, 213 Ind. 542, 13 N.E.2d 229 (1938), **40**

L

Lafayette v. Jenner, 10 Ind. 70 (1858), **135**
Lafayette, M. & B.R. Co. v. Geiger, 34 Ind. 185 (1870), **147**
Lake County Council v. Arredondo, 266 Ind. 318, 363 N.E.2d 218 (1977), **121**
Lake Erie W.R. Co. v. Watkins, 157 Ind. 600, 62 N.E. 443 (1902), **125**
Langdon v. Applegate, 5 Ind. 327 (1854), **18**
Lawrence v. State, 259 Ind. 306, 286 N.E.2d 830 (1972), **91**
Lewis v. State, 148 Ind. 346, 47 N.E. 675 (1897), **92**
Lohm v. State, 380 N.E.2d 561 (Ind. App. 1978), **99**
Loyd v. State, 272 Ind. 404, 398 N.E.2d 1260 (1980), cert. den'd, 449 U.S. 881 (1980), **49**
Lucas v. McAfee, 217 Ind. 534, 29 N.E.2d 588 (1940), **72**
Lutz v. Arnold, 208 Ind. 480, 193 N.E. 840 (1935), **81, 91, 92**
Lynch v. Indiana State University Bd. of Trustees, 378 N.E. 2d 900 (Ind. App. 1978), cert, den'd, 441 U.S. 946 (1978), **40, 41, 42**
Lynk v. State, 271 Ind. 445, 393 N.E.2d 351 (1979), **56**
Lyons v. Bd. of Comm'rs of Perry County, 165 Ind. 197, 73 N.E. 916 (1905), **95**

M

Manlove v. Curtis, 180 Ind. 191, 102 N.E. 827 (1913), **169** In re Marriage of Lopp, 268 Ind. 690, 378 N.E.2d 414 (1978); cert, den'd, 439 U.S. 1116 (1978), **124**
Martin v. Louis, 208 Ind. 346, 195 N.E. 881 (1935), **60**
Martin v. State, 264 Ind. 444, 346 N.E. 2d 581 (1976), **95** In the Matter of J.H., 468 N.E.2d 542 (Ind. App. 1984), **142**
Matter of Lawrence, 579 N.E.2d 32 (Ind. 1991), **122**
Matthews v. State, 237 Ind. 677, 148 N.E.2d 334 (1958), **62**
Maxey v. State, 251 Ind. 645, 244 N.E.2d 650 (1969), cert, den'd, 397 U.S. 949 (1970), **47**
May v. State, 364 N.E.2d 172 (Ind. App. 1977), **47**
McClelland v. State ex rel. Speer, 138 Ind. 321, 37 N.E. 1089 (1894), **98**
McComas v. Krug, 81 Ind. 327 (1882), **119**
McCool v. State, 23 Ind. 127 (1864), **60**
McCulloch v. State, 11 Ind. 424 (1859), **89, 97**
McDermott v. Bicanic, 550 N.E. 2d 93 (Ind. App. 1990), **119**
McKinley v. Britton, 55 Ind. App. 21, 103 N.E. 349 (1913), **58**
McManamon v. Felger, 230 Ind. 185, 102 N.E.2d 369 (1951), **73**
Mellot v. State, 219 Ind. 646, 40 N.E.2d 655 (1942), **78**
Miles v. Department of Treasury, 290 Ind. 172, 199 N.E. 372 (1936), **149**
Milharcic v. Metropolitan Bd. of Zoning Appeals of Marion Co., 489 N.E.2d 634 (Ind. App. 1986), **42** Ex Parte Milligan, 72 U.S. (4 Wall.) 2 (1866), **48**
Miranda v. Arizona, 348 U.S. 436 (1966), **52**
Misenheimer v. State, 268 Ind. 274, 374 N.E.2d 523 (1978), **110**
Mitchell v. Pilgrim Holiness Church Corp., 210 F.2d 879 (7th Cir. 1954), cert, den'd, 342 U.S. 1013 (1954), **41**
Mitsch v. City of Hammond, 234 Ind. 285, 125 N.E.2d 21 (1955), **139**
Mogilner v. Metropolitan Planning Commission of Marion County, 236 Ind. 298, 140 N.E.2d 220 (1957), **93, 120**

Monroe v. State, 242 Ind. 14, 175 N.E.2d 692 (1961), **50**
Montgomery v. State, 115 Ind. App. 189, 57 N.E.2d 943 (1944), **124**
Moran v. State, 625 N.E.2d 1231 (Ind. App. 1993), **47**
Morris v. Powell, 125 Ind. 281, 25 N.E. 125 (1890), **70**
Morthland v. Lincoln National Life Insurance Co., 216 Ind. 689, 25 N.E.2d 325 (1940), **78**
Muncie v. Pizza Hut of Muncie, Inc., 357 N.E.2d 735 (Ind. App. 1976), **39**

N

Northern Indiana Bank & Trust Co. v. State Bd. of Finance, 457 N.E.2d 527 (Ind. 1983), **155**

O

Orbison v. Welsh, 242 Ind. 385, 179 N.E.2d 727 (1962), **146**, **155**

P

Palmer v. Adams, 137 Ind. 72, 36 N.E. 695 (1894), **47**
Parker v. State, 400 N.E.2d 796 (Ind. App. 1980), **61**
Parker v. State ex rel. Powell, 133 Ind. 178, 32 N.E. 836 (1892), **84**
Patrons of Noble County School Corp. v. School, City of Kendalville, 244 Ind. 675, 194 N.E.2d 718 (1963), **84**
Peachey v. Boswell, 240 Ind. 604, 167 N.E.2d 48 (1960), **39**
Pennington v. Stewart, 212 Ind. 553, 10 N.E.2d 619 (1937), **82**
Perkins v. Hayward, 124 Ind. 445, 31 N.E. 670 (1890), **131**
Petition of the Justice of the Peace Ass'n of Indiana, 237 Ind. 436, 147 N.E.2d 16 (1958), **118** In re Petition to Transfer Appeals, 202 Ind. 365, 174 N.E. 812 (1931), **125**
Phillips v. Stern, 145 Ind. App. 628, 252 N.E.2d 267 (1969), **136**
Pitman v. State, 436 N.E.2d 74 (Ind. 1982), **52**
Platter v. Bd. of Comm'rs of Elkhart County, 103 Ind. 360, 2 N.E. 544 (1885), **142**
Pommerehn v. Sauley, 233 Ind. 140, 117 N.E.2d 556 (1954), **172**

Q

Quick v. Springfield Township, 1 Ind. 636 (1856), **19**
Quick v. White Water Township, 7 Ind. 570 (1856), **137**

R

Randolph v. State, 234 Ind. 57, 122 N.E.2d 860 (1955), cert. den'd, 350 U.S. 889 (1955), **57**
Relender v. State, 149 Ind. 283, 49 N.E. 30 (1898), **118**
Remster v. Sullivan, 36 Ind. App. 385, 75 N.E. 860 (1905), **69**
Reynolds v. Bank of Indiana, 18 Ind. 467 (1862), **153–54**
Reynolds v. Sims, 311 U.S. 533 (1964), **83, 84, 85, 86**
Rhoton v. State, 575 N.E.2d 1006 (Ind. 1991), **132**
Ristine v. State, 20 Ind. 328 (1863), **145**
Roberts v. State ex rel. Jackson County Bd. of Comm'rs, 151 Ind. App. 83, 278 N.E.2d 285 (1972), **111**
Robertson v. State, 109 Ind. 79, 10 N.E. 582 (1886), **103**
Robinson v. Schenck, 102 Ind. 307, 1 N.E. 698 (1885), **136**
Robinson v. State, 453 N.E.2d 280 (Ind. 1983), **50**

Roche v. State, 596 N.E.2d 896 (Ind. 1992), **55**
Rodriguez v. State, 179 Ind. App. 464, 385 N.E.2d 1208 (1979), **56**
Roeschlein v. Thomas, 258 Ind. 16, 280 N.E.2d 581 (1972), **89**
Rogers v. Calumet Nat'l Bank of Hammond, 213 Ind. 576, 12 N.E.2d 261 (1938), **168**
Rosencranz v. Evansville, 194 Ind. 499, 143 N.E. 593 (1924), **95**
Roth v. Local Union No. 1460 of Retail Clerks Union, 216 Ind. 363, 24 N.E.2d 280 (1939), **46**
Ruge v. Kovach, 461 N.E.2d 673 (Ind. 1984), **91**
Russell v. State, 111 Ind. 623, 87 N.E. 13 (1909), **168**
Russell v. State, 270 Ind. 55, 383 N.E.2d 309 (1978), **51**

S

St. Mary's Medical Center of Evansville, Inc. v. State Bd. of Tax Comm'rs, 571 N.E.2d 1247 (Ind. 1991), **144**
Sarlls v. State, 201 Ind. 88, 166 N.E. 270 (1929), **64, 95**
Schneck v. City of Jeffersonville, 152 Ind. 204, 52 N.E. 212 (1898), **96**
School, City of Gary v. State ex rel. Gary Artists' League, Inc., 253 Ind. 697, 256 N.E.2d 909 (1970), **136**
School City of Terre Haute, of Vigo County v. Honey Creek School Tp. of Vigo County, 184 Ind. 754, 112 N.E. 518 (1916), **138**
Schultz v. State, 417 N.E.2d 1127 (Ind. App. 1981), **82**
Schwomeyer v. State, 193 Ind. 99, 138 N.E. 823 (1923), **61**
Selch v. Letts, 792 F.Supp. 1502 (S.D. Ind. 1992), **119**
Selvage v. Talbott, 175 Ind. 648, 95 N.E. 114 (1911), **60**
Shack v. State, 259 Ind. 450, 288 N.E.2d 155 (1972), **54**
Sheets v. Bray, 125 Ind. 33, 24 N.E. 357 (1890), **56**
Sherelis v. State, 452 N.E.2d 411 (Ind. App. 1983), **55**
Shoemaker v. Dowd, 232 Ind. 602, 115 N.E.2d 443 (1953), **63**
Shoemaker v. Smith, 37 Ind. 122 (1871), **139**
Shortbridge v. Court of Appeals, 468 N.E.2d 214 (Ind. 1984), **125**
Shupe v. Bell, 127 Ind. App. 292, 141 N.E.2d 351 (1957), **39**
Slenker v. Burch, 226 Ind. 579, 82 N.E.2d 258 (1948), **83**
Smith v. Moody, 26 Ind. 299 (1866), **23, 71, 161**
Smith v. State, 465 N.E.2d 1105 (Ind. 1984), **55–56**
Smith v. Stephens, 173 Ind. 564, 91 N.E. 167 (1910), **144**
South Bend Transportation Corp. v. South Bend, 428 N.E.2d 217 (Ind. 1981), **91**
Stansberry v. McCarty, 238 Ind. 338, 149 N.E.2d 683 (1958), **40**
State v. Allen, 21 Ind. 516 (1863), **111**
State ex rel. Batchelet v. Dekalb Circuit Court, 229 Ind. 126, 95 N.E.2d 838 (1967), **84**
State v. Bear, 135 Ind. 701, 34 N.E. 877 (1893), **131**
State ex rel. Black v. Burch, 226 Ind. 445, 80 N.E.2d 560 (1948), **78**
State ex rel. Blieden v. Gleason, 224 Ind. 142, 65 N.E.2d 245 (1946), **93**
State Bd. of Tax Comm'rs v. Carrier Corp., 266 Ind. 615, 368 N.E.2d 1153 (1977), **145**
State Bd. of Tax Comm'rs v. Pioneer Hi-Bred International, Inc., 477 N.E. 939 (Ind. App. 1985), **144**
State Bd. of Tax Comm'rs v. Wright, 139 Ind. App. 370, 215 N.E.2d 57 (1966), **144**
State v. Buxton, 238 Ind. 93, 148 N.E.2d 547 (1958), **47**
State ex rel City of Terre Haute v. Kolsem, 130 Ind. 434, 29 N.E. 595 (1891), **95**
State v. Clark, 247 Ind. 490, 217 N.E.2d 588 (1966), **84**
State ex rel. Collet v. Gorby, 122 Ind. 17, 23 N.E. 678 (1890), **167**
State v. Comer, 157 Ind. 611, 62 N.E. 452 (1902), **52**

180 ■ TABLE OF CASES

State v. Dearth, 201 Ind. 1, 164 N.E.2d 489 (1939), **119, 131**
State Election Bd. v. Bartolomei, 434 N.E.2d 74 (Ind. 1982), **69**
State Election Bd. v. Bayh, 521 N.E.2d 1313 (Ind. 1988), **103**
State ex rel Fares v. Karger, 226 Ind. 48, 77 N.E.2d 746 (1948), **169**
State ex rel Fox v. La Porte Circuit Court, 236 Ind. 69, 138 N.E.2d 875 (1956), **51**
State v. Goldthait, 172 Ind. 210, 87 N.E.2d 133 (1909), **70**
State ex rel Handley v. Superior Ct. of Marion County, 238 Ind. 421,
    151 N.E.2d 508 (1958), **113**
State v. Haworth, 122 Ind. 462, 23 N.E. 946 (1890), **81**
State v. Hedges, 177 Ind. 589, 98 N.E. 417 (1912), **55**
State ex rel Holt v. Denny, 118 Ind. 449, 21 N.E. 274 (1888), **89**
State ex rel Johnson v. Boyd, 217 Ind. 348, 28 N.E.2d 256 (1940), **44**
State v. Johnston, 101 Ind. 223 (1885), **132**
State ex rel Kopsinski v. Grzeskowiak, 223 Ind. 189, 59 N.E.2d 110 (1945), **111**
State ex rel Kostas v. Johnson, 224 Ind. 540, 68 N.E.2d 592 (1946), **78**
State v. Kuebel, 241 Ind. 268, 172 N.E.2d 45 (1961), **46**
State v. Levitt, 246 Ind. 275, 203 N.E.2d 821 (1965), **39, 46**
State v. Market, 158 Ind. App. 192, 302 N.E.2d 528 (1973), **132**
State ex rel Mass Transp. Auth. of Greater Indianapolis v. Indiana Revenue Bd., 144 Ind. App. 63,
    242 N.E.2d 642 (1968), **108**
State ex rel McClure v. Marion Superior Court, 239 Ind. 472, 158 N.E.2d 264 (1959), **117**
State ex rel McGonigle v. Madison Circuit Court for the Fiftieth Judicial District, 244 Ind. 403,
    N.E.2d 242 (1963), **70**
State ex. rel Morgan v. Workingmen's Bldg. Loan Fund and Savings Ass'n, 152 Ind. 278, 53 N.E.
    168 (1895), **145**
State ex rel. Ocborn v. Eddington, 208 Ind. 160, 195 N.E.2d 92 (1935), **117**
State v. Owings, 622 N.E.2d 948 (Ind. 1993), **51**
State v. Patterson, 181 Ind. 660, 105 N.E. 228 (1914), **82, 119**
State v. Pease, 521 N.E.2d 1207 (Ind. App. 1988), **122, 126**
State ex rel. Pitman v. Tucker, 46 Ind. 355 (1874), **126**
State ex rel Post-Tribune Pub. Co. v. Porter Superior Court, 274 Ind. 408, 412 N.E.2d 748
    (1980), **50**
State v. Richcreek, 167 Ind. 217, 77 N.E. 1085 (1906), **151**
State ex rel. Scobey v. Wheadon, 39 Ind. 520 (1872), **147**
State ex rel. Sendak v. Marion County Superior Ct., No. 2, 268 Ind. 3,
    373 N.E.2d 145 (1978), **101**
State ex rel. Snoke v. Blue, 122 Ind. 600, 23 N.E. 963 (1889), **136**
State ex rel. Steers v. Holovachka, 236 Ind. 565, 142 N.E.2d 593 (1957), **132**
State v. Swift, 69 Ind. 505 (1880), **21, 22, 25**
State ex rel. Taylor v. Mount, 151 Ind. 679, 51 N.E. 417 (1898), **167**
State ex rel. Todd v. Hatcher, 158 Ind. App. 144, 301 N.E.2d 766 (1973), **96**
State ex rel. Wadsworth v. Wright, 211 Ind. 41, 5 N.E.2d 504 (1937), **168**
State v. White, 454 N.E.2d 87 (Ind. 1983), **52**
State v. Williams, 173 Ind. 414, 90 N.E. 754 (1910), **98**
State ex rel. Wilson v. Monroe Superior Court IV, 444 N.E.2d 1178 (Ind. 1983), **60**
Stith Petroleum Co. v. Dept. of Audit and Control of Indiana, 211 Ind. 400,
    5 N.E.2d 517 (1937), **91–92**
Stocking v. State, 7 Ind. 326 (1855), **126**
Stone v. Fritts, 169 Ind. 361, 82 N.E. 792 (1907), **135**
Stout v. Bd. of Commr of Grant County, 107 Ind. 343, 8 N.E. 222 (1886), **97**

Strebin v. Lavengood, 163 Ind. 478, 71 N.E. 494 (1904), **75**
Stults v. State, 336 N.E.2d 669 (Ind. App. 1975), **46**
Sumpter v. State, 264 Ind. 117, 340 N.E.2d 764 (1976), cert. den'd, 425 U.S. 952 (1976), **52**
Suter v. State, 227 Ind. 648, 88 N.E.2d 386 (1949), **53**
Swain v. State, 215 Ind. 259, 18 N.E.2d 921 (1931); cert, den'd, 306 U.S. 660 (1931), **169**
Swank v. Tyndall, 226 Ind. 204, 78 N.E.2d 535 (1948), **169**

T

Taylor v. Mount, 151 Ind. 679, 51 N.E. 417 (1898), **76**
Teamsters, Local No. 364 of the A.F. of L. v. Stewart's Bakery of Rochester, 125 Ind. App. 179, 123 N.E.2d 468 (1955), **65**
Teperich v. North Judson-San Pierre High School Bldg. Corp , 257 Ind. 516, 275 N.E.2d 814 (1971), cert. den'd, 407 U.S. 921 (1971), **147**
Thomas v. City of Indianapolis, 195 Ind. 440, 145 N.E. 550 (1924), **67**
Thomas v. Rev. Bd. of the Indiana Employment Security Division, 391 N.E.2d 1127 (Ind. 1979); rev'd, 450 U.S. 707 (1981); 421 N.E.2d 642 (Ind. App. 1981), **41**
Threats v. State, 582 N.E.2d 396 (Ind. 1991), **50**
Tinkle v. Wallace 167 Ind. 382, 79 N.E. 355 (1906), **72** In re Todd, 208 Ind. 168 193 N.E. 865 (1935), **25, 27, 33, 171**
Todd v. Davidson, 215 Ind. 324, 19 N.E.2d 236 (1939), **154**
Tomlinson v. Marion County Planning Commission, 234 Ind. 88, 122 N.E.2d 852 (1955), **120**
Tucker v. State, 218 Ind. 614, 35 N.E.2d 270 (1941), **78, 107, 111, 112, 115**
Tyson v. State, 593 N.E.2d 179 (Ind. 1992), **126**

U

U.S. v. Bixby, 9 F. 78 (D.C.Ind. 1881), **117**
U.S. v. Bd. of School Comm'rs, City of Indianapolis, 368 F.Supp. 1191 (D.C.Ind. 1973), affi m'd, 483 F.2d 1406 (1973), **135**
U.S. ex rel. Conrad v. Hoffman, 435 F.2d 1273 (7th Cir. 1970), **158**
U.S. v. Garvin, 438 F.2d 109 (7th Cir. 1971), **158**
U.S. v. Kime, 188 F.2d 677 (7th Cir. 1951?); cert, den'd, 342 U.S. 823 (1951), **158**
U.S. v. Leon, 368 U.S. 897 (1984), **47**
U.S. v. Norris, 341 F.2d 527 (7th Cir. 1965); cert. den'd., 382 U.S. 850 (1965), **157**

V

Vonnegut v. Baun, 206 Ind. 172, 188 N.E. 677 (1934), **42**

W

Warren v. Indiana Telephone Co., Ill Ind. 93, 26 N.E.2d 399 (1940), **48**
Washington Nat'l Bank v. Daily, 166 Ind. 631, 77 N.E. 53 (1906), **144**
Weinzorpfl in v. State, 7 Blackf. 186 (1844), **52**
Welch v. Sells, 244 Ind. 423, 192 N.E.2d 753 (1963), **93**
Welch v. State, 126 Ind. 71, 25 N.E. 883 (1890), **166**
Wells v. State, 175 Ind. 380, 94 N.E. 321 (1911), **111**
Werber v. Hughes, 196 Ind. 542, 148 N.E. 149 (1925), **70**
Wheeler v. State, 255 Ind. 395, 264 N.E.2d 600 (1970), **43**

Whitehead v. State, 444 N.E.2d 1253 (Ind. App. 1983), **52**
Wilkins v. Malone, 14 Ind. 153 (1860), **52**
Williams v. Citizen's Enterprise Co., 153 Ind. 496, 55 N.E. 425 (1899), **156**
Willsey v. Newlon, 161 Ind. 332, 316 N.E.2d 290 (1974), **118**
Winters v. Mowery, 836 F. Supp. 1419 (S.D. Ind. 1993), **59**
Wizniuk v. State, 241 Ind. 638, 175 N.E.2d 1 (1979), **50**
Wood v. State, 592 N.E.2d 740 (Ind. App. 1992), **47**
Wright v. Fultz, 138 Ind. 594, 38 N.E. 175 (1894), **58**
Wright v. State, 614 N.E.2d 959 (Ind. 1992), **49**

Y

Yick Wo v. Hopkins, 118 U.S. 356 (1886), **61**
Young v. State, 272 Ind. 1, 375 N.E.2d 772 (1979), **50**
Youngblood v. Marr, 253 Ind. 412, 254 N.E.2d 868 (1970), **111**, **120**
Youngblood v. Warrick Circuit Court of Carwick Co., 208 Ind. 594, 196 N.E. 254 (1935), **122**

Z

Zemel v. Rusk, 381 U.S. 1 (1965), **79**
Zoercher v. Agler, 202 Ind. 214, 172 N.E. 186 (1930), **144**

State Attorney General Opinions
1874 Op. Atty. Gen. p. 38, **110**
1888 Op. Atty. Gen. p. 134, **113**
1900–1902 Op. Atty. Gen. p. 108, **146**
1909–1910 Op. Atty. Gen. p. 160, **107**
1915–1916 Op. Atty. Gen. p. 415, **107**
1917–1920 Op. Atty. Gen. p. 188, **137**
1917–1920 Op. Atty. Gen. p. 582, **137**
1917–1920 Op. Atty. Gen. p. 658, **126**
1921–1922 Op. Atty. Gen. p. 105, **99**
1927–1928 Op. Atty. Gen. p. 145, **111**
1929–1930 Op. Atty. Gen. p. 242, **117**
1931–1932 Op. Atty. Gen. p. 75, **117**
1933 Op. Atty. Gen. p. 14, **104**
1933 Op. Atty. Gen. p. 32, **45**
1933 Op. Atty. Gen. p. 133, **98**
1934 Op. Atty. Gen. p. 140, **116**
1935 Op. Atty. Gen. p. 75, **87**
1936 Op. Atty. Gen. p. 17, **157**, **158**
1936 Op. Atty. Gen. p. 155, **73**
1937 Op. Atty. Gen. p. 123, **100**
1937 Op. Atty. Gen. p. 252, **73**
1939 Op. Atty. Gen. p. 19, **86**
1940 Op. Atty. Gen. p. 239, **157**
1942 Op. Atty. Gen. p. 74, **145**
1943 Op. Atty. Gen. p. 10, **99**
1944 Op. Atty. Gen. No. 58, **118**
1944 Op. Atty. Gen. No. 81, **101**

1944 Op. Atty. Gen. No. 362, **106**
1945 Op. Atty. Gen. No. 28, **111**
1947 Op. Atty. Gen. No. 30, **73**
1947 Op. Atty. Gen. No. 142, **88**
1947 Op. Atty. Gen. No. 327, **132**
1948 Op. Atty. Gen. No. 35, **135**
1948 Op. Atty. Gen. No. 141, **146**
1948 Op. Atty. Gen. No. 153, **106, 111**
1948 Op. Atty. Gen. No. 377, **106, 158**
1949 Op. Atty. Gen. No. 179, **99**
1951 Op. Atty. Gen. No. 312, **117**
1952 Op. Atty. Gen. No. 72, **116**
1954 Op. Atty. Gen. No. 18, **145**
1957 Op. Atty. Gen. No. 3, **138**
1958 Op. Atty. Gen. No. 7, **113**
1959 Op. Atty. Gen. No. 65, **120**
1962 Op. Atty. Gen. No. 37, **156**
1962 Op. Atty. Gen. No. 60, **100**
1966 Op. Atty. Gen. No. 15, **113**
1966 Op. Atty. Gen. No. 49, **93**
1967 Op. Atty. Gen. No. 1, **83, 169**
1967 Op. Atty. Gen. No. 3, **44**
1967 Op. Atty. Gen. No. 40, **116**
1969 Op. Atty. Gen. No. 6, **110**
1970 Op. Atty. Gen. No. 2, **117**
1970 Op. Atty. Gen. No. 5, **116**
1972 Op. Atty. Gen. No. 12, **46**
1972 Op. Atty. Gen. No. 33, **140**
1977 Op. Atty. Gen. No. 29, **88, 90, 97**
1978 Op. Atty. Gen. No. 8, **156**
1979 Op. Atty. Gen. No. 24, **78**
1979 Op. Atty. Gen. No. 29, **46**
1982 Op. Atty. Gen. No. 8, **88, 97**
1991 Op. Atty. Gen. No. 91-15, **84, 86**

■ INDEX

Absolute majority, 10–1, 20–1, 27, 97
Accused, 6, 132, 166, 48–56, 64, 90
Adams, John, 4
Adjournment, 87, 108–9
Admission to the bar, 24n, 16, 25
Amending process, 16–20, 22, 24, 26, 28, 32–3, 172
Amendments, 3, 12, 17, 21–8, 30–1, 35, 84, 86, 98–9, 109, 121, 156, 161, 171–2. *See* Constitutional amendment
Appellate jurisdiction, 75
  of Court of Appeals, 121, 124
  of Supreme Court, 121–2, 124, 30
Appointment, gubernatorial, 15, 102, 117
  legislative power of, 120, 142, 152
Appropriation, 145–6
Armed forces, 65, 70–1, 106–7
Arms, 158. *See* Right to bear arms
Article I (The Bill of Rights), 37–67
Article II (Suffrage and Elections), 24, 69–76
Article III (Distribution of Powers), 77–9
Article IV (Legislative), 81–100
Article V (Executive), 101–13
Article VI (Administrative), 115–20
Article VII (Judicial), 121–133
Article VIII (Education), 135–40
Article IX (State Institutions), 141–2
Article X (Public Finance), 143–9
Article XI (Corporations), 151–6
Article XII (Militia), 157–9
Article XIII (Municipal Debt), 161–3
Article XIV (Boundaries), 165–6
Article XV (Miscellaneous), 167–70
Article XVI (Amendments), 171–2
Auditor, 15, 73–4, 113–6. *See* County Auditor; State Auditor

Bail, 6, 53–5
Bias, 50
Bicameral legislature, 6, 81, 97
Bill of Rights, 6, 30, 37–8, 49, 51.
  See Article I

Blacks, 14, 21–2
Branch banks, 153
Bribery, 71–2

Call for constitutional convention, 7–11, 16–7, 19, 27–30, 37
  for special legislative session, 84, 87, 95, 101
Census, 5, 21, 84, 110. Enumeration
Chief Executive, 101, 106, 109–10
Chief Justice, 123–4, 127
Circuit Court, 6, 8, 15, 116, 119, 121–2, 126. *See* Trial court
Civil cases, 57
Clerk of the Circuit Court, 15, 116
Clerk of the Supreme Court, 15
Coerced confession, 53
Common school fund, 12, 18, 43, 136–9
Common schools, 16, 18, 136, 138. *See* Public school system
Compensation, 59, 60, 73, 88, 95, 96, 99–100, 112, 127, 132, 139. *See* Pay
Confront witness, right to, 51
Conscientious objector, 157–8
Constituents, 75, 118, 131
Constitution of 1816, 6, 3–4, 13
Constitution of 1851, 12–13
Constitutional amendment, 19, 21, 26, 30, 32, 70, 71, 93, 171.
  See Amendments
Constitutional Convention, 7, 4–5, 11–2, 24, 16–8, 26–8, 35, 93, 171
Constitutional interpretation, 32–3
Convention delegates, 6
Coordinate branches, 78
Coroner, 15, 116
Corydon, 5, 7
County Auditor, 15, 73
County Coroner, 15
County Officers, 126, 116–7
County offices, 15, 117, 120
County Recorder, 15. *See* Recorder
County Sheriff, 15

185

County Surveyor, 15
County Treasurer, 15, 117. *See* Treasurer
Court of Appeals, 41, 96, 119, 121, 123–9
Cruel and unusual punishment, 53–4

Debt, 11, 12, 14, 20, 22, 60, 137, 145–6, 161–2. *See* Public debt
Declaration of Independence, 6, 38
Defendant, 47, 49, 51–2, 126
Deficit, 11, 14
Delegates, 5–6, 11–3
Democrats, 7, 18, 85, 10–2
Disabilities, 94, 104, 107
Districts, 15, 11–2, 24, 30, 70, 82–4, 125
Divorces, 8, 94
Domicile, 103
Double Jeopardy, 51–3
Due Process of Law, 48, 144

Education, 6, 16, 25, 44, 135–7, 141. *See* Public school system
Elections, 15–6, 20–1, 28, 30, 69–72, 75, 85, 94, 100–112, 123. *See* Special election
Electors, 7, 9–10, 14, 20–2, 24–5, 27–8, 69, 74–5, 82, 116–7, 171–2. *See* Voters
Enumeration, 83–4. *See* Census
Ex Post Facto, 61
Excessive force, 53
Exclusionary rule, 47–8
Executive order, 110
Expulsion, 90

Felonies, 50
Franchise, 13–4, 18, 24, 28, 69–70. *See* Right to vote; Suffrage
Free elections, 69
Free Exercise Clause, 40–1
Free thought, 45
Fundamental law, 29

General Assembly, 6–8, 10–1, 14–8, 21–2, 24–7, 29, 31, 60–2, 64, 66, 71–3, 75–6, 81–4, 86–7, 89–91, 94, 96, 98–112, 115, 117–21, 123–8, 130–2, 135–48, 151–3, 155–6, 159, 163, 168, 170–1. *See* Article IV; Legislature
General jurisdiction, 6, 122
General welfare, 39, 41, 65
Good faith exception, 47–8

Governor, 4–8, 10–1, 14, 20–1, 26, 31, 62, 74, 78, 84, 87, 89, 98–9, 101–13, 115–7, 127–8, 130–1, 141, 157–8, 169. *See* Article V
Grand Jury, 132

Habeas corpus, 58, 63
Harrison, William Henry, 4
House of Representatives. *See* Indiana House of Representatives

Illinois, 5, 13, 166
Impairment of contract, 61
Impartial jury, 49–50
Impeachment, 8–9, 13, 110, 118–9, 131. *See* Removal
Inalienable rights, 38–9
Income tax, 26, 32, 148–9. *See* Taxation
Indentures, 6
Indiana House of Representatives, 6, 10, 81–2, 91, 102–3, 113, 118
Indiana Senate, 6, 15, 85, 87, 92, 97, 107, 112–3, 118, 104–5, 81–3, 26–7, 10–2
Indiana University, 16, 135, 137
Indianapolis, 7, 41, 58, 170
Inherent powers, 127, 158
Insurrection, 106, 146
Intangible property, 145
Interim appointment, 111
Internal improvements, 11, 14
Invasion, 63, 106, 146, 161
Involuntary servitude, 6–7, 67

Jacksonian Democracy, 9
Joint resolution, 92–3, 97, 118
Joint session, 102–3, 105. *See* Legislative sessions
Journal, 88–9, 97–8
Judicial circuit, 126, 132
Judicial discretion, 54
Judicial nominating commission, 31, 123, 127–8
Judicial power, 121–2, 131
Jurisdiction, 6, 15, 30–1, 75–6, 116, 118, 121–2, 124–7, 162, 166, 168
Jury, 43, 48–50, 52, 56–8, 61, 132, 169
Jury duty, 61
Jury instructions, 56
Just compensation, 59, 144
Juvenile offenders, 142

Kentucky, 5–6, 9, 51, 166

Lawyers' amendment, 24–5
Legal counsel, 50
Legal profession, 16, 30
Legislative session, 8, 13, 18, 31, 87, 89, 100
    Annual session, 8, 14, 87
    Biennial session, 11, 14, 8–9, 29, 87
    Special session, 21, 27, 84, 87, 100, 104, 108. *See* Session
Legislature, 5–12, 14, 16, 18, 20–2, 24–7, 29, 32, 39, 45, 54, 56, 58, 60–3, 65–6, 70–2, 78, 81–7, 89–92, 94, 98–9, 101, 103, 107, 110–1, 117–8, 120, 122, 124, 131, 141, 143–4, 146, 148, 150, 152, 157–8, 167–8. *See* Article IV; General Assembly
Lieutenant Governor, 14, 74, 87, 102–8, 115, 111–3
Local and special legislation, 8–9, 11
Local legislation, 12. *See* Special legislation
Lottery, 170

Mexico, 9
Militia, 6, 65, 73, 106, 157–8
Miranda rights, 52–3
Misdemeanors, 50, 94
Mississippi, 5
Mistrial, 52
Municipal debt, 23, 161. *See* Article XIII
Municipal government, 147
Municipality, 147

Necessary and Proper, 62
"Negroes, Mulattoes and Indians," 6
Northwest Ordinance of 1787, 4
Northwest Territory, 4

Oaths, of office, 83, 169
    of witnesses, 44–5
Obligation of contract, 61
Ohio, 5–6, 10, 51, 95, 165–6
Ohio River, 5, 165–6
Oregon, 9
Organic act, 4, 6, 13, 24, 30, 16–7, 33, 37, 56, 94
Original jurisdiction
    of Circuit Courts, 15, 124
    of Courts of Appeals, 124–5
    of Supreme Court, 124

Pardons, 110–1
Pay, 59, 64, 73–4, 86, 95, 99, 132, 139, 145–6, 148, 152–4, 159. *See* Compensation
Peremptory challenge, 50
Personal liberties and rights, 31. *See* Bill of Rights
Petition, 58, 63–4, 161
Plenary authority, 81, 90–1, 141–2
Plurality, 9–10, 25, 97
Police power, 39, 41, 60–2, 65, 91, 144, 146, 149, 151
Political sovereigns, 6, 38
Presentment, 107–9
President pro tempore, 104–5
Property, 39–40, 46, 48, 59–60, 64, 91, 107, 136, 143–5, 148–9, 161–2, 170
Property tax, 143–5, 148–9. *See* Taxation
Prosecuting attorney, 119, 131–2
Public access, 118
Public debt, 12, 145. *See* Debt
Public defense, 145
Public education, 6, 16
Public funds, 43, 74, 146, 155
Public indebtedness, 162
Public Law, 98
Public school system, 16, 136. *See* Common schools
Public trial, 49–50
Punishment, 6, 53–5, 67, 90, 94

Quartering of soldiers, 66
Quorum, 88, 97, 123, 127

Race, 69–70
Recorder, 15, 73, 116
Recount Commission, 103
Referendum, 26
Regulations, 11, 106, 110, 143–4, 158
Removal, 8–9, 13, 110, 118–9, 131. *See* Impeachment
Representative government, 118
Reprieves, 110–1
Residency, 14, 18, 24, 71, 84–6, 103, 117–8
Revenue bills, 91
Right to bear arms, 6, 65
Right to vote, 6, 24, 69–71. *See* Franchise; Suffrage
Right to worship, 39–40

Search warrant, 48. *See* Warrant
Searches and seizures, 6, 47
Secondary education, 16, 135
Secret ballot, 7. *See* Voice vote
Secretary of State, 15, 21, 99, 103, 108, 115, 169
Self-incrimination, privilege against, 51–2
Senate. Indiana Senate
Separation of powers, 78, 91, 101, 109, 112
Session, 8–9, 13–4, 18, 20, 29, 31, 83–4, 87, 97. *See* Legislative session
Sheriff, 15, 116, 120
Slavery, 6–7, 9, 66–7, 161
Sovereign immunity, 96
Speaker of the House, 97, 104–5, 113
Special election, 22
Special legislation, 9, 11, 13, 18, 95, 151. *See* Local legislation
Speech, 45–6, 85, 117
State Auditor, 115
State party convention, 102
State Superintendent of Public Instruction, 16, 139
State Treasurer, 115
State university, 6, 40, 137, 156
Statehood, 3, 5, 165
Stockholders, 153, 155–6
Succession, 101, 104–6, 111
Suffrage, 12, 14, 24, 69, 72. *See* Franchise; Right to vote
Supreme Court, 6, 8, 15–6, 25–8, 30–3, 38, 18–22, 40–1, 44, 58, 61, 64, 66, 70–1, 75, 83–5, 46–52, 103, 105, 121–6, 141, 148, 161, 168, 128–33
Surveyor, 15, 116

"Take care" provision, 110
  duties, 116
Taking of property, 59, 144
Tangible property, 145
Taxation, 91, 96, 143–4. *See* Income tax; Property tax

Term limitations, 14, 131
Term of office, 101–2, 104, 111, 118, 130–2, 139, 168, 74
Territorial Governor, 4
Territorial Legislature, 4
Territorial stage, 4
Titles of nobility, 66
Treason, 54–5, 63–4, 74–5, 86, 110–1
Treasurer, 15, 115–8. *See* County Treasurer
Treasurer of the State, 15
Trial court, 21, 30, 50, 55, 46, 122, 124, 126, 127. *See* Circuit Court
Trust fund, 139, 155

United States Constitution, 4, 13, 40, 63, 72, 85, 103

Vacancies, 21, 83, 104–7, 111, 117, 119–20, 169
Veto, 107–9
Voice vote, 7, 75. *See* Secret ballot
Voters, 3, 6–14, 16–7, 19–22, 24–8, 30, 32, 69, 74–5, 82, 116–7, 171–2. *See* Electors

Wabash and Erie Canal, 20, 148
Wabash River, 10, 165
War of 1812, 5
Warrant, 31, 47, 49, 72. *See* Search warrant
Whigs, 7, 11
Wisconsin, 13
Witness, 41, 44–5, 49–51, 59
  compulsory process for, 49
  confrontation of, right to, 51
  treason, 63
Women, 14, 18, 24
Women's suffrage, 24

Zoning, 41

About the Author

WILLIAM P. McLAUCHLAN is Associate Professor of Political Science at Purdue University. He has been teaching public law and judicial process for more than twenty years. His research interests focus on court case loads, lawyers and the legal profession, and constitutional law.

Printed in the USA/Agawam, MA
August 25, 2014

595820.052